ADMINISTRATIVE REGULATION BEYOND THE NON-DELEGATION DOCTRINE

The importance of administration in the EU has been growing progressively together with the development of EU competences and tasks in the internal market. From the original model of a Community leaving enforcement with the Member States, the EU has become a complex legal order where administrative tasks are spread among different actors, including EU institutions, EU agencies and national administrations. Within this complex administrative law landscape, agencies and their powers have been essentially 'upgraded'. This volume asks whether any such 'upgrade' is compatible with EU law and its principles. Exploring both the case law of the CJEU and the regulation relating to EU agencies, the volume asks a crucial question about the legitimacy of the ever-increasing role of agencies in the enforcement of EU law.

Volume 88 in the Series Modern Studies in European Law

Modern Studies in European Law

Recent titles in this series:

The EU and Nanotechnologies: A Critical Analysis
Tanja Ehnert

Human Rights Between Law and Politics:
The Margin of Appreciation in Post-National Contexts
Edited by Petr Agha

The European Union and Social Security Law
Jaan Paju

The Rule of Law in the European Union: The Internal Dimension
Theodore Konstadinides

The Division of Competences between the EU and the Member States: Reflections on the Past, the Present and the Future
Edited by Sacha Garben and Inge Govaere

Unity in Adversity: EU Citizenship, Social Justice and the Cautionary Tale of the UK
Charlotte O'Brien

The Use of Force and Article 2 of the ECHR in Light of European Conflicts
Hannah Russell

Environmental Crime in Europe
Edited by Andrew Farmer, Michael Faure and Grazia Maria Vagliasindi

Questioning EU Citizenship: Judges and the Limits of Free Movement and Solidarity in the EU
Edited by Daniel Thym

The European Union under Transnational Law: A Pluralist Appraisal
Matej Avbelj

Illegally Staying in the EU: An Analysis of Illegality in EU Migration Law
Benedita Menezes Queiroz

Social Legitimacy in the Internal Market: A Dialogue of Mutual Responsiveness
Jotte Mulder

The EU Better Regulation Agenda: A Critical Assessment
Edited by Sacha Garben and Inge Govaere

Administrative Regulation Beyond the Non-Delegation Doctrine: A Study on EU Agencies
Marta Simoncini

For the complete list of titles in this series, see 'Modern Studies in European Law' link at www.bloomsburyprofessional.com/uk/series/modern-studies-in-european-law

Administrative Regulation Beyond the Non-Delegation Doctrine

A Study on EU Agencies

Marta Simoncini

•HART•
OXFORD • LONDON • NEW YORK • NEW DELHI • SYDNEY

HART PUBLISHING
Bloomsbury Publishing Plc
Kemp House, Chawley Park, Cumnor Hill, Oxford, OX2 9PH, UK

HART PUBLISHING, the Hart/Stag logo, BLOOMSBURY and the Diana logo are trademarks of Bloomsbury Publishing Plc

First published in Great Britain 2018

A catalogue record for this book is available from the British Library.

Library of Congress Cataloging-in-Publication data

Names: Simoncini, Marta, author.

Title: Administrative regulation beyond the non-delegation doctrine : a study on EU agencies / Marta Simoncini.

Description: Portland, Oregon : Hart Publishing, 2018. | Series: Modern studies in European law ; volume 88 | Includes bibliographical references and index.

Identifiers: LCCN 2018000422 (print) | LCCN 2018000942 (ebook) | ISBN 9781509911721 (Epub) | ISBN 9781509911745 (hardback : alk. paper)

Subjects: LCSH: Administrative agencies—European Union countries. | Administrative procedure—European Union countries. | Administrative law—European Union countries.

Classification: LCC KJE5794 (ebook) | LCC KJE5794 .S56 2018 (print) | DDC 342.24/06—dc23

LC record available at https://lccn.loc.gov/2018000422

ISBN: HB: 978-1-50991-174-5
ePDF: 978-1-50991-171-4
ePub: 978-1-50991-172-1

Typeset by Compuscript Ltd, Shannon
Printed and bound in Great Britain by TJ International Ltd, Padstow, Cornwall

To find out more about our authors and books visit www.hartpublishing.co.uk. Here you will find extracts, author information, details of forthcoming events and the option to sign up for our newsletters.

To the magic memory of my Grandma, Rosy, and her sparkling vitality

Acknowledgements

This volume is the final output of my post-doctoral research fellowship sponsored by the Research Foundation Flanders (FWO), and co-hosted by the University of Antwerp, Faculty of Law and King's College London, the Dickson Poon School of Law. I would like to thank all these institutions and the people therein for their support, guidance and inspiration. I have special thanks for my mentors at the University of Antwerp: Alexia Herwig, who genuinely promoted my FWO fellowships (and my first move to Belgium) and thoroughly nurtured my research skills; and Gert Straetmans, who has always encouraged my research choices. My gratitude is also for Takis Tridimas, who welcomed me at King's College London and engaged me in invaluable discussion sessions and great opportunities for professional growth.

I have published previous studies related to the topic of this volume in the *Yearbook of European Law* (2015) and *European Public Law* (2015). These articles substantially contributed to the development of this study and I want to thank the Journals for having provided me with remarkable feedback. I would also like to thank Hart Publishing for accepting this volume within the 'Modern Studies in European Law' series, the anonymous referees of my book proposal for their inspiring remarks, and the people who worked on the production of this volume.

I also had several occasions to present and discuss the partial findings of my research in national and international conferences and seminars, as well as in informal fora. I would like to thank all those colleagues and friends who offered me their feedback and contributed in some way towards bringing out the best in my research. Amongst my friends, I particularly thank Jacques Pelkmans, who was the first to bring to my attention the still fashionable character of the *Meroni* doctrine. I also want to sincerely thank Edoardo Chiti, my dearest friend Giuseppe Martinico, and Alberto Massera, who offered their thorough and detailed comments on the first draft of this work, giving me extremely useful food for thought. I also thank Chris Gorman for his very professional proofreading service.

Finally, I am grateful to my parents, Anna and Sandro, who have always supported me and my commitment to research (with all that comes with it!) and Nicola, who offers me incessant opportunities to discuss the politics of law (sic!) and tolerated me as I strived towards completing the final draft of this volume.

Contents

Abbreviations

ACER	Agency for the Cooperation of Energy Regulators
AG	Advocate General
AMC	acceptable means of compliance
ANAC	Autorità nazionale anticorruzione (Italy)
ANEC	European Association for the Co-ordination of Consumer Representation in Standardisation
ANS	air navigation services
ATM	air traffic management
BEREC	Body of European Regulators for Electronic Communication
BoA	Board of Appeal
CEBS	Committee of European Banking Supervisors
CEIOPS	Committee of European Insurance and Occupational Pensions Supervisors
CEN	Comité Européen de Normalisation
CENELEC	Comité Européen de Normalisation en Électronique et en Électrotechnique
CESR	Committee of European Securities Regulators
CJEU	Court of Justice of the European Union
CPVO	Community Plant Variety Office
CRA	credit rating agency
CRD	Comment Response Document
CS	certification specification
EAR	European Agency for Reconstruction
EASA	European Aviation Safety Agency
EBA	European Banking Authority
EBU	European Banking Union
EC	European Community
ECB	European Central Bank
ECHA	European Chemicals Agency
ECOS	European Environmental Citizens Organisation for Standardisation
ECSC	European Coal and Steel Community
EDIS	European Deposit Insurance Scheme
EDPS	European Data Protection Supervisor
EEC	European Economic Community
EFSA	European Food Safety Authority
EIOPA	European Insurance and Occupational Pensions Authority
EMA	European Medicines Agency
EMSA	European Maritime Safety Agency

ERA	European Union Agency for Railway
ERG	European Regulators Group
ESA	European Supervisory Authority
ESFS	European System of Financial Supervision
ESM	European Stability Mechanism
ESMA	European Securities and Markets Authority
ESRB	European Systemic Risk Board
ETSI	European Telecommunication Standards Institute
ETUC	European Trade Union Confederation
EU	European Union
EUIPO	European Union Intellectual Property Office
FAB	functional airspace block
GM	guidance materials
GMMOs	genetically modified micro-organisms
HFT	high-frequency algorithmic trading
ICAO	International Civil Aviation Organization
JAA	Joint Aviation Authority
NPA	Notice of Proposed Amendment
OHIM	Office for Harmonisation of the Internal Market
POG	product oversight and governance
SES	Single European Sky
SME	small and/or medium-sized enterprise
SRB	Single Resolution Board
SRM	Single Resolution Mechanism
SSM	Single Supervisory Mechanism
TEU	Treaty on European Union
TFEU	Treaty on the Functioning of the European Union
TSO	Transmission System Operator

Introduction

In the Trap of EU Agencies' Powers: Perspectives for an Analysis

INTERNAL MARKET INTEGRATION in the European Union (EU) has created cross-border interdependencies between markets and regulatory regimes, as market creation often also requires regulation. Services that depend on physical or logical networks constitutively rely on such interdependencies. The effective operation of transport, electronic communications, energy supply or financial markets has steadily assumed cross-border functional dimensions. Individual states with their limited jurisdictional reach cannot adequately govern such interdependencies and the risks that they generate. Their regulation is bound to fail where dangers do not come from the origin of the concerned activities, but rather from interlinkages on which isolated actors have no sufficient view. Where the openness of the internal market and the density of interactions therein no longer make one-level interventions sufficient, the EU subsidiary intervention may better achieve the integration objectives.[1]

EU intervention generally operates through the establishment of complex systems of governance that aim to keep under control the risks of these interdependencies and favour the correct functioning of the network. This, however, does not prevent failures and regulatory paradoxes. As Black observed, no system of regulatory governance can escape this reality, because the vulnerability of network systems based on their 'internal contradictions and tensions' generates mutable performances.[2] Complexity is therefore the justification of EU intervention and the reason for its possible regulatory failure. The most efficient governance of complexity is therefore the objective of EU regulation and the organisation of the governance is key to improving the functioning of networks and reducing their risks of failure.

This EU regulatory effort has been accompanied by the establishment of 'buffer' supranational agencies facilitating the cross-border, sector-specific cooperation between national regulatory authorities and the EU institutions, as well as amongst those national administrations in the framework of EU integration policies. Being placed in the intersection of different regulatory regimes, EU agencies face the

[1] See M Kumm, 'Constitutionalising Subsidiarity in Integrated Markets: The Case of Tobacco Regulation in the European Union' (2006) 12 *European Law Journal* 503.

[2] J Black, 'Paradoxes and Failures: "New Governance" Techniques and the Financial Crisis' (2012) 75 *Modern Law Review* 1037, 1038.

concrete issues of integration, its spill-overs and setbacks. However, they often do this from a backward position. Internal market integration in network services passes through EU agencies, but their powers are generally limited. Legally speaking, they are not more than advisory and monitoring expert bodies working for the Commission and in close cooperation with national competent authorities. In practice, however, their advice cannot be ignored and has the factual strength to contribute to shaping integration.

Especially in the last decade, EU agencies have been acquiring sounder voice in the integration process. Even if their range of powers is not uniform and their regulatory regimes are quite differentiated, some common trends can be identified. In some cases, they have been allocated powers increasingly relevant to the executive rule-making and may also bring significant input to the legislative process. In addition, most of them have developed the traditional recommendatory and advisory powers into standardisation practices, which are increasingly able to constrain the decision-making process of both the EU institutions and the Member States. In other specific cases, EU agencies have also been allocated a few formal regulatory powers. Especially in the financial sector, the wider reach of powers conferred on the European Supervisory Authorities (ESAs) has generated a hybrid organisational model, which shares many characteristics of agencies, yet moves towards an embryonic independence in the structure of organisation.[3] The logical incoherence between the growing relevance of agencies in the integration process and their difficult emergence as a centre of regulation has been the distinctive mark of EU agencies' governance. The result is that EU agencies' responsibilities and tasks are generally limited, but legally uncertain. The main evidence of EU agencies' governance by uncertainty has been the steady development of non-binding powers aimed at generating regulatory effects.

This gap between law and reality is troublesome. The framework strategy for a European Energy Union has considered the necessity to enhance the Agency for the Cooperation of Energy Regulators' (ACER) powers, 'in order to enable it to effectively oversee the development of the internal energy market and the related market rules as well as to deal with all cross-border issues necessary to create a seamless internal market'.[4] This intention has become part of the winter package on a clean energy economy that is aimed to facilitate the transition to a low carbon economy by 2050.[5] The European Commission proposed to confer

[3] See E Chiti, 'European Agencies' Rulemaking: Powers, Procedures and Assessment' (2013) 19 *European Law Journal* 93, 94; C Franchini, 'Le fasi e i caratteri del processo evolutivo dell'organizzazione amministrativa europea' (2017) 27 *Rivista Italiana di Diritto Pubblico Comunitario* 375, 383.

[4] Communication from the Commission to the European Parliament, the Council, the European Economic and Social Committee, the Committee of the Regions and the European Investment Bank, *Energy Union Package: A Framework Strategy for a Resilient Energy Union with a Forward-Looking Climate Change Policy*, COM(2015)80 final (25 February 2015), 9.

[5] Communication from the Commission to the European Parliament, the Council, the European Economic and Social Committee, the Committee of the Regions and the European Investment Bank, *Clean Energy for All Europeans*, COM(2016)080 (30 November 2016).

wider functions on ACER and to partially reform its organisation in light of the enhanced competence.[6] The Commission recognised that while ACER has thus far played a key role in the coordination, advising and monitoring of energy markets, the fragmentation of regulatory oversight and the management of cross-border issues concerning grid operation and electricity trading require these powers to be strengthened so as to make the pursuit of the regulatory goals more effective. Under the Commission's proposal, ACER particularly acquires more powers in the draft of a network code to be adopted by the Commission, may decide the regional relevance of some issues and may adopt individual decisions concerning technical and regulatory issues which require regional coordination.[7] Although the negotiation process is still long, this proposal shows that there is increasing awareness about the key role that EU agencies may play in internal market integration. Hancher and Winters, however, remarked that the reinforcement of powers still 'shies away from centralising regulatory powers in the hands of ACER'.[8] Indeed, these powers are not sufficient to create an independent regulator, but they may nonetheless change the legal position of the Agency in the Energy Union. This change will not come without legal challenges.

The legal explanation of the existing dichotomy between law and practice, in fact, lies in the constitutional position of EU agencies in the EU legal order. As the 1972 Vedel Report emphasised, 'once the Community institutions began to function, practice quite naturally gave birth to bodies for which no provision was made initially'.[9] Although the Report referred to the new establishment of committees and intergovernmental organs, the same issue concerns EU agencies. Their insecure constitutional seat in the structure of the Treaties as interpreted by the Court of Justice of the European Union (CJEU) as at the origin of the conundrum that affects their powers. In a nutshell, the judicial doctrine of non-delegation as developed in the 1958 leading case *Meroni*[10] has prevented the delegation of regulatory competences involving discretionary powers to independent bodies other than the EU institutions. This prohibition aims to protect the democratic accountability of the EU legal order and to prevent the allocation of EU responsibilities to bodies other than the legitimate EU institutions. The constitutional engineering reason is that agencies would unlawfully interfere with the powers conferred upon the institutions by the Treaties and would alter the institutional balance of public powers as set out in the Treaties.

[6] Proposal for a Regulation of the European Parliament and of the Council of 23 February 2017 establishing a European Union Agency for the Cooperation of Energy Regulators (recast), COM(2016)863 final, 7–8.

[7] Proposal of Regulation annexed to COM(2016)863 final/2, COM(2016)863 final/2, 22, recitals 13, 14 and arts 4–6.

[8] L Hancher and BM Winters, *The EU Winter Package: Briefing Paper* (Allen & Overy LLP, February 2017) 11.

[9] 'Report of the Working Party Examining the Problem of the Extension of the Powers of the European Parliament of 25 March 1972' [1972] 4 *Bulletin of the European Economic Community* 7, 27.

[10] 9/56 and 10/56 *Meroni & Co., Industrie Metallurgiche, SAS v High Authority of the European Coal and Steel Community* [1958] ECR 53.

As regards targeting the discretionary content that is at the core of administrative powers, in practice this doctrine has kept EU administrative integration through EU agencies in this conundrum for almost 60 years and still prevents the transformation of ACER into a sort of independent regulator enforcing the Energy Union. Recently the CJEU has revisited the *Meroni* doctrine. In the *ESMA Short Selling* case concerning the allocation of specific regulatory competences to the European Securities and Markets Authority (ESMA) in the trade of securities, futures and other derivative contracts,[11] the CJEU better circumscribed the application of this doctrine and contributed to mitigating the gap between law and practice. However, the validity of the non-delegation principle as the constitutional rule governing the establishment and the functioning of EU agencies has been confirmed. No institutional innovation in the competence of EU agencies can take place without meeting the *Meroni* requirements, even in their updated version. This represents the constitutional foundation of EU agencies' responsibilities and tasks.

The *Meroni*-based legality of delegation is only part of a wider issue related to the distribution of powers in the EU.[12] It is the formal institutional evidence of substantive regulatory dilemmas. Internal market integration in services clearly moves national interests as well as EU institutions' preferences. The establishment of supranational independent regulators governing the structure of a market comes with the acceptance of the reduction of national powers, as well as with the de-politicisation of market integration. Magnette significantly explained that even though every decision depends on a specific political context, both national governments and EU institutions are reluctant to renounce (part of) their powers in favour of independent regulators. On the one hand, governments 'will generally prefer to keep a given field under their control rather than delegate it to an independent agency', but if necessary, they would rather accept 'a weakly independent agency to a true regulatory body' and a national independent regulator to a supranational one. Supranational agencies are therefore the institutional evidence that Member States 'fear the consequences of non-coordination'. On the other hand, 'EU institutions will only support an independent and supranational regulator if they think this widens EU competences and the new regulator will not undermine their own existing and potential powers'.[13]

The establishment of the Body of European Regulators for Electronic Communication (BEREC) remarkably reflects this fierce political negotiation behind the structure and the powers of EU agencies. To address the fragmentation and

[11] C-270/12 *United Kingdom v Council of European Union and European Parliament* ECLI:EU:C:2014:18.

[12] See E Chiti, 'An Important Part of the EU Institutional Machinery: Features, Problems and Perspectives of European Agencies' (2009) 46 *Common Market Law Review* 1395, 1405.

[13] P Magnette, 'The Politics of Regulation in the European Union' in D Geradin, R Muñoz and N Petit (eds), *Regulation Through Agencies in the EU: A New Paradigm of European Governance* (Elgar Publishing, 2005) 3, 10.

the inconsistent regulation of the electronic communication market, the Commission proposed to establish a European authority 'working in close cooperation with the national regulatory authorities (NRAs) and the Commission' in substitution of the informally operating network of national regulators established in the European Regulators Group (ERG).[14] Although few hard powers were allocated to the proposed EU agency, negotiations could only bring about a weird body, not even an agency, but more like a common substation of national regulators. As such, BEREC has no legal personality,[15] but it has an Office with legal personality, which assists and supports the Body of Regulators.[16] BEREC has the responsibility of assisting national regulators for ensuring the consistent application of the EU regulatory framework.[17] As it has been emphasised, it culminated in being an enhanced version of the ERG self-regulation forum.[18]

The political shipwreck of an EU agency shows the harshness of the interests behind their establishment and hints at the political challenges behind the apparent regulatory inconsistencies and paradoxes. The legal discourse therefore cannot ignore consideration of the political reasons concerning the opportunity of delegation. The two levels of analysis, however, can be distinguished and functionally separated for the clarity of the investigation. Clearing out the political issues, this study focuses on the legal aspects of the complex phenomenon of *agencification*. The elucidation of the legal debate may produce positive spillovers on political arguments, making the relevant stakeholders more aware of the potential and the limits of EU agencies as administrative entities. The objective is to investigate the constitutional position of EU agencies' administrative powers in the EU legal order. I aim to question the unavoidability of the legal conundrum that restrains EU agencies' powers and to engage in a reasoned discussion of the *Meroni* non-delegation doctrine in the current framework of the Treaties and the administrative practice. The question is to what extent EU agencies as a model of administration in expansion can contribute to the administrative exercise of regulatory functions.

Legal scholarship has widely debated the *Meroni* doctrine and studies on EU agencies have been flourishing in recent decades. Yet, EU administrative law has not effectively addressed the gap between law and practice and has not clearly responded to the questions concerning the legitimacy and the scope of EU administrative action. In 2000, Vos recognised that the growth of administration

[14] Proposal for a Regulation of the European Parliament and of the Council of 13 November 2007 establishing the European Electronic Communications Market Authority, COM(2007)699 final, 2.

[15] Regulation 1211/2009/EC of the European Parliament and of the Council of 25 November 2009 establishing the Body of European Regulators for Electronic Communications (BEREC) and the Office, recital 6.

[16] Ibid art. 6.

[17] Ibid art. 1(3).

[18] See M Mester, 'Independent NRAs in European Electronic Communications Policy-making and Regulation: The Road to BEREC and Beyond' (2010) 147 *Studia Iuridica Auctoritate Universitatis Pecs Publicata* 113, 124 and 129.

questions the strict application of the *Meroni* doctrine and requires 'searching for additional means to enhance administrative legitimacy'.[19] Dehousse also advocated the inapplicability of the *Meroni* case law in the context of the European Community (EC), as it concerned the powers of the High Authority in the *traité loi* of the European Coal and Steel Community (ECSC) and cannot effectively control the new *traité cadre* of the EC embedding a different system of governance.[20] In 2005, Geradin reached the conclusion that:

> the restrictive interpretation of Meroni followed by the EU institutions fails to resist serious legal analysis. Its main implication, which is to prevent the delegation of regulatory powers to European agencies, fails in turn to satisfy the needs of a modern administrative state.[21]

More recently, scholars have engaged in the search for the compatibility of the *Meroni* doctrine with the changed framework of the Lisbon Treaty. Griller and Orator particularly aimed to reconcile this doctrine with administrative practice and supported its 'cautious reassessment', where the prerogatives of the legislature, the Commission and accountability are secured.[22] Chiti argued that the principle of institutional balance should not preclude 'the inventiveness of a Community authority' where the assessment of the individual case suggests that no undue interference with other EU institutions' powers occurred.[23] Chamon discussed the sustainability of EU agencies' powers in the context of the Lisbon Treaty and concluded that the process of agencification is still based 'on shaky legal grounds'.[24] Maybe more pragmatically, some Italian scholarship recognised that the reference in the Lisbon Treaty to agencies, offices and bodies matches up the recognition of the autonomous existence of such administrative entities under the Treaties and the end of the delegation relationship on which the *Meroni* doctrine is based.[25] Nonetheless, the *Meroni* doctrine is still governing the broad phenomenon of agencification and the *ESMA Short Selling* case confirms that this remains the current legal justification for the legitimate allocation of powers to EU administrative entities.

[19] E Vos, 'Reforming the European Commission: What Role to Play for EU Agencies?' (2000) 37 *Common Market Law Review* 1113, 1123.

[20] R Dehousse, 'Misfits: EU Law and the Transformation of European Governance' in C Joerges and R Dehousse (eds), *Good Governance in Europe's Integrated Market* (Oxford University Press, 2002) 207, 221.

[21] D Geradin, 'The Development of European Regulatory Agencies: Lessons from the American Experience' in D Geradin, R Muñoz and N Petit (eds), *Regulation Through Agencies in the EU: A New Paradigm of European Governance* (Elgar Publishing, 2005) 215, 222.

[22] S Griller and A Orator, 'Everything Under Control? The "Way Forward" for European Agencies in the Footsteps of the *Meroni* Doctrine' (2010) 35 *European Law Review* 3, 31.

[23] Chiti, 'An Important Part of the EU Institutional Machinery' (n 12) 1424.

[24] M Chamon, 'EU Agencies Between *Meroni* and *Romano* or the Devil and the Deep Blue Sea' (2011) 48 *Common Market Law Review* 1055, 1075.

[25] D Sorace, 'Una nuova base costituzionale europea per la pubblica amministrazione' in MP Chiti and A Natalini (eds), *Lo spazio amministrativo europeo. Le pubbliche amministrazioni dopo il Trattato di Lisbona* (Il Mulino, 2012) 45, 56.

The problematic fit between law and practice prevents legal scholarship from definitely closing the discussion on the *Meroni* doctrine and dooms it to reassess the compatibility of EU agencies' powers any time new powers involving some regulatory content are conferred upon them. The poor wording of the Treaties and the ambiguity of the case law do not favour the substantive advancement of the legal discourse. The evidence is that the legal analysis on the compatibility of EU agencies' powers has slightly changed from the issues that Lauwaars examined in his 1979 comment on the powers of the European Monetary Cooperation Fund, which lately flowed into the European Central Bank and indirectly acquired the status of an EU institution.[26] He recognised that where 'delegation to third parties is necessary for the attainment of one of the objectives of the Community', an exception to the execution of such tasks and responsibilities by EU institutions will be made; but such delegation must comply with the Treaties and be limited to executive powers.[27] By building institutional innovation on the necessity requirement, Lauwaars correctly pointed to the proportionality test in the establishment of agencies. What Lauwaars could not resolve, and is still unsolved in the application of the *Meroni* doctrine, is the discretionary content of EU agencies' powers. He conceived the exercise of some discretion by the European Monetary Cooperation Fund 'with a view to the special nature' of its tasks and 'albeit only by way of a provisional measure which, ultimately at the time of the definitive arrangement of the European Monetary System, has to be object of Treaty revision'.[28] He could do nothing but admit an exception to the rigidity of the *Meroni* doctrine.

This is the very vulnerable issue in the application of such a doctrine. It portrays the delegation of purely executive tasks as in the Weberian 'transmission-belt' administration, which does not fit with the complex reality of integration. Vos significantly characterised 'the functioning of EU agencies in the "grey zone" between "pure" administration and politics'.[29] In my view, this is the key issue in which the consolidated discussion on the *Meroni* doctrine needs to be originally engaged. This study aims to discuss the very nature of EU agencies' powers with the aim of getting out of the loop in which the strict interpretation of the *Meroni* doctrine has trapped the discourse on EU agencies and has stretched law and practice apart. The novelty of my study is that the dead-end to which the interpretation of the *Meroni* doctrine has confined the EU agencies' competence is not inescapable and the concerns on delegation addressed in this doctrine need to be considered from another perspective, which does not reject the very nature of administrative powers.

The centrality of the *Meroni* doctrine in the assessment of the constitutional legitimacy of EU agencies' powers has consolidated even though the delegation

[26] RH Lauwaars, 'Auxiliary Organs and Agencies in the E.E.C.' (1979) *Common Market Law Review* 365.

[27] Ibid 372.

[28] Ibid 386–87.

[29] Vos, 'Reforming the European Commission' (n 19) 1130.

of the High Authority's powers under *Meroni* does not completely match the conferral of powers by the legislature to EEC agencies under *Romano*. The subsequent case law has not significantly distinguished these cases, probably because the *Meroni* ruling set a series of requirements for lawful delegation that may also apply in the case of conferral. Conceptually the distinction is relevant, because administrative delegation and legislative conferral necessarily rest on different legitimacy premises. The scope of the allocation of powers is therefore necessarily different. Apart from the preservation of the institutional balance, the legislative conferral enjoys more opportunities than administrative delegation, as the legal source of power has higher (democratic) legitimacy. This is the way public administration is considered democratically compatible in national legal orders: the principle of legality guides and limits administrative powers. Where administration delegates its own competence to another administration, clearly it cannot delegate more powers than those it retains, and some further limitations may apply according to the public interests that the legal order aims to protect. The *Meroni* ruling was seriously concerned with the protection of the ECSC institutions' prerogatives and accordingly limited the possibility of administrative delegation. Nonetheless, *Meroni* is still considered good law that also applies to the cases of conferral. My study recognises this judicial approach, but holds this legitimate as long as *Meroni* points to the substantive issues in the allocation of administrative powers; that is, the administrative nature of the power and its justiciability, which can be extensively considered as the set of legal guarantees that will direct its exercise.

My study therefore identifies in these substantive issues the key questions for the assessment of the tenability of EU agencies' powers. My reading, however, refreshes the substance of the constitutional rule embedded in the *Meroni* doctrine, but dismisses its formalistic interpretation. With regard to the nature of the power, I contend that the *Meroni* doctrine's approach has trapped EU agencies in an unreal dichotomy between technical powers of pure execution and political powers embedding wide discretion. Although the principles of legality and institutional balance play essential roles in the functioning of EU administrative law, the rule of law has no legitimising function. Legitimacy tends to derive from the output of the enforced policies; that is, from the technical effectiveness of their impact. This functional approach of EU administrative law has created some false myths, such as the supposed purely technical nature of EU administrative action and the existence of neutral instruments for EU policies' implementation. Although recognising a circumscribed margin of discretion that is not political in nature, the *ESMA Short Selling* case has not unequivocally wiped out such a myth and it is still difficult to predict how EU courts will review such discretion.

I demonstrate that EU agencies' enforcement powers have a necessary content of discretion that under specific conditions may reconcile with the non-delegation principle. This brings me to identify administrative discretion as a particular category of discretion based on the legislative establishment of objectives, priorities and hierarchy of interests, which may be acceptable in a democratic legal order under a specific conception of the rule of law. The innovative character of this approach is that it challenges the consolidated approach of EU administrative law, which has not yet consistently characterised discretion beyond the political sphere. When dealing with administrative powers, EU administrative law has focused on how to functionalise them to the implementation of EU law, but it has not been concerned with the establishment of a conceptual framework aimed at justifying their exercise in conformity with the democratic principle. This means that EU administrative law could not mature a theoretical justification to the existence of supranational administrative powers. Only recently has some legal scholarship started to emphasise the importance of discretion in EU administrative action.[30] My study follows the pattern of this scholarship and ambitiously aims to confer legal relevance to the notion of administrative discretion under EU law.

Where such discretionary content of the power is accepted, the search is for legal instruments that make administrative action compatible with the democratic principle:

> No society can be considered truly democratic if its citizens are denied the possibility of vindicating their legal rights in judicial proceedings, whether against the oppressive acts of a powerful legislature—even a democratically elected one—or against the unlawful practices of an overweening administration.[31]

Insofar as arbitrary powers are not legitimate in democratic societies, effective legal mechanisms must ensure that no abuse or misuse of such discretion occurs. Legal guarantees are necessary to safeguard and control the exercise of administrative powers. My analysis therefore focuses on the existing accountability instruments and aims to understand whether they create a cogent system of check-and-balances that prevent EU agencies from escaping the rule of law and democratic rule. Insofar as both binding and not binding instruments operate in the EU administrative space and diversify the allocation of legal responsibilities, the study searches for those key mechanisms of control that entrench administrative action and secure its democratic compatibility. The legal guarantees of EU agencies' status; their implementation of the principle of good administration; the accountability mechanisms that connect their activities to EU institutions; and the justiciability of their acts, are examined as the crucial issues in the assessment of the tenability of their administrative powers.

This approach aims to reduce the gap between the traditional interpretation of the *Meroni* doctrine and administrative practice. However, the reinterpretation of the doctrine does not aim to justify reality, but to offer a key to (lawfully) read and lead the phenomenon of *agencification*. I engage in an objective discussion on the sustainability of the *Meroni* doctrine, which may provide insights into the state of

[30] J Mendes, 'Discretion, Care and Public Interests in the EU Administration: Probing the Limits of Law' (2016) 53 *Common Market Law Review* 419; E Chiti, 'Is EU Administrative Law Failing in Some of Its Crucial Tasks?' (2016) 22 *European Law Journal* 576.

[31] F Mancini, *Democracy and Constitutionalism in the European Union: Collected Essays* (Hart Publishing, 2000) 39.

administrative powers in the EU and the still poor equipment of EU administrative law to govern them. The under-conceptualisation of the institutional relationships and the generous acceptance of the existing models of administrative governance are the key obstacles to the advancement of the EU administrative identity and the key reasons for its fragmentation. The issue of the institutional balance between EU agencies' powers and the Commission's non-legislative competence remains particularly difficult to unravel theoretically. Pragmatic distinctions, however, suggest that the pluralisation of administrative powers does not necessarily encroach on the institutional balance.

In addition, the silences and the meagre provisions of the Treaties on EU administration did not favour the elaboration of an accomplished administrative law discourse. Monnet's approach to indirect administration has also relieved the urgency of such need. The Lisbon Treaty has, however, recognised this growth of administrative competences at the EU level. By extending the number of rules referring to administration, the Lisbon Treaty has embraced the pillars that govern and make legitimate the decisions of contemporary administrations: independence, transparency and efficiency in decision-making and judicial review of the decisions taken.[32] The Charter of Fundamental Rights has also reflected this model by recognising citizens' rights to good administration and access to documents, as well as the rights to act against EU acts, including administrative decisions. EU administrative law scholarship has focused on this modern system of administration, showing its potential and limits. Beyond the procedural rights discourse, however, no constitutional conceptualisation of the administrative power has strongly emerged. By elaborating on the categories identified in the *Meroni* doctrine, this study aims to contribute to the evolution of EU administrative law in this direction. In my view, the justification of EU administrative powers is a preliminary condition to understand the originality and the problems of the administrative instruments. My innovative reading of the *Meroni* doctrine offers the opportunity to question the foundations of EU administrative powers and to open a broader discussion on EU administrative identity.

The deeper understanding of EU agencies' powers beyond the label of their technical nature and their coherent entrenchment in the democratic values of the EU legal order would enhance the legal protection under EU administrative law and the comprehension of administrative integration led by EU agencies. It is not by chance that some research studies have begun to consider the possible participation of the United Kingdom in EU agencies in a post-Brexit scenario.[33] The UK interest in EU agencies beyond the withdrawal from EU membership attests the strategic importance of EU agencies in administrative cooperation, especially in those network services that would be heavily affected by the UK exit of the internal market. If the role of EU agencies as centres of regulatory cooperation was

[32] See, respectively, Treaty on the Functioning of the European Union (TFEU), Arts 298 and 263.

[33] House of Commons, *EU Agencies and Post Brexit Options*, Briefing Paper no 7957 (2017).

strongly enhanced, the correct understanding of the justification and the framing of EU agencies' powers would be a necessary condition for the wise engagement in meaningful cooperation beyond internal market integration.

This study is conducted as a critical investigation of the existing case law, literature and administrative practice. Openness to interdisciplinary insights helped to disclose the dynamics of allocation of powers in the EU. The political science scholarship on the role of EU agencies and the economic literature on the risks and benefits of independent regulation in internal market integration particularly framed the legal analysis of regulatory mechanisms and institutional arrangements. The research question is addressed through the examination of significant case studies that exemplify the incoherence of the dominant interpretation of the *Meroni* doctrine. The analysis therefore focuses on two different but complementary phenomena: the reinforcement of the EU agencies' powers and the allocation of comparable powers to hybrid administrations, whose legal status is situated in between powerful agencies and independent authorities. The European Aviation Safety Agency (EASA) is taken as an example of the first tendency, whereas the European Supervisory Authorities in the financial markets (ESAs) are identified as the most prominent examples of the second phenomenon. Unlike EU agencies, the ESAs enjoy wider organisational autonomy from the Commission, which is functional to the allocation of stronger powers of adjudication and rule-making. However, the legal constraints on the exercise of such powers do not allow them to be considered fully independent regulators. As in the case of EU agencies, the *Meroni* doctrine still limits their capability to produce sector-specific regulation. The ESAs share with EU agencies the constitutional horizon and they can be considered as heterogeneous bodies operating in the same constitutional space. From the perspective of the powers, the ESAs cannot be permanently disconnected from the diversified model of EU agencies. Powerful agencies such as the EASA and the ESAs, in fact, cover a range of administrative powers that clearly reverse the idea of purely advisory bodies and show the as yet legally hidden regulatory content of their competence. This power-based approach justifies the reference to these bodies under the general label of EU agencies and it is functional to outline the limits to the allocation of regulatory competences to those administrative entities established under EU law. Insofar as the analysis aims to provide a methodology to understand the powers of those heterogeneous bodies labelled as EU agencies, its findings can be extended beyond the examined case studies. In addition, the analysis does refer to and does not ignore other relevant experiences of EU agencies.

To better understand the nature of the model in question, the analysis also compares it with other EU systems of administrative governance which have been developed beyond the black letter provisions of the Treaties. I particularly focus on two different cases that highlight by contrast the peculiar characteristics of EU agencies' governance in the performance of harmonisation and supervisory tasks: the standardisation bodies under the so-called New Approach to technical harmonisation and standardisation in the internal market on the one hand, and the European Central Bank (ECB) under the Single Supervisory Mechanism

(SSM) instituting the Banking Union, on the other. The goal of this comparison is to emphasise the precise nature of EU agencies' administrative discretion and to point out how institutional arrangements affect the nature of regulation.

The analysis proceeds as follows. Chapter 1 critically elaborates on the non-delegation doctrine and the specific limits that its consolidated interpretation under the *Meroni* and *Romano* case law established for EU agencies. The chapter particularly proposes an innovative reading of the *Meroni* doctrine which builds upon the ambiguity of the judgment and those aspects that were not developed in the subsequent legal interpretation. This 'dark side' of the *Meroni* ruling is used to explain some logical continuity with the *ESMA Short Selling* case that has revisited the *Meroni* doctrine and to identify the substantive concerns at the core of the non-delegation doctrine. Yet, the Court of Justice has not firmly settled the problem of the entrenchment of EU agencies' acts in the rule of law and the democratic principle. It failed to identify the nature of administrative powers and to derive clear legal effects from the constitutional status of EU agencies.

Chapter 2 thus focuses on the responsibilities and tasks that are allocated to EU agencies with the aim of understanding the substance of the exercised powers. The chapter illustrates the legal taxonomy of EU agencies' powers and reveals the pragmatic existence of quasi-regulatory powers that structure sector-specific regulation in informal ways. The analysis of the powers of the EASA and the ESAs shows that adjudication functions have significant regulatory impact; the participation in the formal rule-making of the Commission hides the leading position of these agencies; and soft law standardisation creates legally not-binding but pragmatically compelling effects on sector operators and national administrations.

To understand the substantive compatibility of these quasi-regulatory powers with the *Meroni* doctrine, Chapter 3 investigates the nature of such powers. This analysis aims to go beyond the *Meroni* dichotomy between political and technical powers that has generated the paradoxical stretch of the notion of technical powers to cover the growth of administrative tasks with regulatory impact. The nature of EU agencies' governance is investigated from two distinct but complementary standpoints: the identification of a discretionary content of such powers, and the comparison of this institutional model of governance with other models that present similar challenges with regard to internal market harmonisation and sector-specific supervision.

As anticipated, the compatibility of the discretionary content of EU agencies' powers with the *Meroni* doctrine passes through the recognition of the administrative nature of such discretion reconstructed as a different category from political discretion. Policy-making as priority setting is an activity that must be institutionally precluded to EU agencies. Implementation of such policies with some margin of appreciation in the concrete application of legislation is the peculiar task of administration that also characterises EU agencies' action. This constitutive limit to EU agencies' decision-making distinguishes their system of governance from the ECB's supervision of the Banking Union. Although more similarities can be identified in the standardisation functions of EU agencies and the standardisation bodies under the New Approach, the legal personality of EU agencies as public law entities brings significant legal effects related to their participation in the public function. Administrative governance through EU agencies therefore presents distinctive, functional and institutional significance that is relevant for the correct understanding of their constitutional status.

Insofar as EU agencies exercise administrative powers that may cover some degree of administrative discretion, how EU agencies may legitimately participate in the regulatory function depends on the existence of checks-and-balances that entrench the exercise of powers. Chapter 4 analyses the sustainability of EU agencies' powers in light of their accountability and pins down the essential legal tools that prevent the allocation of regulatory tasks to EU agencies from transforming them to leviathan creatures without a strong entrenchment in the democratic principle. The focus is on the capability of EU agencies as public entities with mixed organisational settings to adopt acts that effectively satisfy the fundamental rights related to the exercise of administrative powers in democratic systems. Autonomy and accountability are considered as two sides of the same coin that empower EU agencies to act in a fair and impartial way. Procedural rights to good administration and effective judicial protection emerge as key issues that ensure the compatibility of EU agencies' discretionary powers. In this context, the introduction of an EU administrative law that legislatively fixes the rules of participation and transparency is welcomed as a means to remove the evaluation of the relevance of the competing rights and interests from the administrative availability. In addition, the issues in the institutional structure of EU agencies' action and the institutional environment where they operate are critically examined. The analysis reveals that the complexity of the mechanisms governing accountability fails to provide a clear-cut and coherent system of administration and leaves some fundamental issues of accountability open. The compatibility of administrative discretion with the non-delegation doctrine is not supported by the existence of consolidated mechanisms to control administrative power. This affects the possibility of reaching definitive conclusions on the capability of EU agencies to exercise regulatory powers, but clearly indicates the roadmap leading there.

1

The Non-Delegation Doctrine and the Limits to EU Agencies' Powers

I. INTRODUCTION

IN THE EUROPEAN UNION, the development of internal market integration has boosted the growing importance of administration at the supranational level. From the original model of a Community reserving administration to the Member States, the EU has become a complex legal order where administrative tasks are increasingly allocated to institutions, agencies and bodies of the EU. In addition, these tasks have evolved to include some regulatory content. Yet most of these developments occurred in the silence of the Treaties. EU agencies as administrative structures in particular grew in the absence of significant Treaty provisions. Neither has the factual development of EU administrative action been supported by a general theory about the nature, the reach and the limits of EU executive powers. However, structural principles elaborated by the Court of Justice of the European Union (CJEU) on the grounds of the system of the Treaties have directed the patchy growth of agencies' powers. Those structural principles refer to the articulation of the executive power in the EU and its checks-and-balances in the institutional framework of the Treaties.[1]

60 years ago, the CJEU developed the so-called *Meroni* doctrine concerning the non-delegation of regulatory powers to agencies in an attempt to answer the key question of the compatibility of agencies' action with the law emerging from the Treaties. Yet the sectional character of the European Coal and Steel Community (ECSC) did prevent the judicial elaboration of an organic theory of administrative power in the same way as states. Although different solutions were legitimate beyond the state, this doctrine could only aim to contain the expansion of supranational administrative agencies and bodies in the absence of clear standards for the legality of their action. After the establishment of the European Community and the development of a general legal order,

[1] See T Tridimas, *The General Principles of EU Law*, 2nd edn (Oxford University Press. 2006) 3–4, who includes these principles amongst the 'systemic principles which underlie the constitutional structure of the Community and define the Community legal edifice'; see also G Falcon, 'Qualche sottolineatura in tema di principi generali del diritto dell'Unione europea' (2017) 27 *Rivista Italiana di Diritto Pubblico Comunitario* 364, 367–69.

no theoretical elaboration could, however, govern the supranational expansion of administrative bodies and the *Meroni* doctrine settled as the paradigm for the sustainability of agencies' powers under the system of the Treaties. This has structurally affected the growth of EU administration as a mature administrative system, but has not stopped the proliferation of administrative tasks at the EU level nor the frequent waves of *agencification*, endowing EU agencies with stronger powers. As Dehousse observed, 'quantitatively and qualitatively, the mushrooming of specialized European agencies is one of the most interesting developments in the functioning of the EU bureaucracy in the post-Maastricht years'.[2] The result is a crippled system of EU administrative law, where legal protection is not built on a substantive idea of the powers, and administrative reality may not perfectly fit within the legal framework designed by the non-delegation doctrine.

The legal difficulty to reconcile the constitutional principle conveyed in this doctrine and the factual reality of the allocation of further tasks and considerable responsibilities to EU agencies is precisely due to the weakness of the EU administrative law discourse on the nature of administrative powers. As legal scholarship has started to point out, so far EU administrative law has not thoroughly framed the key elements of administrative power within the rule of law and the democratic principle, namely, discretion and accountability.[3] This failure has affected the effective understanding of administrative power as a law-based power within the existing hierarchy of the sources of law and blended it into a blurred system of administration. Discretion has been reserved to institutional policy-making, legally covered by the Treaties and the supposedly pure executive nature of administrative tasks has relieved the accountability demand. Administration has been considered a technical task, neutral to the balance of interests. Delegation has therefore developed as a methodology aimed at responding to complex technical issues with specialised skills.

I contest the validity of this consolidated narrative and I argue that EU agencies' powers also need to be understood as a phenomenon of administrative discretion beyond the dichotomy between political and technical powers. Although I recognise the special nature of the administrative discourse in the EU in comparison to the state model, I claim that the consolidation of a specific legal interpretation has favoured the restrictive interpretation of administrative tasks in the EU. This chapter particularly demonstrates that the *Meroni* doctrine contained the seeds for the development of a theory of administrative power at the EU level and an alternative reading of its constitutional principles may be possible. The chapter outlines how this doctrine has so far constrained the competence of EU agencies

[2] R Dehousse, 'Misfits: EU Law and the Transformation of European Governance' in C Joerges and R Dehousse (eds), *Good Governance in Europe's Integrated Market* (Oxford University Press, 2002) 207, 216.

[3] See E Chiti, 'Is EU Administrative Law Failing in Some of Its Crucial Tasks?' (2016) 22 *European Law Journal* 576, 588.

and proposes a different approach to the investigation of the nature, the reach and the limits of EU agencies' powers.

After the definition of the pillars of the non-delegation doctrine (section II), the chapter focuses on the constitutional relevance of the *Meroni* doctrine for EU agencies' action (section III). When portraying the key issues of the *Meroni* doctrine, the analysis shows that the (mis)construction of the ruling has contributed to freezing the potential development of administrative regulation. Emphasising the existence of an unexplored 'dark side' of the *Meroni* doctrine, section IV highlights the existence of margins of compatibility between *Meroni* and administrative action with regulatory impact. The most recent revision of the *Meroni* doctrine in the *ESMA Short Selling* case is thus analysed with a view to providing evidence of the consistency of the proposed argument (section V). By setting the conditions for the allocation of some regulatory powers to EU agencies, the *ESMA Short Selling* case has started to pave the way towards administrative regulation. The revisited *Meroni* doctrine can no longer escape the fundamental question of administrative law; that is, how administrative powers can be legitimately exercised according to the democratic principle and the rule of law. The chapter therefore focuses on the conferral of such powers to EU agencies by analysing how to anchor them to the framework of the Treaties and to position their acts in the hierarchy of the sources of law (section VI). Against this backdrop, the chapter identifies the legal variables that may entrench EU agencies' powers and assesses their sustainability in the light of the *Meroni* doctrine: the nature of the exercised powers and their accountability framework (section VII).

II. PILLARS OF THE NON-DELEGATION DOCTRINE IN THE EU

Sovereignty finds a fundamental qualification in the allocation of public powers. How these powers are distributed and exercised affects the nature of sovereignty itself. In the EU, the principle of conferral characterises the nature of European sovereignty and the limits of the European legal order. The Treaties recognise that the Member States have renounced some national sovereignty in favour of EU institutions in order to pursue common values and shared objectives of integration aimed at peace, security and prosperity in the European continent.[4] This has happened according to the democratic rule expressed both in Article 10(2) of the Treaty on European Union (TEU), which founds the EU on representative democracy expressed through different modalities by the European Parliament, the Council and the European Council, and in Article 11 TEU, which promotes public participation as an essential component of democracy. On these grounds, the Treaties limit the reach, the content and the procedures of EU institutions' powers. Articles 5(2) and 13(2) of the TEU lay down these constitutional

[4] Article 3 TEU.

limitations to the exercise of powers, by setting the limits of competence, respectively, with regard to the Member States and to other institutions.

The principle of conferral emerges as the rule of thumb holding that EU institutions may legally exercise only expressly attributed powers.[5] In addition, those articles clarify the effects of the principle of conferral both vertically with regard to the competence of Member States and horizontally with regard to the exercise of the conferred competence to EU institutions. On the one hand, Article 5(2) TEU holds that competences not conferred upon the Union in the Treaties remain in the competence of the Member States. On the other hand, in the horizontal relations between EU institutions 'mutual sincere cooperation' should guide the exercise of their conferred powers. The case law of the CJEU has qualified the nature of inter-institutional cooperation at the EU level in the principle of institutional balance, according to which 'each institution must exercise its powers with due regard for the powers of other institutions'.[6] Recent case law has also clarified that the powers conferred by the Treaties on each institution also set the limits to sincere cooperation, so that 'the obligation resulting from Article 13(2) TEU is therefore not such as to change those powers'.[7]

Aiming to avoid any confusion and overlap of powers, the principle of conferral outlines a justiciable rule on the distribution of powers that has been said to recall the Montesquieu's fundamental principle of separation of powers. Although the analogy is not misplaced, a structural difference distinguishes these principles. The EU has no organic distinction between public powers, as they appear at state level. Yet, the principle of conferral outlines an ultra vires doctrine of legality, according to which every EU institution cannot act beyond the powers conferred in the Treaties and the exercise of the related functions is only possible according to the rules as envisaged in the Treaties. The principle of institutional balance develops the principle of separation of powers through this ultra vires doctrine.[8]

This means that in the EU, the separation of powers cannot be structured on the organisation of public powers, but on the distinction of the public functions.[9]

[5] It should be added that to some extent a doctrine of implied powers is also accepted in the framework of the Treaties. According to Article 352 TFEU, if action by the Union in the internal market should prove necessary to attain a Treaties' objective and the Treaties have not provided the necessary powers, the unanimity of the Council, on a proposal from the Commission and after obtaining the consent of the European Parliament, shall adopt the appropriate measures.

[6] C-70/88 *European Parliament v Council (Chernobyl)* [1991] ECR I-04529, para 22; C-403/05 *European Parliament v Commission* [2007] ECR I-09045, para 49; C-133/06 *European Parliament v Council* [2008] ECR I-03189, para 57; C-409/13 *Council v Commission (MFA)* [2015] ECLI:EU:C:2015:217, para 64; C-73/14 *Council v Commission (ITLOS)* ECLI:EU:C:2015:663, para 61; C-660/13 *Council v Commission (Swiss Memorandum of Understanding)* ECLI:EU:C:2016:616, para 32.

[7] C-48/14 *Parliament v Council* ECLI:EU:C:2015:91, paras 57–58; C-73/14 *ITLOS* (n 6) para 84.

[8] See J-P Jacqué, 'The Principle of Institutional Balance' (2004) 41 *Common Market Law Review* 383, 384; G Conway, 'Recovering a Separation of Powers in the European Union' (2011) 17 *European Law Journal* 304, 319.

[9] See K Lenaerts, 'Some Reflections on the Separation of Powers in the European Community' (1991) *Common Market Law Review* 11, 13–14, who considered that 'whereas the legislative powers are performed almost entirely by the Community organs themselves … the executive and judicial

This functional approach sets the bottom rule for an effective separation of powers. As Advocate General Trstenjak observed in the Opinion in *Audiolux*, institutional balance concerns 'a principle of separation of functions, whereby the Community's functions are intended to be exercised by the organs which are best placed to perform them under the Treaties'.[10] According to Lenaerts and Verhoeven, the *ratio* of the institutional balance can therefore be interpreted against Montesquieu's paradigm only if it is considered 'as the necessary institutional frame within which different interests can discuss with each other in order to achieve solutions that are acceptable to all and do not unduly abridge the liberties of anyone'.[11]

In addition, if the Montesquieu principle of separation of powers aimed to protect individuals against the abuse of public powers, the reach of institutional balance is less clear. This is evident when considering that the CJEU has been swinging between the imperative of individual protection and the mere maintenance of the distribution of powers between the institutions, with no individual actionability.[12] After the *Chernobyl* case, it appeared that institutional balance might be interpreted as a justiciable principle which could be invoked by private parties. Conversely, in the 1990s, the CJEU limited the reach of the principle to the maintenance of the distinction of competence between the institutions.[13] In fact, the CJEU has used the principle to support its (teleological) interpretation of the Treaties' rules and not as an autonomous ground of review.[14] It mainly helps to contextualise the settlement of conflicts when issues of competence arise.

Delegation of powers does not necessarily represent a break with the established framework of sovereign powers. In principle, it introduces 'a change in the constitutionally established allocation of powers', but that change may not necessarily be in contrast to 'the constitutionally established order in the distribution of competences'.[15] Delegation can be a mode of exercise of the Treaties' conferred powers, a functional deviation aimed to deal more effectively with the concrete implementation of policies. In the silence of the Treaties, the legal theory of delegation of powers in EU law has been significantly based on the judicial interpretation of the constitutional framework on the distribution of powers.

functions are performed to the larger extent by the Member States acting on behalf of Community interests'; G Guillermin, 'Le principe de l'équilibre institutionnel dans la jurisprudence de la Cour de justice des Communautés européennes' (1992) 119 *Journal de droit international* 319, 344, who also considered that the separation of powers is a politico-philosophical principle, whereas the institutional balance is the product of a specific polity. See also M Chamon, 'The Institutional Balance, an Ill-Fated Principle of EU Law?' (2015) *European Public Law* 371, 374–75.

[10] C-101/08 *Audiolux and others* [2009] ECR I-9823, Opinion of Advocate General Trstenjak, para 104.

[11] K Lenaerts and A Verhoeven, 'Institutional Balance as a Guarantee for Democracy in EU Governance' in C Joerges and R Dehousse (eds), *Good Governance in Europe's Integrated Market* (Oxford University Press, 2002) 35, 42–43.

[12] Jacqué, 'The Principle of Institutional Balance' (n 8) 384–85.

[13] C-282/90 *Vreugdenhil BV v Commission* [1992] ECR I-1937, paras 20–22.

[14] See Chamon, 'The Institutional Balance, an Ill-Fated Principle of EU Law?' (n 9) 386.

[15] HCH Hofmann, GC Rowe and AH Türk, *Administrative Law and Policy of the European Union* (Oxford University Press, 2011) 223.

In order to be lawful, delegation needs to comply with the principle of conferral and not to alter its vertical and horizontal dimensions. This means that delegation needs to be accompanied by adequate guarantees that maintain the responsibility on the delegating institution and ensure the balance of powers according to the framework of the Treaties. Delegation cannot become a means to abdicate the competence allocated with the Treaties nor to seize further competences not envisaged in the Treaties from Member States or from other EU institutions.

On these grounds, the CJEU has developed the so-called non-delegation doctrine as a constitutional principle aimed at keeping any delegation of powers within the constitutional boundaries set in the Treaties. The case law of the CJEU characterises the non-delegation doctrine as a two-faced theory. On the one hand, in order not to seize undue powers, secondary law adopted by the competent EU institutions cannot amend or change the decision-making procedures established in the Treaties. On the other hand, in order not to abdicate their mandate, the conferred EU institutions should not transfer their competence on policy choices to other entities. The following sub-sections will analyse these two pillars of non-delegation.

A. Non-Delegation as Non-Interference with Powers

The decision-making rules are set out in the Treaties. Any deviation from these rules not explicitly authorised in the Treaties themselves, but only provided by secondary law, would be an undue appropriation of legislative power beyond the limits of the Treaties' constitution-like framework.[16] Changes would impair the competence of the institutions authorised by the Treaties to take particular decisions and the balance of powers would therefore be affected. Deviation from the Treaties' procedural rules would affect the exercise of any EU institutions' own powers with due regard for the powers of other institutions. In other words, any undue change by an institution in procedural aspects leads to substantive deprivation of competence of another institution.

The choice of the legal basis for the adoption of measures is therefore a key issue for the legal assessment of the actual compliance with the principle of institutional balance.[17] The case law is particularly meaningful as the CJEU has consistently held that the choice of the legal basis for a measure must be based on 'objective factors which are amenable to judicial review' and which 'include in particular

[16] 68/86 *United Kingdom v Council* [1988] ECR 855, para 24; C-316/91 *Parliament v Council* [1994] ECR I-625, para 14; C-327/91 *France v Commission* [1994] ECR I-3641, para 36; C-426/93 *Germany v Council* [1995] ECR I-3723, para 21; C-363/14 *European Parliament v Council (Europol)* ECLI:EU:C:2015:579, para 43; C-133/06 *European Parliament v Council (Refugee Status)* EU:C:2008:257, paras 54–56; C-317/13 and C-679/13 *Parliament v Council* EU:C:2015:223, paras 42–43; C-540/13 *European Parliament v Council* EU:C:2015:224, paras 32–33; C-660/13 *Swiss Memorandum of Understanding* (n 6) para 43.

[17] See Jacqué, 'The Principle of Institutional Balance' (n 8) 386.

the aim and content of the measure'.[18] The resort to a dual legal basis is possible 'where an institution's power is based on two provisions of the Treaty',[19] but not where 'the use of both provisions as a joint legal basis would divest the … procedure of its very substance'.[20]

In addition, the CJEU has consistently affirmed that mere institutional practice on the choice of the legal basis cannot derogate the rules set out in the Treaties and 'cannot therefore create a precedent binding on Community institutions with regard to the correct legal basis'.[21] More generally, the case law has consistently held that institutional practice is not a suitable means to change the institutional balance derived from the Treaties. The reason is that practice 'cannot deprive the other institutions of a prerogative granted to them by the Treaties themselves'.[22] Therefore, soft law measures should also comply with the principle of conferral and their adoption requires to take into account 'the division of powers and the institutional balance established by the Treaty'.[23]

Alongside the choice of the legal basis, the infringement of essential procedural requirements also leads to disruptions in the institutional balance. The decision-making rules set out in the Treaties 'are not at the disposal of the Member States or of the institutions themselves'.[24] 'The Treaty alone may … empower an institution to amend a decision-making procedure established by the Treaty',[25] therefore secondary legislation cannot derogate from the Treaties. This is particularly relevant when the infringement from an institution encroaches the prerogatives of other EU institutions. The failure to comply with procedural rules breaches the principle of sincere cooperation among institutions and affects the competence of individual institutions. On these grounds, the CJEU held that when subjecting the implementing powers of the Commission to the supervision of a committee composed of representatives of the Member States, the comitology procedure was compatible with the principle of institutional balance, because it was aimed 'to ensure permanent consultation in order to guide the Commission in the exercise of the powers conferred on it by the Council and to enable the latter to substitute its own action for that of the Commission', and not 'to take a decision in place of the Commission or the Council'.[26]

[18] 45/86 *Commission v Council* [1987] ECR 1493, para 11; C-70/88 *Chernobyl* (n 6) para 9; C-300/89 *Commission v Council (Titanium Dioxide)* [1991] ECR I-2867, para 10; C-338/01 *Commission v Council* [2004] ECR I-4829, para 54; C-176/03 *Commission v Council* [2005] ECR I-7879, para 45; C-94/03 *Commission v Council* [2006] ECR I-1, para 34; C-155/07 *European Parliament v Council* [2008] ECR I-8103, para 34; C-130/10 *European Parliament v Council* [2012] ECLI:EU:C:2012:472, para 42.

[19] 165/87 *Commission v Council* [1988] ECR 5545, para 11.

[20] C-300/89 *Titanium Dioxide* (n 18) para 18.

[21] 68/86 *United Kingdom v Council* (n 16) para 24; C-426/93 *Germany v Council* (n 16) para 21; C-271/94 *European Parliament v Council* [1996] ECR I-1689, para 24; C-84/94 *United Kingdom v Council* [1996] ECR I-5755, para 19; C-133/06 *European Parliament v Council* (n 6) para 60.

[22] 149/85 *Roger Wybot v Edgar Faure* [1986] ECR 2391, para 23; 68/86 *United Kingdom v Council* (n 16) para 24; C-426/93 *Germany v Council* (n 16) para 21; C-133/06 *Refugee Status* (n 16) para 60.

[23] C-233/02 *France v Commission* [2004] ECR I-2759, para 40.

[24] 68/86 *United Kingdom v Council* (n 16) para 38.

[25] C-133/06 *Refugee Status* (n 16) para 55.

[26] C-25/70 *Einfuhr- und Vorratsstelle für Getreide und Futtermittel v Köster* [1970] ECR 1161, para 9.

On the basis of the principle of the institutional balance, the CJEU has also pointed out that the power of the Commission to withdraw legislative proposals 'ha[s] to be supported by cogent evidence or arguments' insofar as 'such a decision prevents the Parliament and the Council from exercising, as they would have indeed, their legislative functions under Articles 14(1) TEU and 16(1) TEU'.[27] The Court also recognised the substantive prerogative of the Parliament to consultation under the EEC Treaty as 'an essential factor in the institutional balance intended by the Treaty' that 'reflects at the Community level the fundamental democratic principle that people should take part in the exercise of power through the intermediary of a representative assembly'.[28] Similarly, the prerogatives of the European Parliament in the co-decision procedure have been recognised against the implementing powers of the Council under Article 202 of the EC Treaty.[29]

In order to maintain the institutional balance, the CJEU has also gone beyond the black letter provisions of the Treaties and recognised standing rights to the European Parliament in the action for annulment only for the protection of its own prerogatives, as long as no effective legal remedies were available to ensure that the parliamentary prerogatives were defended.[30] Because of the principle of institutional balance, therefore, the formal rules of the Treaties needed to be interpretatively changed in order to preserve their substance. Even if this does not mean that the CJEU can act in favour of a particular institution, the dynamic character of the principle is exposed to the changes in the conceptions of the Treaties.[31]

In the current framework of the Treaties, the European Parliament and the Council have equal powers under the ordinary legislative procedure. As legal scholarship has pointed out, this may raise questions about the legal limits of resorting to international agreements among the Member States outside the EU framework, as they may encroach the prerogatives of the Parliament under the ordinary legislative procedure.[32] So far, the CJEU has not brought up the institutional balance as a ground for reviewing the exercise of such intergovernmental

[27] C-409/13 *MFA* (n 6) paras 76–77.

[28] 138/79 *SA Roquette Frères v Council* [1980] ECR 3333, para 33 and 139/79 *Maizena v Council (Isoglucose)* [1980] ECR 3393, para 34; C-65/93 *European Parliament v Council* [1995] ECR I-00643, paras 21–23. See also C-317/13 and C-679/13 *European Parliament v Council* EU:C:2015:223, para 63; C-540/13 *European Parliament v Council* EU:C:2015:224, para 53; C-363/14 *Europol* (n 16) para 82.

[29] C-133/06 *Refugee Status* (n 16) paras 58–59.

[30] C-70/88 *European Parliament v Council (Chernobyl)* [1990] ECR I-02041, para 20. According to the Court (para 15), this interpretation does not contradict its previous decision in 302/87 *European Parliament v Council (Comitology)* [1988] ECR 5615, because in that case other legal remedies could ensure the prerogatives of the Parliament. In the 1990 *Chernobyl* case, the Court realised that 'the various legal remedies provided for both in the Euratom Treaty and in the EEC Treaty, however effective and diverse they may be, may prove to be ineffective or uncertain' (para 16).

[31] See Lenaerts and Verhoeven, 'Institutional Balance as a Guarantee for Democracy in EU Governance' (n 11) 38–39 and 46.

[32] P Craig, 'The Stability, Coordination and Governance Treaty: Principle, Politics and Pragmatism' (2012) 37 *European Law Review* 231, 241–45; F Fabbrini, 'A Principle in Need of Renewal? The Euro-Crisis and the Principle of Institutional Balance' (2016) 50 *Cahiers de Droit Européen* 285, 298.

powers. In *Pringle*, the CJEU recognised that the European Stability Mechanism (ESM) did not infringe the provisions of EU law on the competence of EU institutions, but it emphasised that nonetheless it should 'not alter the essential character of the powers conferred on those institutions by the EU and FEU Treaties'.[33] As Craig noted, if a reference to the institutional balance is embedded in the CJEU's statement, it is still difficult to give a relevant interpretation to the notion of 'essential character of the powers'.[34] Similarly, the reach and the justiciability of the institutional balance also seem to be uncertain with regard to the powers of EU agencies. In the *ESMA Short Selling* case, when asked to distinguish between the powers of the Commission under Article 291 of the Treaty on the Functioning of the European Union (TFEU) and the competence of the European Securities and Markets Authority (ESMA), the CJEU did not even refer to this principle.[35] According to Chamon, this is further proof of the fact that the principle of institutional balance is not an actionable principle of EU law.[36]

B. Non-Delegation as Limits on Delegation

As long as political decisions fall within the responsibility of the conferred EU institutions, delegation can concern only implementing measures that do not affect policy choices. In the words of the CJEU in *Köster*, 'the basic elements of the matter' must be reserved to the appraisal of the delegating authority in the act authorising the delegation of powers, in accordance with the relevant Treaty rules on the procedure for their adoption.[37] This would preserve the institutional balance, as the legislator has no right to renounce its power to legislate.[38]

When covering the delegated acts of the European Commission, this approach is confirmed by Article 290(1) TFEU, which holds that 'the essential elements of an area shall be reserved for the legislative act and accordingly shall not be the subject of a delegation of power'. The principle of *Köster*, however, is broader as it also reasonably applies to delegation of powers contained in non-legislative acts.[39]

[33] C-370/12 *Thomas Pringle v Government of Ireland, Ireland and the Attorney General* ECLI:EU:C:2012:756, para 162.

[34] See P Craig, '"Pringle" and Use of EU Institutions Outside the EU Legal Framework: Foundations, Procedure and Substance' (2013) 9 *European Constitutional Law Review* 263, 277–81.

[35] Chamon, 'The Institutional Balance, an Ill-Fated Principle of EU Law?' (n 9) 389–90.

[36] M Chamon, 'The Empowerment of Agencies under the Meroni Doctrine and Article 114 TFEU: Comment on United Kingdom v. Parliament and Council (Short Selling) and the Proposed Single Resolution Mechanism' (2014) *European Law Review* 380, 397.

[37] C-25/70 *Köster* (n 26) para 6. See also C-46/86 *Romkes* [1987] ECR 2671, para 16; C-417/93 *European Parliament v Council* [1995] ECR 1-1185, para 30.

[38] J-P Jacqué, 'The Evolution of the Approach to Executive Rulemaking in the EU' in C F Bergström and D Ritleng (eds), *Rulemaking by the European Commission* (Oxford University Press, 2016) 21, 31.

[39] See D Ritleng, 'The Reserved Domain of the Legislature: The Notion of "Essential Elements of an Area"' in C F Bergström and D Ritleng (eds), *Rulemaking by the European Commission* (Oxford University Press, 2016) 133, 147.

As the Court has lately clarified, the *Köster* 'classification must be reserved for provisions which are intended to give concrete shape to the fundamental guidelines of Community policy'.[40] However, in that case the Court considered the system of penalties in the aid scheme introduced by the Commission on delegation by the Council as a non-essential element, because it was designed to ensure the implementation of the fundamental guidelines of Community policy.[41] By and large, the case law has been swinging between a generous identification of these essential elements, leaving to the legislative branch the determination of what might be essential, and a more restrictive approach aimed at strictly reviewing the validity of the enabling provisions.[42]

On the one hand, the CJEU admits broader justifications of the implementing powers by restraining its review of the conditions for delegation, whereas in the second scenario it imposes more rigorous requirements on delegation. It therefore came about that in competition law, the rules laying down the hearing procedure, 'however important they may be', were considered to be legitimately adopted by the Commission since the Council had recognised the right to be heard as a principle in Regulation 17/62/EEC;[43] and that the inclusion of genetically modified micro-organisms (GMMOs) in the measures implementing Regulation 2092/91/EEC establishing a framework of Community rules on production, labelling and inspection for the protection of organic farming did not exceed the limits of delegation, because the aim of the enabling regulation was not to lay down new rules permitting the use of GMMOs in organic farming.[44] At the same time, the particular policy field allowed more extensive interpretation of the reach of the implementing powers of the Commission: the Common Agricultural Policy particularly allowed for wide interpretation of these powers,[45] placing their limits directly in the 'basic general objectives of the organization of the market' and not exclusively 'the literal meaning of the enabling word'.[46]

On the other hand, in *Central-Import Münster*, the CJEU held that in order to be valid, an enabling provision 'must be sufficiently specific—that is to say, the Council must clearly specify the bounds of the power conferred on the Commission':[47]

> Those provisions thus determine the situations in which protective measures may be taken, the criteria for assessing whether such a situation exists, the kind of measures to

[40] C-240/90 *Germany v Commission* [1992] ECR I-05383, para 37.
[41] Ibid.
[42] See Hofmann, Rowe and Türk, *Administrative Law and Policy of the European Union* (n 15) 227–30.
[43] 41/69 *Chemiefarma v Commission* [1970] ECR 661, para 65.
[44] C-156/93 *European Parliament v Commission* [1995] ECR I-02019, paras 23–26.
[45] 22/88 *Vreugdenhil and others v Minister van Landbouw en Visserij* [1989] ECR 2049, paras 16–17.
[46] 23/75 *Rey Soda v Cassa Conguaglio Zucchero* [1975] ECR 1279, para 14.
[47] C-291/86 *Central-Import Münster GmbH & Co KG v Hauptzollamt Münster* [1988] ECR 3679, para 13.

> be adopted and the period of their validity. The power conferred on the Commission is delimited by those factors in a sufficiently specific manner.[48]

This approach has been upheld in *Alliance for Natural Health*, where the CJEU specified that if the Community legislature wishes to delegate its power to modify the list of vitamins and minerals which can be used in food supplements as set out in Annex I of Directive 2002/46/EC:

> it must ensure that that power is clearly defined and that the exercise of the power is subject to strict review in the light of objective criteria (see, to that effect, Case 9/56 Meroni v High Authority [1958] ECR 133, at p. 152) because otherwise it may confer on the delegate a discretion which, in the case of legislation concerning the functioning of the internal market in goods, would be capable of impeding, excessively and without transparency, the free movement of the goods in question.[49]

After the Lisbon Treaty, the Court has fully embraced this stricter interpretation of the scope of delegation, so that today the identification of the inalienable political choices cannot be left only to the political appreciation, but should be based on 'objective factors amenable to judicial review' and on 'the characteristics and particular features of the field concerned'.[50] In these later judgments, the protection of fundamental rights has been clearly included under the shelter of the essential elements. The *Schengen Borders Code* case recognised that the provisions on conferring powers of public authority on border guards may interfere with the fundamental rights of the persons concerned 'to such an extent that the involvement of the European Union legislature is required'.[51] Similarly, the *Europol* case recognised the delegation to this Agency of the power to amend the list of police and judicial cooperation with third countries, as long as these relations comply with the objectives and take place in the legal framework that were defined by the EU legislature.[52] Particularly, the transmission of personal data must remain subject to an authorisation agreement to be adopted by the Council, as it 'may interfere with the fundamental rights of the persons concerned, and some of those interferences may be so serious that intervention by the EU legislature becomes necessary'.[53] The Court admitted that when performing the tasks conferred by secondary law, some discretion involving 'certain compromises with technical and political dimensions' may be allocated to EU agencies.[54] Political choices that cannot be delegated therefore covered the interference with the exercise of fundamental rights (ie, data protection) and not the sensitive establishment of cooperative relations with third countries.

[48] Ibid para 15.
[49] C-154/04 and C-155/04 *Alliance for Natural Health* [2005] ECR I-6451, para 90.
[50] See also C-355/10 *European Parliament v Council (Schengen Borders Code)* EU:C:2012:516, paras 64–68; C-363/14 *Europol* (n 16) para 47.
[51] C-355/10 *Schengen Borders Code* (n 50) para 77.
[52] C-363/14 *Europol* (n 16) para 50.
[53] Ibid paras 53–57.
[54] Ibid para 51.

As Ritleng has pointed out,[55] this case law is not in conflict with the earlier judgment in *Germany v Commission*, where the CJEU accepted that the EU executive (the Commission) and not the EU legislative (the Council) had the power to impose (administrative) penalties on traders.[56] According to Ritleng, the choice of the legal basis for the limitation of fundamental rights depends on the degree of the interference. The system of penalties in the Commission's aid scheme could be lawfully delegated, because it did not affect to a serious extent the protection of fundamental rights. The restriction of fundamental rights can thus either be an essential element to be established by the EU legislature, or a simple measure implementing the principles established in the basic regulations.[57] The case roughly sketches the distinction between the administrative activity of policy-implementation and the legislative activity. Ritleng correctly pointed out that 'the threshold beyond which the interference with fundamental rights will be a matter for the legislature may only be determined on a case-by-case basis'.[58] This approach also confirms that the content and the reach of these essential rules cannot be identified in the abstract, but they need to be concretely spotted in every single policy-making process and legislative act. This confers a certain degree of flexibility in the assessment of the reach of the non-delegation principle. Broadly speaking, the reserved political choices will depend on the legal basis of the act concerned and the essential elements will cover both legal and factual aspects of the regulated matter.[59] This broad approach implies a residual definition of the reach of delegation and leaves to the practice the concrete identification of what can be lawfully delegated.

III. THE *MERONI* DOCTRINE

The so-called *Meroni* doctrine represents a specific application of the non-delegation principle to agencies' tasks and responsibilities. It concerns whether EU institutions can delegate powers to agencies and, if so, to what extent such delegation is feasible. The doctrine has been developing in two distinct rulings of the CJEU: *Meroni* and *Romano*.[60] Although held in very different stages of growth of the EU legal order, these judgments have elaborated the constitutional rule about the delegation of powers to agencies, which still represent a strong legacy.

The *Meroni* case questioned the validity of Decision 14/55 of the High Authority establishing a financial arrangement for ensuring a regular supply of ferrous

[55] Ritleng, 'The Reserved Domain of the Legislature' (n 39) 153.
[56] C-240/90 *Germany v Commission* (n 40).
[57] Ibid para 39.
[58] Ritleng, 'The Reserved Domain of the Legislature' (n 39) 154.
[59] See ibid 149 and 154.
[60] 9/56 and 10/56 *Meroni & Co, Industrie Metallurgiche, SAS v High Authority of the European Coal and Steel Community* [1958] ECR 53; C-98/80 *Romano* [1981] ECR 1241.

scrap for the common market. The applicant, Meroni company, challenged *inter alia* that this general decision delegated powers for the financial operation of the ferrous scrap regime to two cooperative undertakings established under Belgian commercial law: the Joint Bureau of Ferrous Scrap Consumers and the Imported Ferrous Scrap Equalization Fund, better known under the label of Brussels agencies. According to Meroni, these bodies were ill-qualified to adopt compulsory equalization arrangements on the ground of the delegation from the High Authority, which allowed the Fund to fix the rate of contributions and the accounting periods and the Joint Bureau to propose to the Fund the essential data for calculating the rate of contributions, namely, the tonnage of ferrous scrap to be imported, the maximum import purchase price and the equalisation price.

The *Romano* case questioned the validity of Decision 101/75 of the Administrative Commission on Social Security for Migrant Workers, establishing *inter alia* the rate of currency conversion to be applied by national authorities to social security schemes of employed persons and their families moving within the Community, on the basis of a competence delegated by the Council in article 107 of Regulation 574/72/EEC. As Romano was severely penalised by the administrative rate in the calculation of his invalidity pension in comparison to the market rate,[61] he advocated that the application of that rate was an illegal transfer of legislative powers from the Council to the Agency established by article 80 of Council Regulation 1408/71/EEC.

The legal doctrine has correctly underlined that these judgments refer to different types of delegation with regard to both the delegating authorities and the delegated agencies.[62] In *Meroni*, the High Authority under the European Coal and Steel Community (ECSC) Treaty delegated its powers to bodies of a private law nature, whereas in *Romano* the Council delegated its own powers to an administrative body established under EEC secondary law. In addition, the grounds of invalidity of the delegation were different: in *Meroni* the problem was the delegation of the High Authority's powers to bodies outside the ECSC Treaty, whereas in *Romano* it was the delegation of powers to a body other than that provided by the EEC Treaty, that is the Commission, whose prerogatives therefore were prejudiced. Nevertheless, the issue at stake was actually the same: the discretionary nature of the delegated power affected the Treaty-conferred responsibilities of the delegating authorities and impacted on the placement of the delegated agencies within the functioning of the EU legal order. This is the reason why, in the literature, these rulings have been considered as a unique mainstreaming doctrine.[63]

[61] Romano particularly contended that in the proportionate reduction of his Belgian invalidity pension by the amount of the pension received under Italian law, 'whatever exchange rate had to be applied for conversion, the amount of provisional benefit which was recovered might never exceed the amount of arrears of pension due under the foreign scheme in respect to the period in which the benefits overlapped' in accordance with art 7 of Regulation 574/72/EEC (C-98/80 *Romano* (n 60) para 9).

[62] M Chamon, 'EU Agencies Between Meroni and Romano or the Devil and the Deep Blue Sea' (2011) 48 *Common Market Law Review* 1055, 1060–61, 1063.

[63] See D Geradin, 'The Development of European Regulatory Agencies: What the EU Should Learn from the American Experience' (2004) 11 *Columbia Journal of European Law* 1, 10; A von Bogdandy,

Generally speaking, the *Meroni* doctrine holds that only 'clearly defined executive powers' can be delegated from the EU institutions to agencies and their use must be entirely subject to accountability mechanisms; namely, the supervision of the delegating institution and judicial review.[64] In doing this, *Meroni* pointed to the key elements that must anchor administrative powers to the rule of law and the democratic principle: discretion and accountability. It thus set down the necessary principles and conditions under which the delegation of powers could be lawful.[65]

The requirements for the existence of a delegated power were laid down. The delegation of powers must be explicit,[66] so as to ensure legal certainty. It must be in line with the principle of conferred competences: the delegation must be within the limits of the powers that the delegating authority retains under the Treaties. Tridimas has emphasised the importance of proportionality of delegation as a further condition for its lawfulness.[67] According to *Meroni*, in fact, in light of Article 53 of the ECSC Treaty, delegation should also be recognised by the delegating authority as necessary for the accomplishment of its tasks.[68]

Meroni also sketched the conditions for the accountability of such delegated power.[69] The exercise of the delegated tasks by the agency will then be performed under the same conditions under which the delegating authority would have performed them directly. This means that the execution of the delegated tasks will be subject to the same legal guarantees as applied by the delegating authority as a necessary condition for its legitimacy. More specifically, the agency should be subject to the duty to state reasons for its decisions and to refer to any opinions which were required to be obtained; the duty to publish annually a general report on its activities and its administrative expenses; the duty to publish such

F Arndt and J Bast, 'Legal Instruments in European Union Law and their Reform: A Systematic Approach on an Empirical Basis' (2004) 23 *Yearbook of European Law* 91, 132; S Griller and A Orator, 'Everything Under Control? The "Way Forward" for European Agencies in the Footsteps of the *Meroni* Doctrine' (2010) 35 *European Law Review* 3, 18; R Schütze, '"Delegated" Legislation in the (New) European Union: A Constitutional Analysis' (2011) 74 *Modern Law Review* 661, 674.

64 10/56 *Meroni v High Authority* (n 60) 173.

65 9/56 *Meroni v High Authority* (n 60) 151–52; 10/56 *Meroni v High Authority* (n 60) 171–73.

66 See also C-154/04 and C-155/04 *Alliance for Natural Health* (n 49) para 90; C-301/02P *Tralli v ECB* [2005] ECR I-4071, paras 42–52; T-311/06 *FMC Chemical SPRL v European Food Safety Agency (EFSA)* [2008] ECR II-88, para 66, where the General Court rejected the argument that the Commission had delegated to EFSA its powers to adopt decisions having binding effects on third parties on the grounds that 'powers cannot be presumed to have been delegated and that, even when empowered to delegate its powers, the delegating authority must take an express decision to that effect'.

67 T Tridimas, 'Financial Supervision and Agency Power: Reflections on ESMA' in N Nic Shuibhne and L W Gormley (eds), *From Single Market to Economic Union, Essays in Memory of John A. Usher* (Oxford University Press, 2012) 55, 60. On the 'effet utile' of the establishment of an agency for the pursuit of the objectives provided in the legal basis on which it is founded see also K Lenaerts, 'Regulating the Regulatory Process: "Delegation of Powers" in the European Community' (1993) *European Law Review* 23, 42.

68 9/56 *Meroni v High Authority* (n 60) 151; 10/56 *Meroni v High Authority* (n 60) 172.

69 See M Scholten, *The Political Accountability of EU and US Independent Regulatory Agencies* (Brill Nijhoff, 2014) 83, who considers the accountability requirements set in *Meroni* insufficient, as the CJEU did not clarify 'who should hold agencies to account and with what mechanisms (in quantitative and qualitative terms) in order to pass the delegation test' (85).

data as could be useful to governments or to any other parties concerned. Finally, the exercise of the delegated powers must be subject to judicial review and to the supervision of the delegating authority. According to *Meroni*, these conditions aim to avoid that delegation 'in reality gives the Brussels agencies more extensive powers than those which the High Authority holds from the Treaty'.[70] They aim to ensure that delegation is not a means to circumvent 'the balance of powers' set out in the Treaties.

The main controversial issue of the *Meroni* legacy concerns the nature of the powers that can be delegated according to the mentioned conditions. The case pointed out that delegation of 'discretionary power, implying a wide margin of discretion which may, according to the use which is made of it, make possible the execution of actual economic policy' is not lawful, because it 'brings about an actual transfer of responsibility'.[71] Only 'clearly defined executive powers the exercise of which can, therefore, be subject to strict review in the light of objective criteria determined by the delegating authority' can be delegated.[72] This has been interpreted as holding that no kind of regulatory power can be delegated to agencies without a prejudice to the design of powers as set in the Treaties. By further circumscribing the nature of agencies' tasks, *Romano* made a significant contribution in this direction.

In *Romano*, the Court of Justice added that having regard to the system of delegated acts as provided in Article 155 of the EEC Treaty and judicial system created by the EEC Treaty, and in particular Articles 173 and 177 thereof, 'the Administrative Commission may not be empowered by the Council to adopt acts having the force of law'.[73] National authorities therefore cannot be required to apply certain methods and interpretative rules in the implementation of EEC law: agencies can only 'provide an aid' to national authorities responsible for applying EEC law.[74] This ruling has usually been interpreted as meaning that agencies can only provide recommendatory acts, not generally binding on national authorities. As Chamon has correctly observed, this has left open the possibility to adopt binding acts in individual cases.[75] In fact, *Romano* has not stopped the development of EU agencies' adjudication powers.

The consolidated interpretation of *Meroni* and *Romano* has led EU institutions to design regulatory frameworks where EU agencies can only adopt pure management decisions and advise EU institutions and national authorities. As a consequence, the development of administrative regulation by agencies in the path of national experiences has been frozen at the EU level. Soon after the *Meroni* ruling, legal scholarship gave a rigid interpretation to the notion of non-discretionary

[70] 10/56 *Meroni v High Authority* (n 60) 171–72.
[71] Ibid 173.
[72] Ibid 173.
[73] 98/80 *Romano* (n 60) para 20.
[74] Ibid para 20.
[75] M Chamon, *EU Agencies: Legal and Political Limits to the Transformation of the EU Administration* (Oxford University Press, 2016) 255.

powers and very much restricted the possibilities to delegate powers to bodies not envisaged in the EEC Treaties.[76] However, today, at a different stage of EU integration, it can be noticed that the consolidated interpretation of the *Meroni* doctrine has ignored significant parts of this case law, as it did not take into account the full array of the reasons behind the restriction of agencies' powers. The rulings of the CJEU were much more open to recognising the possibility to delegate a range of administrative tasks to agencies than the consolidated interpretation of cases actually permitted.

IV. 'DARK SIDE' OF THE *MERONI* DOCTRINE

Some key aspects of the *Meroni* case law have been underestimated in the understanding of the compatibility of delegation of administrative powers with the system of the Treaties. As Schütze has effectively underlined, 'constitutional folklore continues to pay homage to a "Meroni Doctrine"' where no discretionary power can be delegated to agencies, 'while this expansive reading may not have been originally intended'.[77] If these aspects left in the dark by the *Meroni* and *Romano* cases would have been emphasised, EU administrative law would probably by now have been more advanced. Institutional arrangements and legal scholarship might have been able to push the Court of Justice to clarify its statements about the nature of the powers that EU agencies may legitimately exercise.

A different reading of *Meroni* shows that the CJEU and Advocate General Roemer in his Opinion were ready to recognise the delegation of powers of agencies as it happens in the national legal order. They had no ideological opposition to the delegation of powers to bodies not envisaged in the Treaties; they were rather concerned with the evaluation that the delegation act would be compatible with the current system of the Treaties and would not exceed the powers of the delegating institution.

I consider it to be very significant that Advocate General Roemer based his analysis of the delegation of powers to the Brussels agencies on the delegation of powers of a public authority to private associations in national law.[78] After a brief summary of the main reasons that could favour delegation of administrative powers in national legal orders, he inferred the basic conditions governing such a delegation of powers 'in a modern State founded on the rule of law':

> the delegation must be governed by a law which specifies the content of the delegation precisely and which must guarantee not only sufficient control by the State, but also

[76] See in particular P Pescatore, 'La fusion des institutions et des pouvoirs' (1966) 18 *Revue internationale de droit comparé* 301; H Maas, 'The Administrative Commission for the Social Security of Migrant Workers' (1967) 4 *Common Market Law Review* 51; for a reconstruction of the main positions see Chamon, *EU Agencies* (n 75) 183–85.

[77] Schütze, '"Delegated" Legislation in the (New) European Union' (n 63) 674–75.

[78] 10/56 *Meroni* (n 60), Opinion of AG Roemer, 190.

> complete legal protection against the measures adopted by these associations. Legal protection may be achieved by assimilating the measures adopted by such associations to those of public administrations, so that they may be contested by legal proceedings in accordance with the general rules of administrative law.[79]

Advocate General Roemer considered those conditions also to be relevant for delegation under Community law, as long as the silence of the Treaties about rules concerning delegation does not necessarily involve a prohibition of delegation, although the competence to delegate powers cannot be inferred from the Treaties either. The CJEU further clarified this point by holding that even in the silence of the Treaties, the delegation of powers cannot be excluded:

> Hence the power of the High Authority to authorize or itself to make the financial arrangements mentioned in Article 53 of the Treaty gives it the right to entrust certain powers to such bodies subject to conditions to be determined by it and subject to its supervision.[80]

When determining conditions for delegation, Roemer considered that 'at the very least … legal protection shall continue to exist even in the case of delegation'.[81] In his view, the existence of judicial review for delegated acts is the minimum requirement for delegation. The ruling of the CJEU is more precise, as it fixed a detailed series of conditions for lawful delegation. In particular, the CJEU held that in light of Article 53 of the ECSC Treaty, delegation of powers is legitimate only if the High Authority recognises that it is 'necessary for the performance of the tasks set out in Article 3 and compatible with this Treaty, and in particular with Article 65',[82] namely, if it is necessary for the achievement of the (general) objectives set out in Article 3 of the ECSC Treaty and if it complies with Article 65 of the same Treaty on the authorisation of agreements and concentration of enterprises under competition law. In my view, this part of the ruling has been severely underestimated, but it contains the rule to identify and circumscribe the powers that can be lawfully delegated. It allows the proper understanding of the distinction between wide discretionary powers and 'clearly defined executive powers' which is at the core of the *Meroni* doctrine.

In this part of the ruling, the Court of Justice emphasised that:

> in the pursuit of the objectives laid down in Article 3 of the Treaty, the High Authority must permanently reconcile any possible conflict which may be implied by these objectives when considered individually, and when such conflict arises must grant such priority to one or other of the objectives laid down in Article 3 as appears necessary having regard to the economic facts or circumstances in the light of which it adopts its decisions. Reconciling the various objectives laid down in Article 3 implies a real

79 Ibid.

80 10/56 *Meroni* (n 60) 172.

81 10/56 *Meroni* (n 60), Opinion of AG Roemer, 190, 194 and 196.

82 10/56 *Meroni* (n 60) 172.

> discretion involving difficult choices, based on a consideration of the economic facts and circumstances in the light of which those choices are made.[83]

It is this kind of discretion directly related to priority-setting and policy choices that cannot be delegated to agencies, as it would involve a transfer of (political) responsibility. It can be inferred therefore that the 'clearly defined executive powers' that can be delegated are all those necessary administrative powers that exclude priority-setting, must conform to pre-determined criteria and are subject to supervision and judicial review. In light of the non-delegation doctrine, this means that the *Köster*'s 'basic elements of a matter' cannot be delegated.[84] Although the two cases remain autonomous, the CJEU has applied the *Köster* condition in close connection with the *Meroni* doctrine.[85] According to Chamon, the relationship between *Köster* and *Meroni* is still unclear in the case law and Advocate General Jääskinen has contributed to blurring it in his Opinion in the (withdrawn) *Bankers' Bonus Cap* case, when inferring the (technical) reach of the European Banking Authority (EBA)'s draft standards from the fact that the delegation criteria set out in the IV Credit Requirements Directive aimed to define the strategic and political choices as essential elements for the adoption of the Commission's regulatory technical standards.[86]

This framework outlines the very nature of administrative powers, which do not automatically exclude some degree of (administrative) discretion proportionate to the task to be performed, but necessarily preclude the exercise of legislative choices. As the relevance of the nature of discretion will be thoroughly analysed in Chapter 3, it suffices here to say that the *Meroni* ruling did not intend to limit delegation to purely management powers of execution, but it rather aimed to identify the guarantees for the exercise of administrative powers.

The same concern for the existence of effective legal guarantees for the delegation of powers to agencies emerges in the *Romano* ruling. Although the Court did not refer to *Meroni*, the judgment further elaborated on the conclusions of the

[83] Ibid 172–73.

[84] See HCH Hofmann and A Morini, 'Constitutional Aspects of the Pluralisation of the EU Executive Through "Agencification"' (2012) 37 *European Law Review* 419, 425; Schütze, '"Delegated" Legislation in the (New) European Union' (n 63) 674.

[85] C-164/98P *DIR International Film Srl and others v Commission* [2000] ECR I-447, para 27; C-154/04 and 155/04 *Alliance for Natural Health* (n 49) paras 90–92.

[86] Chamon, *EU Agencies* (n 75) 241. C-507/13 *United Kingdom v European Parliament and Council* ECLI:EU:C:2014:2394, Opinion of AG Jääskinen, para 62. Jääskinen considers that the EBA's power to draft regulatory technical standards specifying the classes of instruments that satisfy the conditions set out in Directive 2013/36/EU and the quantitative and qualitative criteria to identify categories of staff whose professional activities have a material impact on the institution's risk profile does not involve any strategic/political choice, because this choice was made in the Directive that had delegated the Commission to adopt binding regulatory technical standards under Art 290 TFEU drafted by the EBA. Note that, the UK having withdrawn its action for annulment under Art 263 TFEU, the Court of Justice did not rule on the case and, particularly, on the limits of the EBA's powers. See C-507/13 *United Kingdom v European Parliament and Council* ECLI:EU:C:2014:2481, Order of the President of the Court of 9 December 2014.

Meroni case and further circumscribed agencies' actions under the EEC Treaty: agencies cannot adopt acts with the force of law under the existing framework of the Treaties and in the absence of a system of judicial review applicable to their acts. The Opinion of Advocate General Warner in *Romano* is particularly meaningful, as it pointed out the relevance of the absence of an effective system of judicial review in the decision to declare the invalidity of the decision of the Administrative Commission. The Treaties recognised the jurisdiction of the Court to review the legality of the acts of the Council and the Commission and to rule on the validity and interpretation of acts of the Community's institutions, but the Administrative Commission was not an institution:

> So it would seem that this Court has no jurisdiction to pronounce, except indirectly, upon the lawfulness of an act of the Administrative Commission—and therefore indeed no jurisdiction to answer directly the question referred to it by the Tribunal in the present case. The idea that there may be set up for the Community an administrative body empowered to make binding decisions, but whose decisions are, in themselves, incapable of review by this Court seems to me incompatible with the scheme of the Treaty. Nor does it seem to me that the concept of an administrative body whose decisions are incapable of judicial review is reconcilable with constitutional principles that are accepted in all the Member States and, I think, in every other civilized country.[87]

As the issue of judicial protection was already addressed in the *Van der Vecht* case law, Chamon has pointed out that the originality of *Romano* is found in the requirement of compliance with Article 155 of the EEC Treaty on the conferral of delegated powers on the Commission by the Council. In his view, this might also have significant implications on the current validity of the *Romano* principle under the Lisbon Treaty, which has further developed the delegated acts of the Commission under Articles 290 and 291 TFEU.[88] How Article 155 of the EEC Treaty limits agencies' action and therefore articulates their non-interference in the Commission' powers, however, remains uncertain in *Romano*. It is relevant that Advocate General Warner did not consider Article 155 of the EEC Treaty an obstacle to the delegation of similar powers to a body like the Administrative Commission.[89] However, he did not elaborate on this point and the Court of Justice did not follow him. On the basis of Article 155 of the EEC Treaty, the Court rather refused to recognise the legitimacy of the Administrative Commission's powers, but it did not analyse the relationship between the delegation of powers to the Commission under Article 155 EEC and the impossibility of agency delegation.

[87] 98/80 *Romano* (n 60), Opinion of AG Warner, 1265. AG Warner supports his statement with the evidence provided by the case law of the CJEU itself about the interpretation of secondary law concerning judicial protection with the Treaties (19/67 *Van der Vecht* [1967] ECR 345) and the admissibility of the Management Committee procedure on the grounds that the legislative powers were reserved to the Commission and so neither Art 155 of the EEC Treaty nor the jurisdiction of the Court were impaired (25/70 *Köster* (n 26) and 30/70 *Scheer* [1970] 2 ECR 1197).

[88] Chamon, *EU Agencies* (n 75) 253–54, 257–58.

[89] 98/80 *Romano* (n 60), Opinion of AG Warner, 1264.

This is, however, a key point to discern the reach of EU agencies' competence with due regard to the institutional balance of the Commission's delegated acts.

Recently, all these aspects of the *Meroni* and *Romano* case law have become more apparent inasmuch as the CJEU has been asked to pronounce on the compatibility of an EU agency's powers with the *Meroni* doctrine. These uncharted requirements for delegation therefore have had to emerge from the limbo to which they have been relegated for years and the CJEU had to provide an updated interpretation of these old principles.

V. *MERONI* DOCTRINE REVISITED: *ESMA SHORT SELLING* CASE

In 2014, the CJEU was again called to rule on the legitimacy of an EU agency's powers.[90] This long-awaited ruling represents the latest development of the principle of non-delegation with regard to EU agencies, but it is not conclusive about the reach of such delegation. In fact, the CJEU confirmed the validity of the *Meroni* ruling, but somehow 'mellowed' it in light of the different framework of the Lisbon Treaty.[91] On the same grounds, it has probably set aside the *Romano* ruling, but this was done via holding its inapplicability. This judgment can also be read as evidence that the above-mentioned aspects of the *Meroni* doctrine, which had remained for almost 60 years in the dark, are actually going to become central issues in the future delegation of powers to EU agencies.

The United Kingdom was seeking an annulment of Regulation 236/2012/EU's provision empowering the European Securities and Markets Authority (ESMA) to forbid short selling in certain highly specific circumstances and under strict conditions.[92] This provision empowers the ESMA to exercise the proper supervision and prevent financial activities 'that threaten the orderly functioning and integrity of financial markets or the stability of the whole or part of the financial system in the Union' in the specific sector of short selling transactions.[93] The United Kingdom invoked the *Meroni* doctrine and the legal limits to harmonisation in the internal market and employed four arguments in advocating annulment. The CJEU dismissed the case in its entirety.

[90] C-270/12 *United Kingdom v Council of European Union and European Parliament* ECLI:EU:C:2014:18.

[91] See J Pelkmans and M Simoncini, 'Mellowing *Meroni*: How ESMA Can Help Build the Single Market' *Regulatory Policy, CEPS Commentaries* no 1 (2014).

[92] Regulation 236/2012/EU of the European Parliament and the Council of 14 March 2012 on short selling and certain aspects of credit default swaps, art 28 [2012] OJ L 86/1.

[93] Regulation 1095/2010/EU of the European Parliament and of the Council of 24 November 2010 establishing a European Supervisory Authority (European Securities and Markets Authority), amending Decision 716/2009/EC and repealing Commission Decision 2009/77/EC, art 9(5) [2010] OJ L 331. Note that under the current review of ESAs, the European Commission is studying the possibility of converting art 9(5) into a self-standing empowerment, so that ESAs would no longer need sector-specific regulation to provide them with the power in question, but could directly exercise it in any sector of competence. See *Report from the Commission to the European Parliament and the Council on the Operation of the European Supervisory Authorities (ESAs) and the European System of Financial Supervision (ESFS)*, COM(2014)509 (8 August 2014) 8–9.

The United Kingdom contended that in the exercise of supervisory powers on the short selling market, the ESMA had been given 'a very large measure of discretion' which could have a political nature, at odds with *Meroni*.[94] According to the UK, the ESMA would be 'required to take potentially controversial decisions' that would 'involve ESMA in the implementation of actual economic policy and require it to arbitrate between conflicting public interests, make value judgments and carry out complex economic assessments'.[95] The ESMA would have 'a wide range of choices as to which measure or measures to impose and as to any exceptions that may be specified' that would 'have very significant economic and financial policy implications' related, for instance, to 'the impact on liquidity and the level of uncertainty that will be created in financial markets, which, in turn, have long-term consequences as to general overall confidence in the markets'.[96] According to the UK, 'these are "unquantifiable … judgments" and cannot be categorised as decisions made on the basis of set criteria amenable to objective review'.[97] In addition, when deciding which measure should be adopt, the criteria set out in article 28(3) of Regulation 236/2012/EU 'encompass tests which are "highly subjective"'.[98] As a counter-argument, the UK also submitted that even if the ESMA's powers were not such as to involve 'policy choices in the form of decisions on macroeconomic policy', nonetheless they would be too broad to fit the principle established in *Meroni*,[99] and their temporary nature would not make any relevant difference and would not exclude the applicability of *Meroni*.[100]

In my view, the legal pleas of the United Kingdom had the potential to help disclose the precise administrative nature of EU agencies' powers, composed of some degree of discretion, as well as technical evaluations. However, Advocate General Jääskinen qualified the ESMA's powers only as technical evaluations. He dismissed the existence of discretion by identifying them as 'complex technical assessment of facts' to be made 'on an objective and non-political basis' 'dependent on procedural guarantees ensuring that decision makers base their assessments on a broad factual basis and sound methodology, after having consulted the relevant actors'.[101] By relying on the distinction between political and technical powers, Advocate General Jääskinen did not actually answer the United Kingdom's final objection: although not concerning political choices, was the ESMA's capability to choose the measures and the possible exceptions to adopt, as well as to make what were to some extent value judgements, compatible with the *Meroni* doctrine? In other words, can some administrative discretion be allocated to EU agencies?

[94] C-270/12 *United Kingdom v Council of European Union and European Parliament* (n 90) para 28.
[95] Ibid para 29.
[96] Ibid paras 30–31.
[97] Ibid para 31.
[98] Ibid para 32.
[99] Ibid para 34.
[100] Ibid para 33.
[101] C-270/12 *UK v Council of European Union and European Parliament* (n 90), Opinion of AG Jääskinen, paras 99–100.

Unfortunately, the CJEU did not take up the challenge to qualify clearly the nature of administrative powers within the framework of EU law. Nonetheless, the CJEU fitted the ESMA's powers in question into the 'clearly defined executive powers' that can be delegated under the *Meroni* doctrine. Scholten and van Rijsbergen pointed out that the Court avoided labelling the ESMA's powers and ambiguously used the notion of discretion, so as to suggest that although not vested with wide discretion, the ESMA still retains some degree of discretion.[102] As they also observed, however, the taxonomy of EU agencies' powers remains unclear.[103]

The CJEU constructed the legitimacy of the ESMA's powers on two main grounds: the retention within the general competence of the ESMA and the existence of 'various conditions and criteria which limit ESMA's discretion'.[104] On the one hand, the Court pointed out that the power in question actualises a competence established by ESMA's Founding Regulation and it does not exceed the legal boundaries set out therein. On the other hand, the Court identified in the contested provision the circumscribed conditions that should guide the exercise of discretionary powers, so that the ESMA should intervene:

(1) only if a concrete risk to the financial stability is at stake and no competent national authority has intervened;
(2) by taking into account a cumulative number of factors delineated in the Short Selling Regulation so that the ESMA's intervention does not create further risks in the financial markets (eg the risk of regulatory arbitrage, or the risk of a reduction of liquidity, or the creation of further uncertainty in the market);
(3) by limiting the power of intervention to temporary and precise measures as outlined in the Founding Regulation; and
(4) by notifying the competent national authorities.[105]

In addition, according to Regulation 236/2012/EU, delegated acts of the Commission could specify further criteria and factors that the ESMA has to take into account, whereas Regulation 918/2012/EU specified the type of threat and emphasised that the ESMA carried out 'technical factual assessment'.[106]

In my view, the CJEU swung between its traditional distinction between political and technical powers and the recognition that non-political powers may also include a circumscribed margin of discretion, which pertains to the sphere of administrative action. The 'clearly defined executive powers' that can be lawfully

[102] M Scholten and M van Rijsbergen, 'The *ESMA-Short Selling* Case: Erecting a New Delegation Doctrine in the EU upon the *Meroni-Romano* Remnants' (2014) 41 *Legal Issues of Economic Integration* 389, 394–95.

[103] Ibid 394.

[104] C-270/12 *United Kingdom v Council of European Union and European Parliament* (n 90) paras 44–45.

[105] Ibid paras 46–50.

[106] Ibid paras 51–52.

delegated to EU agencies, therefore, cover different sets of non-political powers, which nature is not clearly qualified by the Court. This interpretation of the nature of EU agencies' powers may not be completely unexpected, as those aspects of *Meroni* left in the dark for years were already open to the exercise of administrative discretion by EU agencies. Unlike Scholten and van Rijbergen, I am not fully convinced that the *ESMA Short Selling* ruling 'devastated the *Meroni*'s distinction between *executive* powers ... and *discretionary* powers ... because the Court has accepted the delegation of *executive discretionary* powers subject to certain limits'.[107] The Court rather smashed the consolidated interpretation of *Meroni* and qualified the nature of executive powers as a wider category of implementing powers that may necessarily include some degrees of discretion. They should broadly identify powers administrative in nature and they do not qualify the type of administrative action involved, whether being purely technical or involving some discretionary evaluations. Executive powers belong to the administration, and do not necessarily identify by themselves the absence of discretion.

Alongside these considerations about the nature of the power in contention, in the application of the *Meroni* doctrine the CJEU also raised the key issue of the legal status of the entity which has been delegated the power, yet did not secure certain legal consequences. The Court distinguished the ESMA as 'a European Union entity, created by EU legislature' from the Brussels agencies in *Meroni* which 'were entities governed by private law'.[108] This part of the judgment remains insufficiently explicit as to the reasoning of the Court: it seems that the different nature of the entities in question should affect the application of the *Meroni* doctrine, but how this should happen is not clarified under the *Meroni* ground of review. My understanding is that this statement is relevant under the second ground of review about the breach of the *Romano* ruling.

The United Kingdom also deemed the ESMA's power contrary to the *Romano* principle concerning the prohibition on administrative bodies adopting 'measures of general application having the force of law'. According to the UK, 'a prohibition on short sales affects the entire class of persons engaging in transactions in that instrument or category of instruments', so being 'quasi-legislative measures of general application' 'even if confined to a very limited range of stocks'.[109] According to the CJEU, the contended power required the ESMA 'to adopt measures of general application', which 'may also include rules affecting any natural or legal person who has a specific financial instrument or specific class of financial instruments or who enter into certain financial transactions'.[110] However, the Court did not infer that this was at odds with *Romano*, on the grounds that the TFEU now

[107] Scholten and van Rijsbergen, 'The *ESMA-Short Selling* Case' (n 102) 395.
[108] C-270/12 *United Kingdom v Council of European Union and European Parliament* (n 90) para 43.
[109] Ibid paras 56–57.
[110] Ibid para 64.

covers judicial protection against EU agencies' acts and, in particular, it 'expressly permits Union bodies, offices and agencies to adopt acts of general application'.[111]

When setting the guarantees of judicial review, the TFEU only indirectly recognises the capability of EU agencies to adopt acts of general application. In addressing the plea of illegality by guaranteeing the inapplicability of acts of general application to specific proceedings, Article 277 TFEU implicitly recognises that alongside EU institutions, agencies, bodies and offices of the Union can also issue these acts; whereas Article 263 TFEU simply includes the review of the legality of their acts where 'intended to produce legal effects vis-à-vis third parties', without expressly mentioning acts of general application. Nonetheless, these provisions more or less explicitly admit that acts of general application are now in the domain of EU agencies and bodies; otherwise, as Advocate General Jääskinen noted, 'these Treaty amendments would be meaningless'.[112] The *Romano* constraint on EU agencies' actions appeared out-dated in the reasoning of the CJEU: as long as the TFEU recognised EU agencies' powers, the generally valid *Romano* principle could no longer apply to their specific case. In fact, the CJEU went on to say that only *Meroni* governs the delegation of powers 'to a body such as ESMA'.[113]

Yet the CJEU dismissed the applicability of the *Romano* ruling without clarifying how the case of the ESMA differs from *Romano*'s Administrative Commission. It remains ambiguous in the judgment whether the context of reference has changed or the powers in questions are different. The first case may be substantiated by the centrality of the changed institutional framework in the decision of the Court. *Romano* might have been ruled out because of the recognition of EU agencies' powers in the TFEU and their amenability to judicial review.[114] Considering that the Treaties recognise this protection for all agencies, bodies or offices of the Union, it is very difficult to imagine any residual application of the *Romano* principle. It should therefore be pragmatically held that the Court has (ambiguously) abandoned *Romano*.

The second hypothesis is rationally supported by the fact that the CJEU did not formally dismiss the validity of *Romano*, but it did not apply it. The Court in fact said that the ESMA's powers are not 'at odds with the principle established in *Romano*',[115] but only *Meroni* governed the case. This might hint at the possible distinction between the acts having the force of law under *Romano* and the acts of general application at the disposal of EU agencies. The former category refers to acts normative in nature that innovate the legal framework and have a general normative impact, whereas the latter concerns administrative acts that conform to pre-determined criteria, address specific cases or situations, and

[111] Ibid para 65.
[112] C-270/12 *United Kingdom v Council of European Union and European Parliament* (n 90), Opinion of AG Jääskinen, para 74.
[113] C-270/12 *United Kingdom v Council of European Union and European Parliament* (n 90), para 66.
[114] Ibid paras 79–80.
[115] Ibid para 65.

have no normative reach. The *Romano* constraint to EU agencies' action would not therefore be applicable to the kind of tasks and responsibilities allocated to the ESMA under Regulation 236/2012/EU. However, the pragmatic approach of the Court does not allow the setting of rigid boundaries between these acts and the endorsement of such a formalistic approach.[116] The CJEU assesses the substantive nature of the legal instrument irrespective of its *nomen iuris*. As the CJEU specified, the ESMA's measures of general application 'may also include *rules* affecting any natural or legal person who has a specific financial instrument or specific class of financial instruments or who enter into certain financial transactions' (emphasis added).[117] This suggests that administrative acts of general application may also have some 'force of law', yet circumscribed to a specific sector or category of persons. The existence of some normative powers in the domain of EU agencies therefore cannot be ruled out, and the characterisation of the nature of acts of general application remains ambiguous.

Another possible interpretation of the *Romano* principle emerges in the defence of the Council and in the Opinion of Advocate General Jääskinen. According to the Council, *Romano* prohibited the conferral of legislative powers on bodies other than the EU legislature, and it did not concern 'quasi-legislative' powers or 'measures of general application'.[118] Similarly, Advocate General Jääskinen referred the *Romano* principle to the conferral of legislative powers and clarified the opportunity of the Court's decision in that case in the absence of judicial protection against such delegation in the Treaties.[119] If reading the ambiguous judgment of the CJEU in light of these interpretations, it might be possible to distinguish EU agencies' acts from legislative acts and to prohibit only the latter in light of the Lisbon Treaty.[120] This would open the possibility of recognising some normative power, administrative in nature, to EU agencies within the sector of their action. The reach of the *Romano* ruling is not delineated and its applicability as a test for the legitimacy of EU agencies' powers appears questionable. The result is that *Romano* remains in a limbo. In the absence of securing Treaties' provisions and a structured interpretation of the CJEU, the distinction of EU agencies' powers and their reach in the realm of EU executive powers remains legally complex. However, the *ESMA Short Selling* case tersely held them compatible with the framework of the Treaties. The CJEU considered the ESMA's powers in line with the *Romano* ruling on the grounds that they do not encroach on the powers of the Commission under Articles 290 and 291 TFEU.

[116] See already G De Vergottini, 'Note sugli atti normativi e amministrativi dell'ordinamento comunitario europeo' (1963) *Rivista Trimestrale di Diritto Pubblico* 887.

[117] C-270/12 *United Kingdom v Council of European Union and European Parliament* (n 90) para 64.

[118] Ibid para 60.

[119] C-270/12 *UK v Council of European Union and European Parliament* (n 90), Opinion of AG Jääskinen, para 70.

[120] See Scholten and van Rijsbergen, 'The *ESMA Short Selling* Case' (n 102) 396–98, who point out that the distinction between legislative and quasi-legislative powers relies on procedural criteria, rather than on the nature of the power itself.

According to the CJEU, two sets of reasons justify the possibility to confer the analysed administrative tasks on an EU agency: the first reason is based on the framework of the Treaties, whereas the second one pertains to the legislative context which conferred such powers on the ESMA. With regard to the Treaties, they do not exclude the possibility to confer powers on a Union body, office or agency when presupposing that their acts of general application are subject to judicial review.[121] As a consequence, the delegated powers of the Commission cannot be considered as the exclusive system of delegation. As Bergström has emphasised, the Court has elaborated a regime of delegation of powers to agencies parallel to the regime under Articles 290 and 291 TFEU.[122] By introducing new legitimate actors in the exercise of EU executive powers, this interpretation affects the principle of the separation of powers itself. It fragments implementation powers and recognises the necessity of a plural administrative organisation. With regard to the contended provision, the Court situates the conferred power in the specific context of the close cooperation between national authorities against threats to financial stability, pointing out their need to adopt temporary measures aimed at preventing price falls and to rely on 'a high degree of professional expertise'.[123]

Advocate General Jääskinen made the same attempt to clarify the different reach of these powers. He emphasised the exclusivity of the delegated acts of the Commission under Article 290 TFEU, on the grounds that these non-legislative acts of general application have the capability to change legislative acts by amending or supplementing their non-essential elements. According to the wording of Article 290 TFEU and the principle of democracy as developed under Articles 2, 10 and 11 TEU, the exercise of such an intrusive power presupposes the democratic accountability which is vested in the Commission.[124] Conversely, the Advocate General recognised that the conferral of implementing powers on EU agencies, similar to those allocated to the Commission under Article 291 TFEU, represents 'a midway solution between vesting implementing authority in either the Commission or the Council, on the one hand, or leaving it the Member States, on the other'.[125] The distinction from the powers of the Commission under Article 291(2) TFEU, however, is not straightforward. To some extent, this emerges in a recent case on the European patent system, where the CJEU has clarified that Article 291(2) TFEU applies 'only where uniform conditions for implementing

[121] C-270/12 *United Kingdom v Council of European Union and European Parliament* (n 90) paras 79–80.

[122] CF Bergström, 'Introduction' in CF Bergström and D Ritleng (eds), *Rulemaking by the European Commission* (Oxford University Press, 2016) 1, 15.

[123] C-270/12 *United Kingdom v Council of European Union and European Parliament* (n 90) para 85.

[124] C-270/12 *United Kingdom v Council of European Union and European Parliament* (n 90), Opinion of AG Jääskinen, paras 84–85.

[125] Ibid para 86. This development of agencies 'as an intermediate approach between the extremes of *administration communautaire directe* and *administration communautaire indirecte*' was already recognised by Lenaerts, 'Regulating the Regulatory Process" (n 67) 46.

legally binding Union acts are needed'.[126] The judiciary envisages a distinction of the executive competence between EU agencies and the Commission, demonstrating to accept the pluralisation of executive powers based on the principle of competence. However, the criteria for the allocation of the implementation powers to an EU agency instead of the Commission require further clarification. How to distinguish the general competence of the Commission from the sectional competence of EU agencies may not be straightforward in practice and this may lead to conflicts based on the principle of conferral.

The combined reading of the *ESMA Short Selling* judgment and the Advocate General's Opinion reveals that the conferral of powers on EU agencies is construed as a further organisational option at the disposal of the Member States and the EU legislative branch, when shared competences should be exercised according to the subsidiarity principle. From this point of view, the recourse to an EU agency needs to be based on the requirement of its necessity for the implementation of the task based on the expertise that it may provide. The assessment of necessity which emerged as a key criterion for delegation under the *Meroni* doctrine should therefore amount to a proportionality test aimed at establishing whether other options with the same effectiveness might be used to achieve the implementation goal. In the application of the principle of competence, the proportionality of the organisational solution should legally justify the choice between (very) different branches of the EU executive.

VI. COMPETENCE OF EU AGENCIES IN THE SHADOW OF CONFERRAL

By responding positively to the concerns raised in the *Meroni* and *Romano* cases, the CJEU's judgment in the *ESMA Short Selling* case recognised the possibility to

[126] C-146/13 *Spain v European Parliament and Council* ECLI:EU:C:2015:298, para 77. The difficulty to identify a clear-cut functional distinction between the implementing acts and the delegated acts of the Commission further complicates the situation of EU agencies' acts. In fact, the case law on Commission's acts ambiguously distinguishes the delegated power 'to adopt rules which supplement or amend certain non-essential elements' of a legislative act from the implementing power to 'provide further detail to the content of a legislative act' (C-427/12 *Commission v European Parliament and Council (Biocides)* ECLI:EU:C:2014:170, paras 38–39), and judicial review is limited to manifest errors of assessment (see ibid para 40). The result is that the choice of the legal instrument pragmatically rests upon the bargaining between the Council and the European Parliament. EU institutions therefore agreed on a common understanding on delegated acts aimed at ensuring the fair exercise of Commission's powers and the effective control of the European Parliament and the Council; see Annex to Interinstitutional Agreement between the European Parliament, the Council of the European Union and the European Commission on Better Law-Making [2016] OJ L 123/1. In the literature see P Ponzano, 'The Reform of Comitology and Delegated Acts: An Executive's View' in C F Bergström and D Ritleng (eds), *Rulemaking by the European Commission* (Oxford University Press, 2016) 37; P Craig, 'Comitology, Rulemaking and the Lisbon Settlement: Tensions and Strains' in CF Bergström and D Ritleng (eds), *Rulemaking by the European Commission* (Oxford University Press, 2016) 173; J Mendes, 'The Making of Delegated and Implementing Acts: Legitimacy Beyond Institutional Balance' in CF Bergström and D Ritleng (eds), *Rulemaking by the European Commission* (Oxford University Press, 2016) 233.

allocate powers on EU agencies as long as such powers comply with the criteria laid down in the delegating acts and are subject to judicial review as well as to the supervision of the delegating authority. These pillars of delegation rest on the premise that the Lisbon Treaty has conferred a constitutional status on EU agencies by ensuring judicial protection against their acts. As long as EU agencies have been recognised as legitimate actors in the EU legal order, the CJEU acknowledged that they can exercise to some extent some regulatory functions. The Court therefore admits some administrative regulation performed by EU agencies under specific conditions.

As mentioned, however, the Court has not developed an organic theory on the structure and the limits of EU agencies' powers. Despite some significant clarification on the reach and relevance of the *Meroni* doctrine, some fundamental issues related to the separation of powers still remain obscure. Significantly, the Court of Justice does not conceptualise the relation of subordination between legal sources that is at the core of administrative law. The result is a cherry-picking approach to administrative law that applies some typical categories of administrative law in the absence of a reference framework. The lack of solid provisions in the Treaties about EU agencies' regulatory competence is actually a significant *vulnus* in the reconstruction of their powers, which is going to affect the legal tenability of the increasing importance of far-reaching powers of EU agencies in the internal market.[127] From this point of view, the requirement of proportionality of delegation becomes central, as it assists the maintenance of the institutional balance in the absence of an express legal basis in the TFEU for the allocation of competence to EU agencies.

EU agencies must act within the limits of the mandate provided by the secondary law (regulations) that establishes their competence and the conditions for their action. However, it is not clear if this hierarchy of powers represents an institutional relationship of conferral or delegation between the EU legislature and the EU agency in question. Under EU law, in fact, these notions have been used quite interchangeably without identifying distinct legal regimes.[128] For instance, under the Treaties and the case law the Commission may be 'delegated' powers by the legislature,[129] whereas the Administrative Commission in *Romano* was considered by the Court to be 'empowered by the Council'.[130]

[127] See R van Gestel, 'European Regulatory Agencies Adrift? Case 270/12' (2014) 21 *Maastricht Journal of European and Comparative Law* 188, 195.

[128] See Lenaerts, 'Regulating the Regulatory Process' (n 67) 24–27, who distinguishes three different forms of delegation: (1) 'the Community executive process' under which the Council in its legislative capacity leaves implementing powers to the Member States or the Commission; (2) 'the transfer of authority by the Community to an international body in whose establishment and operation it participates with one or more third States'; (3) 'the transfer of authority to so-called third parties' not provided in the Treaties, such as agencies and other bodies; see also Hofmann and Morini, 'Constitutional Aspects of the Pluralisation of the EU Executive Through "Agencification"' (n 84) 442; Chamon, *EU Agencies* (n 75) 233–35.

[129] Articles 290 and 291 TFEU (ex Art 155 EEC); see also C-25/70 *Köster* (n 26) para 9.

[130] 98/80 *Romano* (n 60) para 20.

The *ESMA Short Selling* case uses the notion of conferral of powers, but it does not provide any explicit clue about its legal distinction from the case of delegation. As Chamon emphasised, this depends on the CJEU's failure to remark that according to *Meroni*, only the competences that the delegating authority retains can be delegated.[131] Actually, the notion of conferral is borrowed from the ESMA's Founding Regulation, article 1(2) of which provides that 'the Authority shall act within the powers conferred by this Regulation'. On this premise, when addressing the *Romano* ground of review, the CJEU portrayed the allocation of such powers as a case of conferral. However, when discussing the *Meroni* ground of review, it pragmatically avoided qualifying the nature of the allocation of powers and simply referred to 'the powers available to ESMA under Article 28 of Regulation No 236/2012'.[132] The CJEU avoided clarifying the reasons why the *Meroni* ruling concerning the delegation of powers was also relevant in the *ESMA Short Selling* case which relied on the conferral of powers. Conversely, Advocate General Jääskinen clearly qualified *Romano* as a case of conferral, whereas he referred to *Meroni* as a case of delegation.[133] In his analysis, the conferral of powers from the legislature should not be subject to the restrictions set out in the *Meroni* ruling, as 'the EU legislature is not acting as a "delegating authority"', but as 'a constitutional actor exercising its own legislative competence, as conferred on it by the higher constitutional charter, i.e. the Lisbon Treaty'.[134] Therefore, *Meroni* is relevant only when implementing powers are delegated from the delegating authority, be it the Commission or the Council, upon whom they have been conferred by the EU legislature.[135] In his analysis, conferral concerns the legislative allocation of competence of an original (administrative) power, whereas delegation is an administrative allocation of powers within the area of competence of the delegating authority.

Although this might be formally correct,[136] the judgment has not connected any legal effect to this distinction and it conducted the review in the light of *Meroni* and *Romano* on more substantive grounds. More pragmatically, the qualification of the delegation model appears to be based on the legal regime that applies to the institutional relation in question.[137] In addition, by relying on this distinction, it should be admitted that the *ESMA Short Selling* case has indirectly expanded the relevance of the *Meroni* criteria for delegation also to the case of conferral of

[131] Chamon, *EU Agencies* (n 75) 247.

[132] C-270/12 *United Kingdom v Council of European Union and European Parliament* (n 90) para 53.

[133] C-270/12 *United Kingdom v Council of European Union and European Parliament* (n 90), Opinion of AG Jääskinen, paras 70–72.

[134] Ibid para 91.

[135] Ibid para 88.

[136] See Scholten and van Rijsbergen, 'The *ESMA-Short Selling* Case' (n 102) 402, who point out that the delegation of powers from the EU legislature to EU agencies would lead to the non-feasible option that EU agencies should exercise legislative powers under the same obligations and conditions that the EU legislature has to respect.

[137] See Chamon, *EU Agencies* (n 75) 241.

powers on EU agencies. The legal boundaries to EU agencies' action must therefore be identified within the *Meroni* constitutional pattern. The issue at stake is how to apply the principle of conferral and the connected principle of institutional balance, so that the pluralisation of public powers in the EU may remain anchored to the democratic rule laid down in Article 10(2) TEU. EU agencies should fit within the general framework of representative and participatory democracy and cannot be constructed as expert bodies beyond democratic rule.

A. Anchor Requirements for EU Agencies' Powers

The legal status of EU agencies and the nature of the powers that they may exercise are key to anchoring these entities to the democratic rule embedded in the Treaties. From a subjective standpoint, EU agencies enjoy organisational and functional autonomy aimed at infusing the implementation policies of the Commission with sector-specific expertise. When assisting the Commission, agencies have the capacity to take independent decisions, but they are subject to the steering function and supervision of the EU institutions. In the case of the ESAs, such autonomy is particularly qualified and the steering role of the Commission is more feeble. As bodies with varied degree of autonomy, EU agencies represent a deviation from the centralisation of administrative powers in the Commission and an exception to the principle of indirect administration by the Member States.

The conferral of legal personality under EU law on EU agencies supports the pluralisation of the EU executive and complements their legal status under the Treaties. It particularly allows them to be legally responsible for the adoption of acts that produce legal effects on third parties. Legal personality under EU law is fundamental for a coherent integration of EU agencies in the EU institutional setting. It gives legal certainty to EU agencies' action. Given the weak entrenchment of EU agencies in the Treaties, legal personality allows the conferral of powers on EU agencies, while limiting their sphere of action and attributing direct responsibilities for their action to them. According to Ruffert, legal personality should represent the conceptual framework under which EU agencies should act, as it allows the development of coherent inter-institutional relationships, to recognise hierarchical structures within the EU executive branch, to advance legal protection and the rule of law, as well as to maintain a formal and substantive distinction between public and private entities.[138]

The importance of legal personality for EU agencies is to some extent embedded in the *ESMA Short Selling* case, where the Court affirmed that the Authority 'is a European Union entity'. Although this remains only a premise of the Court's reasoning, it implicitly reflects the legal status of 'Union body with legal

[138] M Ruffert, 'Personality under EU Law: A Conceptual Answer Towards the Pluralisation of the EU' (2014) 20 *European Law Journal* 346, 358–66.

personality' recognised in the ESMA's Founding Regulation.[139] This places the ESMA in the realm of secondary-level institutions created by legislative acts within the framework of the Treaties, and to some extent contributes to justifying its conferral of autonomous powers under EU law.

From a functional standpoint, EU agencies' competence should be comprised within this institutional design. The identification of the nature of this competence as administrative allows the understanding of the limits to EU agencies' action and gives them a place in the hierarchy of the sources of law that is compatible with democratic rule. The correct identification of the legal basis according to which EU agencies can exercise their competence is therefore essential, as it represents the backdrop against which the legality of their action has to be ensured. The acts of general application that EU agencies might adopt as a kind of administrative regulation, as well as their individual decisions directed to natural or legal persons, should be in accordance with secondary law and the TFEU.

The *ESMA Short Selling* case has opened significant perspectives on the compatibility of EU agencies' action in internal market regulation. Building upon its previous case law on the generous reach of Article 114 TFEU, the CJEU considered the ESMA's powers as legitimate measures for the approximation of laws in the internal market.[140] The Court particularly referred to the *Smoke Flavouring* case, which left the choice of the method of harmonisation to the discretion of the EU legislature,[141] so that individual measures can also be considered harmonisation measures; and to the *ENISA* case, which considered this Agency able to contribute to harmonisation through its implementing action, so as 'to supplement the EU's institutional structure'.[142] In light of the consistent judicial trend towards an extensive interpretation of Article 114 TFEU,[143] the CJEU recognised that the ESMA's powers are also covered by this provision as far as they contribute to the harmonisation of Member States' supervision and the establishment of a functioning financial internal market.

Advocate General Jääskinen took a more restrictive view of the scope of Article 114 TFEU, which resembles the CJEU's interpretation in the first *Tobacco* case. In that case, harmonisation was strictly connected to the principle of conferral, so that it could not be a means to extend creeping competences.[144] In his view, the ESMA's powers are designed to intervene on the conditions for competition in

[139] ESMA Founding Regulation, art 2 (1).

[140] C-270/12 *United Kingdom v Council and European Parliament* (n 90) paras 97–119.

[141] C-66/04 *United Kingdom v European Parliament and Council (Smoke Flavouring)* [2005] ECR I-10553, para 45.

[142] C-217/04 *United Kingdom v European Parliament and Council (ENISA)* [2006] ECR I-3771, para 44. Chamon, *EU Agencies* (n 75) 145.

[143] See S Weatherill, 'The Limits of Legislative Harmonization Ten Years after Tobacco Advertising: How the Court's Case Law has Become a "Drafting Guide"' (2011) 12 *German Law Journal* 827; A Somek, *Individualism: An Essay on the Authority of the European Union* (Oxford University Press, 2008) 114.

[144] C-376/98 *Germany v Parliament* [2000] ECR I-2247, para 83.

a particular market by replacing national decision-making, and not to genuinely improve the conditions for the functioning of the internal market.[145] The correct legal basis for addressing 'the cross-border implications of inadequate Member State action with respect to short selling' was therefore Article 352 TFEU on the unanimity rule for the exercise of implied powers.[146] Clearly, if his position had been upheld by the Court, the ESMA's powers would have been invalid and they would probably not be reinstated on the new legal basis, because of (at least) the opposition of the United Kingdom.

As I have observed elsewhere, the choice between the two legal bases is difficult as long as we look at the administrative powers not explicitly provided in the Treaties from different perspectives: on the one hand, internal market integration and on the other hand, political consensus.[147] If the former supports the role of the EU legislature (the European Parliament and the Council acting in the ordinary legislative procedure under Article 289 TFEU) in the design of the powers of EU agencies, the latter is open to inter-governmental negotiation also in the scope of the powers.[148] Nonetheless, it is the uncertainly broad reach of Article 114 TFEU itself that favours the development of agencies such as the ESMA operating in the internal market with harmonisation functions.[149]

The Hercules columns of the EU agencies' harmonisation competence should therefore be set out: on the one hand, the conferral of such powers by the EU legislature represents the subjective limit to the development of EU agencies' powers; on the other hand, the functioning and/or the construction of the internal market is the objective limit to their responsibilities. If appropriate guarantees do not apply to the exercise of these powers, this serves as a broad regulatory space. Be the tasks purely technical or to some extent discretionary, legal guarantees are required to ensure their compatibility with the framework of the Treaties, so that they do not become a sort of 'modern kings'.[150]

[145] C-270/12 *United Kingdom v Council of European Union and European Parliament* (n 90), Opinion of AG Jääskinen, paras 45–52.

[146] Ibid paras 54–58.

[147] M Simoncini, 'The Erosion of the *Meroni* Doctrine: The Case of the European Aviation Safety Agency' (2015) 21 *European Public Law* 309, 341.

[148] See D Geradin and N Petit, 'The Development of Agencies at EU and National Levels: Conceptual Analysis and Proposals for Reform' (2004) 23 *Yearbook of European Law* 137, 177; van Gestel, 'European Regulatory Agencies Adrift?' (n 127) 192; Chamon, *EU Agencies* (n 75) 148.

[149] See P Van Cleynenbreugel, '*Meroni* Circumvented? Article 114 TFEU and EU Regulatory Agencies' (2014) 21 *Maastricht Journal of European and Comparative Law* 64, 72, who then argues that the open-ended reading of Art 114 TFEU affects the constitutional relevance of the *Meroni* doctrine, as it allows the development of 'operational support structures' through a process of Europeanisation of national functions, instead of delegation at the EU level. *Contra*, Chamon, *EU Agencies* (n 75) 196–97, who criticises the idea that Europeanisation can rule out the relevance of *Meroni* for EU agencies; J-P Schneider, 'A Common Framework for Decentralized EU Agencies and the *Meroni* Doctrine' (2009) *Administrative Law Review* 29, 38.

[150] The definition is borrowed from an unpublished paper by Cassese on the role of independent administrative authorities in national states; see S Cassese, 'Modern Kings: Non-elected Bodies in Modern Democracies' paper presented at the CREA Conference, Ancienne École Polytechnique, Paris, 1998.

In order to ensure the principle of institutional balance of powers in the conferral of regulatory tasks on EU agencies, the *Meroni* requirements become relevant. Accountability mechanisms must apply and ensure their full commitment to the Treaties in line with the safeguard of democratic rule. The CJEU has set the criteria against which the responsibilities of independent agencies at the national level should be identified and required them to be made compatible with democratic rule; namely, with parliamentary oversight in terms of both ex ante controls (conferral of defined powers by the Parliament; appointment of the authority board by the Parliament itself or the government) and ex post accountability mechanisms (activity reports to the Parliament).[151] *Mutatis mutandis*, the same framework should reasonably be applicable to EU agencies. The institutional relationships with both the EU legislature and the Commission should be designed so that their prerogatives are preserved against EU agencies' action.[152] Political accountability and legal accountability structure the legitimate conferral of powers on EU agencies.[153] This means focusing on both institutional relations and judicial review, as the former links administration to the democratic circuit and the latter ensures judicial protection against administrative action.

VII. ADMINISTRATIVE POWERS AND THE NON-DELEGATION DOCTRINE: VARIABLES FOR AN ENQUIRY

In the *ESMA Short Selling* case, the CJEU missed the chance to entrench the legality of EU agencies' acts in the framework of the Treaties. As long as the effects of EU agencies' legal status and the administrative nature of their powers are not thoroughly clarified, their competence to adopt acts with a regulatory impact can be challenged and their compliance with the democratic principle of accountability questioned. Despite gradual changes, discretion and accountability still remain blurred as the Achilles' heel of an establishing administration by EU agencies. As long as these issues are not settled, how EU agencies participate in the EU executive function and ensure the principle of legality remains uncertain. Sooner or later, therefore, the CJEU will be called upon to review EU agencies' powers in light of the *Meroni* doctrine. The *ESMA Short Selling* case has not elucidated the accountability structure behind the rules and the conditions for the legitimate allocation of regulatory competences on EU agencies. If new regulatory powers are allocated to EU agencies, the *ESMA Short Selling* case will probably be only the first of a series of cases which will dispute the legitimacy of their competence.

[151] C-518/07 *Commission v Germany* [2010] ECR I-01885, paras 42–46.

[152] See S Lavrjissen and L Hancher, 'Networks on Track: From European Regulatory Networks to European Regulatory "Network Agencies"' (2009) 36 *Legal Issues of European Integration* 23, 38; Griller and Orator, 'Everything Under Control?' (n 63) 27; Chamon, *EU Agencies* (n 75) 202–3.

[153] See JL Mashaw, 'Accountability and Institutional Design: Some Thoughts on the Grammar of Governance' in MW Dowdle, *Public Accountability: Designs, Dilemmas and Experiences* (Cambridge University Press, 2006) 115, 120–21.

The weak grip of the Treaties on EU agencies may explain the hesitation in the definition of a self-standing accountability model which would secure their place in the EU executive and fully open the development of an extensive administrative regulation by EU agencies within the framework of the Treaties. The CJEU preferred to mellow the *Meroni* doctrine in light of the new framework of the Treaties by emphasising that no shift of responsibilities occurs as long as EU agencies' powers are firmly circumscribed and amenable to judicial review. According to Chamon, the CJEU reduced the *Meroni* doctrine to this 'hollowed-out' single requirement, so that its grip on the growth of EU agencies' powers became 'ethereal'.[154] In my view, the *ESMA Short Selling* case weakened judicial control when it did not clarify the nature of EU agencies' powers, and missed the chance to enlighten whether this *Meroni* requirement replicates the *Köster* principle of non-delegation of 'the essential elements of a matter'.[155] If these issues had been explained, the new interpretation of the *Meroni* requirements concerning the limits to the delegation of powers would have strengthened the understanding of EU executive powers. The grip of *Meroni* would have been qualitatively strengthened as it would have been able to effectively guide administrative rule-making against the backdrop of the (indirect) recognition of EU agencies' powers in the Treaties.

Yet the interpretative exercise remains unavoidable. The *ESMA Short Selling* case produced indecisive findings about the nature of the powers and the limits to administrative action by decentralised agencies. Nonetheless, it indicated some general criteria that should guide their administrative decision-making with regulatory impact. The model of delegation designed in the *ESMA Short Selling* case is based on the implementation of the principle of legality as a hierarchical principle which governs the relations between the legislature and the relevant administration. An autonomous agency established under EU law is empowered by secondary law to take action under specific criteria and conditions in a technical matter and its acts should be amenable to judicial review.

If this judgment has opened a new era for agencification by paving the (still long) way to the recognition of EU agencies' regulatory competence, the development of EU agencies' powers requires further legal qualification. The legal guarantees for their action must be ruled out. The question of the sustainability of EU agencies' regulation needs to respond to two sub-questions that set the reach and the limits to lawful delegation at the core of non-delegation concerns. First, the nature of the delegated powers must be characterised. The question of the compatibility of EU agencies' powers with the non-delegation doctrine should therefore be taken from the perspective of the nature of the discretionary powers exercised. The allocation of regulatory competences to EU agencies requires a substantive clarification of the nature, the reach and the limits of their powers.

[154] Chamon, *EU Agencies* (n 75) 247.

[155] On the mixed use of *Meroni* and *Köster* see C-154/04 and C-155/04 *Alliance for Natural Health* (n 49) paras 90–92. In the literature, see Ritleng, 'The Reserved Domain of the Legislature' (n 39) 148.

In addition, how EU agencies may legitimately participate in the regulatory function without infringing the constitutional principle of non-delegation needs to be ascertained. This second condition focuses on the existence of accountability structures governing the limits and ensuring adequate checks-and-balances to the exercise of administrative powers by EU agencies.

The first variable of the enquiry therefore considers whether EU agencies may participate in the regulatory function. Chapter 3 will specifically address this issue and will frame this *if*-condition. In light of the characterisation of EU agencies' (possible) powers, the second variable allows the understanding of the accountability regime that will frame the exercise of the identified power. Chapter 4 will investigate this other aspect for legitimate delegation and will concern a *how*-condition. These two variables will guide the analysis as roadmap requirements that will allow us to reach provisional conclusions about the current capability to allocate regulatory powers to EU agencies.

2

Killing Me Softly? The Quasi-Regulatory Powers of EU Agencies

I. INTRODUCTION

THE EXPANSION OF AGENCIES' tasks and responsibilities has been connected to the rise and growth of the so-called regulatory state.[1] However, the rise and growth of EU agencies has been strongly influenced by the particular features of the European polity. As illustrated in Chapter 1, the non-delegation doctrine, as a constitutional principle that positions agencies in the EU institutional framework, has remarkably influenced the allocation of competence to EU agencies. The restrictive reading of *Meroni* has particularly reduced the legal chances to develop a model of administration through EU agencies comparable to national administration systems. Nonetheless, EU agencies have grown, and their tasks and autonomy have been (quantitatively and qualitatively)[2] strengthened, raising important legal issues about their status under EU law. This Chapter aims to discuss this ambiguous stance of EU agencies by questioning the quasi-regulatory competence they actually exercise.

Extensive studies have contributed to understanding the reasons for establishing EU agencies. After more than 20 years, the findings of the 1997 Special Issue of the *Journal of European Public Policy* on European agencies remain seminal. In the deadlock of intergovernmental politics, EU agencies responded to the integration

[1] See F Gilardi, *Delegation in the Regulatory State: Independent Agencies in Western Europe* (Elgar Publishing, 2008) 107–8; D Levi-Faur and J Jordana, 'The Rise of Regulatory Capitalism: The Global Diffusion of a New Order' (2005) 598 *Annals of the American Academy of Political and Social Science* 200. On the notion of regulatory state see in particular G Majone, 'The Rise of the Regulatory State in Europe' (1994) 17 *West European Politics* 77; G Majone, 'The Rise of the Regulatory State in Europe' in R Baldwin, C Scott and C Hood (eds), *A Reader on Regulation* (Oxford University Press, 1998) 192; G Majone, *The Regulatory State and its Legitimacy Problems*, IHS Political Science Series no 56 (1998); G Majone, *The Transformations of the Regulatory State*, AIR Paper (2010), available at www.osservatori-oair.it/wp-content/uploads/2010/10/Paper_Majone_RegulatoryState_sept2010.pdf; G Majone, 'From the Regulatory State to a Democratic Default' (2014) 52 *Journal of Common Market Studies* 1216; but see also R Baldwin, M Cave and M Lodge, *Understanding Regulation*, 2nd edn (Oxford University Press, 2011); M Moran, 'The Rise of the Regulatory State' in D Coen, W Grant and G Wilson (eds), *The Oxford Handbook of Business and Government* (Oxford University Press, 2010) 383.

[2] See M Busuioc, *European Agencies: Law and Practices of Accountability* (Oxford University Press, 2013) 15.

demand by neutralising conflicts under the cover of technical expertise. By providing specialised skills, EU agencies support European integration through the development of harmonisation and coordination practices that shape Member States' enforcement policies in light of EU objectives and rules, with no need to further centralise regulatory powers in the EU institutions. According to Dehousse:

> agencies owe their existence to a paradox. On the one hand, increased uniformity is certainly needed; on the other hand, greater centralization is politically inconceivable, and probably undesirable.[3]

According to Shapiro, agencies were conceived as a kind of neo-functionalist experiment, aimed at integrating Europe 'indirectly' by creating 'Europe-wide epistemic communities whose technical truths transcend intergovernmental politics'.[4] Also Kreher saw in agencies a phenomenon of administrative integration.[5] By fostering interdependencies, administrative integration can prosaically contribute to the enhancement of the connections between the different Member States beyond ambitious political projects.

By reducing politics, enforcement of EU law is believed to be less susceptible to variations.[6] This enhances consistency in the implementation of EU law, as it allows EU institutions to outsource operational functions and concentrate on core tasks.[7] As Rittberger and Wonka have pointed out, this phenomenon can be analysed from two different perspectives: the politics of the creation of EU agencies and the functionalist approach to the problem of credible commitment.[8] On the one hand, political strategies determine the establishment of EU agencies and inter-institutional bargaining affects their powers and organisation. On the other hand, EU agencies' design can rationally respond to functional needs. These approaches are not mutually exclusive and contribute to the explanation of different aspects of the European *agencification* process: the political momentum for their establishment and the regulatory objectives that their establishment pursues.

According to the political approach, EU institutions and the Member States pursue different institutional interests that originate conflicts over the allocation

[3] R Dehousse, 'Regulation by Networks in the European Community: The Role of European Agencies' (1997) 4 *Journal of European Public Policy* 246, 259.

[4] M Shapiro, 'The Problems of Independent Agencies in the United States and the European Union' (1997) 4 *Journal of European Public Policy* 276, 281–82.

[5] A Kreher, 'Agencies in the European Community: A Step Towards Administrative Integration in Europe' (1997) 4 *Journal of European Public Policy* 225.

[6] See B Rittberger and A Wonka, 'Introduction: Agency Governance in the European Union' in B Rittberger and A Wonka (eds), *Agency Governance in the EU* (Routledge, 2012) 2, 3.

[7] See Dehousse, 'Regulation by Networks in the European Community' (n 3) 254–55; G Majone, 'The New European Agencies: Regulation by Information' (1997) 4 *Journal of European Public Policy* 262, 272. See also Communication from the Commission to the European Parliament and the Council, *The Operating Framework for the European Regulatory Agencies*, COM(2002)718 (11 December 2002); Communication from the Commission to the European Parliament and the Council, *European Agencies: The Way Forward*, COM(2008)135 (11 March 2008).

[8] Rittberger and Wonka, 'Introduction' (n 6) 4.

of regulatory authority and its distributional effects.[9] The choice to establish EU agencies rests upon a low degree of distributional conflict and, precisely, upon the unpredictability of the distributional consequences of the delegation of authority to an EU body, or the non-existence of a blocking minority of Member States that incur high distributional costs because of the establishment of a supranational body.[10] Agencies give Member States a 'collective agenda-setting power', while the 'decision-making authority is transferred at the supranational level', so that 'the Commission is formally empowered to enact agency recommendations, and the Parliament gains powers to oversee regulation by a European agency in a sector that was previously out of bounds to them'.[11]

Other factors can, however, concur to define the political momentum for the establishment of EU agencies: so far crises have been the most powerful driving force.[12] The establishment of the European Food Safety Authority (EFSA) is remarkable: it finds its roots in the need to rebuild consumer confidence after the spread of BSE in Europe.[13] A crisis scenario was also at the origin of the establishment of the system of the European Supervisory Authorities (ESAs) in the financial markets and it drove the political momentum for their stronger empowerment. Crises change the ordinary structures of institutional interests and create those unpredictable conditions for engaging in significant (institutional and regulatory) reforms that restore (or further develop) the credibility of the Union.[14]

[9] RD Kelemen and AD Tarrant, 'The Political Foundations of the Eurocracy' (2011) 34 *West European Politics* 922, 925. See also MLP Groenleer, *The Autonomy of European Union Agencies: A Comparative Study of Institutional Development* (Eburon, 2009) 100–8, who considers the functional needs and the political motives; P Magnette, 'The Politics of Regulation in the European Union' in D Geradin, R Muñoz and N Petit (eds), *Regulation through Agencies in the EU: A New Paradigm of European Governance* (Elgar Publishing, 2005) 3, 7–10, who reads the need for agencies in light of the Principal-Agent approach.

[10] Kelemen and Tarrant 'The Political Foundations of the Eurocracy' (n 9) 930. As the historical institutionalist analysis has pointed out, the case for delegation of authority needs to take into account also the inherited institutional context that influences and limits institutional reforms. See K Yesilkagit and J Christensen, 'Institutional Design and Formal Autonomy' (2010) 20 *Journal of Public Administration Research and Theory* 53; M Thatcher, 'The Creation of European Regulatory Agencies and Its Limits: A Comparative Analysis of European Delegation' (2011) 18 *Journal of European Public Policy* 790, who compares three cases: the previous formal delegation was to the Commission, which gives poor results for agency creation as in the case of the Body of European Regulators for Electronic Communication (BEREC); the previous delegation to national regulators, which confers limited powers on the new agency, especially related to cross-border questions, such as in the case of the BEREC and the Agency for the Cooperation of Energy Regulators (ACER); and the previous delegation to European networks of regulators, where the agency creation corresponds to the opportunity of the Commission to expand its powers, as in the case of the European Aviation Safety Agency (EASA) built on the regulators' club of the Joint Aviation Authority (JAA).

[11] Kelemen and Tarrant, 'The Political Foundations of the Eurocracy' (n 9) 931.

[12] See Busuioc, *European Agencies* (n 2) 32–33.

[13] See E Vos, 'EU Food Safety Regulation in the Aftermath of the BSE Crisis' (2000) 23 *Journal of Consumer Policy* 227; D Byrne, 'The Genesis of EFSA and the First 10 Years of EU Food Law' in A Alemanno and S Gabbi, *Foundations of EU Law and Policy: Ten Years of the European Food Safety Authority* (Routledge, 2014) 17.

[14] On the establishment of EU agencies as a means to enhance the credibility of EU policies, see G Majone, 'The Credibility Crisis of Community Regulation' (2000) 38 *Journal of Common Market*

The functional approach focuses on the efficiency benefits that arise from the establishment of an EU agency and portrays it as a regulatory option for dealing with issues that require high technical competences and that cannot be addressed through the mere coordination of national regulators.[15] Economists have notably explained this approach through the subsidiarity approach.[16] When a measure falls within the area of shared competence between the EU and the Member States, the limited reach of national jurisdictions may be insufficient to achieve the specific policy goal and the EU should take action.[17] Only when EU action is appropriate on the basis of the subsidiarity test would the policy in question effectively benefit from the supranational intervention. Otherwise, the main cost is a market distortion and too much regulation and/or other forms of centralisation for the internal market, reducing its gains and unduly hindering Member States from pursuing their own policies. According to Pelkmans,[18] a subsidiarity test should begin with identifying the 'need to act in common' based on cross-border externalities and scale. The test should then ascertain whether cooperation between national regulators can be sufficient and credible for market players. If this is not feasible, a shift of the regulatory functions to the EU level should be envisaged and the establishment of an EU agency should be objectively considered according to the proportionality principle.

Such an institutional choice, however, does not indicate the substitution of a supranational administration for the regulatory powers of the national ones. In the European multilevel governance, EU agencies emerged rather as autonomous entities, which contribute to mediating interests and neutralising conflicts between Member States and EU institutions. So far, they have not become independent

Studies 273, 289; S Krapohl, 'Credible Commitment in Non-Independent Regulatory Agencies: A Comparative Analysis of the European Agencies for Pharmaceuticals and Foodstuffs' (2004) 10 *European Law Journal* 518, 523; Busuioc, *European Agencies* (n 2) 25–27.

[15] The establishment of an EU agency requires the impact assessment of all the relevant regulatory options; see Common Approach Annex to the Joint Statement of the European Parliament, the Council of the EU and the European Commission of 19 July 2012 on Decentralised Agencies, paras 2–5. Impact assessment was already required in the Draft Interinstitutional Agreement of the European Commission on the Operating Framework for the European Regulatory Agencies, COM(2005)59 (25 February 2005) para 7.

[16] See J Pelkmans, *Testing for Subsidiarity*, Bruges European Economic Policy Briefings no 13 (2006); J Pelkmans, *Subsidiarity Between Law and Economics*, Bruges Research Papers in Law no 1 (2005); S Ederveen, G Gelauff and J Pelkmans, 'Assessing Subsidiarity' in G Gelauff, I Grilo and A Lejour (eds), *Subsidiarity and Economic Reform in Europe* (Springer, 2008) 19. See also R Van den Bergh, 'The Subsidiarity Principle in European Community Law: Some Insights from Law and Economics' (1994) 1 *Maastricht Journal of European and Comparative Law* 337; G Majone, 'La crescita dei poteri regolativi nella Comunità europea' (1993) 25 *Rivista Italiana di Scienza Politica* 409, 431–32, who exemplifies the subsidiarity approach to agencification with the failure of the national regulators' network for the authorisation and the mutual recognition of pharmaceutical products and the final establishment of the EMA.

[17] See A Estella, *The EU Principle of Subsidiarity and its Critique* (Oxford University Press, 2002) 105; R Schütze, *From Dual to Cooperative Federalism: The Changing Structure of European Law* (Oxford University Press, 2009) 250.

[18] Pelkmans, *Testing for Subsidiarity* and *Subsidiarity Between Law and Economics* (n 16).

regulators, as they do not have the full powers of independent adjudication and rule-making. Alongside political conflict, a legal rationale explains this limitation. As Majone has correctly observed, the European administrative culture developed along the particular constraints of the EU polity: the *Meroni* doctrine and the legislative approach to integration based on national enforcement of EU policies prevented the allocation of broad regulatory tasks and responsibilities to EU agencies.[19] Their powers consist of indirect instruments aimed at committing the relevant actors to common purposes that produce regulatory effects. Traditionally, they cooperate with the Member States and the EU institutions by providing technical advice on regulatory choices. Recently, the intensity of EU agencies' powers has increased, questioning the traditional place of EU agencies under EU law and opening distinctive scenarios for the future developments of the EU agencification process. The reinforcement of EU agencies' powers, on the one hand, and the development of much more autonomous bodies with new competences, on the other, contribute to partially changing the features of EU agencies. Enhanced participation in the rule-making process, stronger standardisation practices and selected regulatory powers have innovated the pattern of EU agencies' powers, potentially widening their scope towards independent regulation.

This Chapter investigates these powers of EU agencies with the aim of understanding how they contribute to sector-specific regulation. In doing so, the Chapter focuses on the powers of the European Aviation Safety Agency (EASA) and of the European Supervisory Authorities in the financial markets (ESAs) as exemplary case studies that challenge the traditional framework of EU agencies' powers and develop different mechanisms of cooperation between the Member States and the EU institutions. As Lavrijssen and Ottow emphasised, the specificity of these agencies consists in the fact that they institutionalise previous cooperative networks between the relevant national authorities.[20] Although the added value of EU agencies has been disputed, they clearly represent an innovative system of governance aimed at enhancing the expertise and the transparency of enforcement. EASA took over the Joint Aviation Authorities (JAAs) cooperation, which could not agree common objectives in a timely manner and did not ensure the implementation of such commitments by member countries;[21] the ESAs substituted the system of

[19] Majone, 'The New European Agencies' (n 7) 263–65.

[20] S Lavrijssen and A Ottow, 'Independent Supervisory Authorities: A Fragile Concept' (2012) 39 *Legal Issues of Economic Integration* 419, 438–40. See also S Lavrijssen and L Hancher, 'Networks on Track: From European Regulatory Networks to European Regulatory "Network Agencies"' (2009) 36 *Legal Issues of Economic Integration* 23, 53–54.

[21] On a critical position regarding the benefit of agencification in aviation, see A Schout, 'Inspecting Aviation Safety in the EU: EASA as an Administrative Innovation?' in E Vos (ed), *European Risk Governance: Its Science, Its Inconclusiveness and Its Effectiveness*, Connex Report Series no 6 (2008) 257, 267–68. Schout particularly shows that although the powers of the Commission were effectively strengthened, the negotiations for the establishment of the EASA failed to centralise powers and invert the previous system (286). See also A Schout, 'Assessing the Added Value of an EU Agency for Aviation Safety' (2011) 31 *Journal of Public Policy* 363.

committees operating in the same financial sectors: the Committee of European Securities Regulators (CESR), the Committee of European Banking Supervisors (CEBS), and the Committee of European Insurance and Occupational Pensions Supervisors (CEIOPS), which inadequately contributed to the complex regulatory process known as the Lamfalussy process with non-binding advice to the Commission on technical matters and ineffective powers to commit Member States to the enforcement of EU law.[22] Unlike the EFSA, for instance, they do not originate from a top-down institutional exercise of EU policies, but they are the product of bottom-up sectorial needs that reject centralisation in the Commission. From an organisational standpoint, however, they design different models of cooperation with the EU executive, which frame their different degree of autonomy from the Commission. By enjoying stronger autonomy in support of their enhanced powers, the ESAs particularly push the organisational model of EU agencies to its limits. Nonetheless, the comparison of their powers functions to demonstrate the prominent decentralisation of administrative powers with regulatory effects in the internal market beyond Treaties' institutions and the Member States. By combining specific adjudication powers with forms of rule-making powers, they are able to push forward the limits to administrative regulation.[23]

After the introduction of a functional taxonomy of EU agencies' powers (section II), the Chapter presents the peculiarity of the EASA's and the ESAs' powers. It does so against the backdrop of the administrative law distinction between adjudication and rule-making (section III). Individual sub-sections address specific supervisory powers, strengthened participation in formal rule-making of the European Commission and independent standardisation practices as the characteristic instruments at the disposal of these EU agencies. Section IV and its sub-sections compare and contrast the identified powers with the aim of disclosing their quasi-regulatory content. The final remarks under section V outline the tensions connected to the 'resistance' of these hybrid instruments to administrative governance.

II. DIVERSITY OF EU AGENCIES AND TAXONOMY OF THEIR POWERS

Being entities with their own legal personality autonomous from EU institutions and governed by EU public law, EU agencies operate as decentralised

[22] See E Posner, 'The Lamfalussy Process: Polyarchic Origins of Networked Financial Rule-making in the EU' in CF Sabel and J Zeitlin (eds), *Experimentalist Governance in the European Union* (Oxford University Press, 2010) 43, 58; A Ottow, 'The New European Supervisory Architecture of the Financial Markets' in M Everson, C Monda and E Vos (eds), *European Agencies in Between Institutions and Member States* (Kluwer, 2014) 123, 127–28; on a more critical position on agencification in the financial sector, see N Moloney, *EU Securities and Financial Markets Regulation*, 3rd edn (Oxford University Press, 2014) 875–78 and 955–56.

[23] HCH Hofmann and A Morini, 'Constitutional Aspects of the Pluralisation of the EU Executive Through "Agencification"' (2012) *European Law Review* 419, 431; Busuioc, *European Agencies* (n 2) 19.

organisations.[24] When they institutionalise a supranational approach to cross-border regulatory issues, they realise the diffusion of responsibilities and tasks outside the European Commission's hierarchy. Decentralisation therefore identifies a composite phenomenon: the centralisation of some responsibilities at the EU level and their delocalisation from the authority of the Commission.[25]

Despite this general definition, any attempt to outline the legal nature of EU agencies has had to face the multiform shapes of the phenomenon. Since 2002, the Commission has meant to rationalise the operating framework of EU agencies by clarifying their organisations, functions, controls and accountability.[26] Legal scholarship has deeply engaged in the possible taxonomy of EU agencies, but EU agencies are far from being completely explained as a legal phenomenon. The different taxonomies had the merit of explaining aspects of their nature, but their place within the EU legal framework still remains uncertain. The reason is that secondary legislation, not Treaties, regulates agencies. This makes the identification of the constitutional limits to their action very difficult. Conversely, when the competence is covered by the Treaties, no general legitimacy issue arises.[27] In addition, when the Treaties refer to the indistinct plurality of agencies and bodies, they

[24] The legal scholarship agrees that these are the minimum legal requirements necessary to identify a body as an EU decentralised agency. See E Vos, 'European Agencies and the Composite EU Executive' in M Everson, C Monda and E Vos (eds), *European Agencies in Between Institutions and Member States* (Kluwer, 2014) 11, 19; M Chamon, *EU Agencies: Legal and Political Limits to the Transformation of EU Administration* (Oxford University Press, 2016) 5–15.

[25] Note that the delocalisation is also physical, as EU agencies have their headquarters throughout Europe and not in Brussels.

[26] See COM(2002)718; COM(2005)59, abandoned by the Council. After this failure, COM(2008)135 aimed to launch an inter-institutional dialogue between the Commission, the European Parliament and the Council and a more coherent approach to EU agencies was stipulated in the 2012 Joint Statement and Common Approach. Although legally non-binding, the 2012 Common Approach guides the initiatives and reforms of individual EU agencies and the rationalization process is monitored with regular progress reports (see *Commission Progress Report on the Implementation of the Common Approach* (10 December 2013); *Commission Progress Report on the Implementation of the Common Approach*, COM(2015)179 (24 April 2015)).

[27] The Treaties mention only few EU agencies and bodies. Under Art 286(2) of the EC Treaty, this was the case of the European Data Protection Supervisor (EDPS) which was recognised as an 'independent supervisory body responsible for monitoring the application of such Community acts to Community institutions and bodies and shall adopt any other relevant provisions as appropriate'. Revisions occurred with the Lisbon Treaty and today Art 16(2) TFEU and Art 39 of the Treaty on European Union (TEU) confer control over the compliance with data protection rules generally on 'independent authorities', giving the impression of referring indistinctly to national authorities and the EDPS. In addition, Arts 85 and 88 TFEU (but before the Lisbon Treaty, Arts 29–31 TEU) respectively cover the mission of Eurojust and Europol, which were established under the former third pillar, respectively by Council Decision 2002/187/JHA of 28 February 2002 setting up Eurojust with a view to reinforcing the fight against serious crime [2002] OJ L 63, and Council Decision 2009/371/JHA of 6 April 2009 establishing the European Police Office (Europol) [2009] OJ L 21/37. Note that according to Chiti, the intergovernmental origin of these agencies makes their functioning different from the decentralised agencies originally established under the first pillar in that inter-state cooperation is voluntary and reserves only a marginal role to the Commission. See E Chiti, 'An Important Part of the EU's Institutional Machinery: Features, Problems and Perspectives of European Agencies' (2009) 46 *Common Market Law Review* 1395, 1398–99. See also Busuioc, *European Agencies* (n 2) 29–30.

are sibylline about their status and competence, so that fundamental questions for the legal analysis remain ambiguous.

The issue is that unlike in national jurisdictions, the source of administrative powers and the position of agencies within the EU legal order are not clearly defined. At the EU level, enforcement has been generally based on the principle of indirect administration through national implementation.[28] Agencies developed beyond this principle. However, the steady expansion of their tasks and responsibilities has been agreed on the basis of specific issues and cannot be understood as a general project aimed at developing the administrative capacity at the EU level.

The taxonomy of EU agencies based on the functions that they are asked to exercise clearly shows the case-by-case approach of the EU legislature to this decentralised model of direct administration. The organisation and competence of EU agencies are designed on the tasks and the responsibilities that they are allocated.[29] As the 2005 Commission draft institutional agreement pointed out, 'they are typified by their diversity'.[30] When reading functions together with the time that EU agencies have been established, the different 'waves' of agencification complement the functional taxonomy by showing a trend in the growth of agencies' powers, which uncovers the substantive growth of the enforcement functions at the EU level.[31]

Many legal scholars engaged in the identification of the functions that EU agencies perform and they observed a number of different activities that show to what extent agencies actually participate in the EU integration process. The first general distinction that should be traced is between these decentralised agencies and the so-called executive agencies. Meant to assist the European Commission in the pure management of EU programmes, executive agencies are created by the Commission itself and operate under its direct administrative responsibility and strict supervision.[32] In contrast, decentralised agencies are established by a legislative act and contribute to regulation and policy implementation as autonomous bodies.[33] For this reason they have been traditionally labelled as regulatory agencies, because they participate to a certain extent in the regulation of specific sectors.[34]

[28] Article 197 TFEU.

[29] See Chamon, *EU Agencies* (n 24) 20.

[30] COM(2005)59, para 1.

[31] See D Geradin and N Petit, 'The Development of Agencies at EU and National Levels: Conceptual Analysis and Proposal of Reform' (2004) 23 *Yearbook of European Law* 137, 181; P Craig, *EU Administrative Law*, 2nd edn (Oxford University Press, 2012) 145–47; Vos, 'European Agencies and the Composite EU Executive' (n 24) 13–17.

[32] The statute of these agencies is regulated by Council Regulation 58/2003/EC of 19 December 2002 laying down the statute for executive agencies to be entrusted with certain tasks in the management of Community programmes [2002] OJ L 11/1. See P Craig, *EU Administrative Law*, 3rd edn (Oxford University Press, 2015) 70.

[33] See COM(2002)718; COM(2008)135.

[34] According to Vos, the identification of these agencies as 'decentralised' instead of 'regulatory' is to be preferred, because it takes account of the level at which they operate in the executive and of their geographical spread in the EU. Moreover, it allows the classification of EU agencies on different grounds rather than only their functions. See Vos, 'European Agencies and the Composite EU Executive' (n 24) 20.

As executive agencies work under the lead of the Commission, the traditional hierarchical model applies. Conversely, decentralised agencies have an autonomous area of competence within the EU legal framework that will be fully explored.

Founding Regulations establish functional relations between institutions, decentralised agencies and Member States, so that the pure hierarchical scheme cannot apply. The result is a (functionally) diversified and polyhedral system of agencies whose functions vary according to the place EU institutions (and the Member States) want to give them within the EU legal framework.

First, decentralised agencies perform information tasks. This is Majone's model of 'regulation by information' that aims to produce and share with the EU institutions and the Member States technical and scientific information in their specific area of expertise.[35] Secondly, they also have a cooperation function aimed at producing best practices and coordinating the networks of the Member States and EU institutions in the relevant area of their expertise. If these are transversal functions common to all the different agencies, there are a few more functions that are allocated only in selected cases. These are further powers that allow EU decentralised agencies to participate proactively in the regulation of the relevant area of their expertise. These powers consist of the capability to assist the European Commission in the formulation of policies through opinions, recommendations and reports, to take binding individual decisions under specific circumstances, and to adopt soft law with a de facto regulatory impact.

The introduction of these powers has been very carefully designed to fill the gap between the functional need to confer powers on specialised administrative organisations not explicitly envisaged in the Treaties, and the legal (constitutional) need to comply with the non-delegation doctrine. By developing these specific instruments, EU agencies' expertise has been acquired for the regulatory process with the aim of limiting their capability to set general rules. Nonetheless, these powers enhance the administrative capacity of EU agencies by making them more mature administrative organisations. Only a few agencies have all these powers and most of them operate in the internal market.

By elaborating on the European Commission's taxonomy of EU agencies' powers,[36] Griller and Orator classified EU agencies 'according to the mode and scope of instruments they dispose' and identified four types of agencies: ordinary agencies, pre-decision-making agencies, genuine decision-making agencies and rule-making agencies.[37] In their taxonomy, all the EU decentralised agencies are included in the first type, as all of them perform either information or cooperation activities. This reflects the idea of transversal functions. Pre-decision-making agencies include those agencies that strongly influence the Commission in the adoption of its own final decisions: this is the case of the European Medicines

[35] Majone, 'The New European Agencies' (n 7).

[36] See COM(2002)718, para 2; COM(2005)59, para 7.2.

[37] See S Griller and A Orator, 'Everything Under Control? The "Way Forward" for European Agencies in the Footsteps of the *Meroni* Doctrine' (2010) 35 *European Law Review* 3, 13–14.

Agency (EMA),[38] the European Food Safety Authority (EFSA),[39] the European Maritime Safety Agency (EMSA)[40] and the European Union Agency for Railway (ERA).[41] This covers the activities of the assistance to the Commission through opinions, recommendations and inspections. As Griller and Orator point out, although EU agencies' decisions are not legally binding, nonetheless they must be taken into account in the Commission's decision-making process and represent 'de facto decision making powers'.[42]

The third category covers those agencies that have the capacity to take decisions legally binding on third parties under specific conditions. This is the case of the Office for the Harmonisation of the Internal Market (OHIM), now the European Union Intellectual Property Office (EUIPO),[43] the Community Plant Variety Office (CPVO),[44] of the European Chemical Agency (ECHA),[45] the European Aviation Safety Agency (EASA)[46] and the ESAs in the financial markets.[47]

[38] Regulation 726/2004/EC of the European Parliament and of the Council of 31 March 2004 laying down Community procedures for the authorisation and supervision of medicinal products for human and veterinary use and establishing a European Medicines Agency [2004] OJ L 136/1.

[39] Regulation 178/2002/EC of the European Parliament and of the Council of 28 January 2002 laying down the general principles and requirements of food law, establishing the European Food Safety Authority and laying down procedures in matters of food safety [2002] OJ L 31/1.

[40] Regulation 1406/2002/EC of the European Parliament and of the Council of 27 June 2002 establishing the objectives and tasks, the internal structure and functioning and the financial requirements of EMSA [2002] OJ L 208/1.

[41] Corrigendum to Regulation 881/2004/EC of the European Parliament and the Council of 29 April 2004 establishing a European railway agency [2004] OJ L 220/3.

[42] Griller and Orator, 'Everything Under Control?' (n 37) 14. See also Chiti, 'An Important Part of the EU's Institutional Machinery' (n 27) 1405–6; E Chiti, *Le agenzie europee. Unità e decentramento nelle amministrazioni comunitarie* (Cedam, 2002) 209–19 (with reference to the EMA).

[43] Council Regulation 40/1994/EC of 20 December 1993 on the Community trade mark [1994] OJ L 011; Regulation 2015/2424/EU of the European Palrliament and of the Council of 16 December 2015 amending Council Regulation (EC) 207/2009 on the Community trade mark and Commission Regulation (EC) 2868/95 implementing Council Regulation (EC) 40/94 on the Community trade mark, and repealing Commission Regulation (EC) 2869/95 on the fees payable to the Office for Harmonisation in the Internal Market (Trade Marks and Designs) [2015] OJ L 341/21.

[44] Council Regulation 2100/1994/EC of 27 July 1994 on Community plant variety rights [1994] OJ L 227/1.

[45] Corrigendum to Regulation 1907/2006/EC of the European Parliament and of the Council of 18 December 2006 concerning the registration, evaluation, authorisation and restriction of chemicals (REACH), establishing a European Chemicals Agency, amending Directive 1999/45 and repealing Regulation 793/93 and Regulation 1488/94, as well as Directive 76/769 and Directives 91/155, 93/67, 93/105 and 2000/21 [2006] OJ L 396/3.

[46] Regulation 1592/2002/EC of the European Parliament and the Council of 15 July 2002 on common rules in the field of civil aviation and establishing a European Aviation Safety Agency [2002] OJ L 240/1.

[47] Regulation 1093/2010/EU of the European Parliament and of the Council of 24 November 2010 establishing a European Supervisory Authority (European Banking Authority), amending Decision No 716/2009/EC and repealing Commission Decision 2009/78/EC [2010] OJ L 331; Regulation 1094/2010/EU of the European Parliament and of the Council of 24 November 2010 establishing a European Supervisory Authority (European Insurance and Occupational Pensions Authority), amending Decision No 716/2009/EC and repealing Commission Decision 2009/79/EC [2010] OJ L 331; Regulation 1095/2010/EU of the European Parliament and of the Council of 24 November 2010 establishing a European Supervisory Authority (European Securities and Markets Authority), amending Decision No 716/2009/EC and repealing Commission Decision 2009/77/EC [2010] OJ L 331.

The last category envisaged is the model of the rule-making agency, which has powers to adopt rules of general application comparable to national regulatory agencies.[48] Griller and Orator emphasise that, so far, no EU agency exercises genuine rule-making powers. However, they indirectly recognise the existence of a grey area of de facto rule-making, which Busuioc identified under the category of quasi-regulatory agencies endowed with particularly strong recommendatory powers.[49] I do recognise the need to address quasi-regulatory powers as a distinct category in the taxonomy of EU agencies' powers and make their regulatory content explicit. By elaborating on Griller and Orator's taxonomy, a further category should be added: the pre-rule-making agencies adopting quasi-regulatory acts. This category aims to cover all those instruments at the disposal of EU agencies which may indirectly contribute to regulating the internal market. Although EU agencies do not have full powers to adjudicate and rule,[50] administrative law can contribute to shedding light on this set of quasi-regulatory activities and so help to understand the limits to the exercise of EU agencies' powers within the EU legal framework.

III. CHALLENGES OF ADJUDICATION AND EXECUTIVE RULE-MAKING

Administrative law distinguishes implementation powers between adjudication and executive rule-making. Adjudication concerns individual decision-making, whereas executive rule-making defines the production of general rules governing the conduct of natural or legal persons. EU decentralised agencies exercise a set of tasks that participate at different levels in these activities. When implementing EU policies, EU agencies have a range of limited administrative powers, which include some forms of adjudication and executive rule-making in sector-specific domains. Agencies can participate in the adjudication activities through their own decision-making process or by issuing opinions extremely relevant in the decision-making process of other institutions. Executive rule-making can be broadly understood, so as to include all those activities that have a regulatory impact. Accordingly, it covers not only formal rule-making procedures resulting in binding acts, but also soft law powers that direct but do not bind their addressees[51] and those supervisory tasks that may involve the exercise of some regulatory functions.[52]

[48] In the same sense see Geradin and Petit, 'The Development of Agencies at EU and National Levels' (n 31) 183.

[49] Busuioc, *European Agencies* (n 2) 41.

[50] To say it with Craig, they are not 'true' regulatory agencies. See P Craig, *EU Law: Texts, Cases and Materials*, 6th edn (Oxford University Press, 2015) 69.

[51] On soft law as de facto rule-making see E Chiti, 'European Agencies' Rulemaking: Powers, Procedures and Assessment' (2013) 19 *European Law Journal* 93, 95–96, 102–3, who identifies a model of 'regulation by soft law' which pairs with the powers of EU agencies in formal rule-making procedures.

[52] This interpretation is in line with the findings of the Court of Justice in the so-called *ESMA Short Selling* case (see below). In fact, the Court considered the ESMA's direct supervision tasks as a kind of regulatory power aimed 'to adopt measures of general application' which 'may also include rules

To explore these sets of activities, the following sub-sections portray administrative powers conferred on the EASA and the ESAs as significant case studies. The outline of their competence aims to set the scene for the analysis of the nature and the limits to the exercise of their quasi-regulatory powers. The analysis proceeds by distinguishing adjudication, participation in the formal rule-making and soft law powers that combine to enforce EU legislation and its goals effectively and consistently. The goal is to make explicit the quasi-regulatory content embedded in every activity that they are called to perform.

A. Competence of the European Aviation Safety Authority

The EASA is bestowed with competences related to the implementation of the Single European Sky (SES), a fundamental European policy aimed at improving air transport in Europe by providing common rules for the efficient management of European airspaces. In order to enhance the capacity of the air infrastructure and the sustainability of increasing air traffic demand in Europe, two packages of EU legislation were introduced with the aim of addressing the gaps in European air traffic management (ATM) and reinforcing safety by restructuring European airspaces and air navigation services (ANS).[53]

The development of the SES regulation can be considered a clear result of the challenges raised in the internal market of air transport. Since efficiency and coordination in aviation are indispensable for the prevention of air traffic congestion, the satisfaction of the future needs in terms of capacity and safety, and the reduction of environmental footprint, the performance of these functions needs to improve the management of airspaces and to rationalise the use of the sky as

affecting any natural or legal person who has a specific financial instrument or specific class of financial instruments or who enter into certain financial transactions' (see C-270/12 *United Kingdom v Council and European Parliament* ECLI:EU:C:2014:18, para 64).

[53] The first package of regulations (so-called SES I) was introduced in 2004 and it consists of four pieces of regulation: Framework Regulation 549/2004/EC of the European Parliament and the Council of 10 March 2004 laying down the framework for the creation of the single European sky [2004] OJ L 96/1; Regulation 550/2004/EC of the European Parliament and the Council of 10 March 2004 on the provision of air navigation services in the single European sky [2004] OJ L 96/10 ('Service Provision Regulation'); Regulation 551/2004/EC of the European Parliament and the Council of 10 March 2004 on the organisation and use of the airspace in the Single European Sky [2004] OJ L 96/20 ('Airspace Regulation'); Regulation 552/2004/EC of the European Parliament and the Council of 10 March 2004 on the interoperability of the European Air Traffic Management network [2004] OJ L 96/26 ('Interoperability Regulation'). In 2009, after many single amendments and the 2007 report on the implementation of such legislation, a second package of measures was delivered (so-called SES II), which aimed to address the growing demand for air transport by improving the performance and sustainability of the European aviation system through the introduction of a new operational concept of airspace, which overcomes national boundaries for the establishment of functional airspace blocks (FABs). See Regulation 1070/2009/EC of the European Parliament and the Council of 21 October 2009 amending Regulations (EC) 549/2004, 550/2004, 551/2004 and 552/2004 in order to improve the performance and sustainability of the European aviation system [2009] OJ L 300/34.

a scant European resource. EU regulation has complemented the jurisdiction of individual states in the attempt to allow the freedom of movement of people and goods more effectively in Europe.

In this framework, the EASA has been progressively bestowed with fundamental tasks for the development of safety and environmental protection within the SES. It is establishing regulation attributed to the Agency with the responsibility for the airworthiness and environmental certification of aeronautical products, parts and appliances.[54] The initial scope of the EASA's responsibilities has been extended by Regulation 216/2008/EC (the so-called Basic Regulation) to air operations (OPS), pilot licencing (FCL) and the safety of third country operators/aircraft.[55] In 2009, the scope was further extended to aerodromes, ATM/ANS (linked to the SES II package) and air traffic controllers, as it is related to the development of a common EU framework for civil aviation.[56] The EASA's responsibilities now effectively cover all main aspects of aviation safety. When developing these tasks, the EASA exercises powers which contribute to shaping the air transport market according to EU regulatory goals. In the context of the aviation strategy for Europe,[57] the Commission has supported the further enhancement of the EASA's mandate and its leading role in aviation safety.[58] Its 2015 legislative proposal aimed to rationalise and strengthen the rules on civil aviation, and it is currently under consideration of the Council (in second reading) in the ordinary legislative procedure. If the current text is passed, the EASA will be in charge of developing, adopting, publishing, and subsequently updating the European Plan for Aviation Safety setting out the necessary measures to mitigate safety risks.[59] Its responsibilities will also be extended to unmanned aircraft,[60] environmental compatibility of

[54] See Regulation 1592/2002/EC.

[55] See Regulation 216/2008/EC of the European Parliament and the Council of 28 February 2008 on common rules in the field of civil aviation and establishing a European Aviation Safety Agency and repealing Council Directive 91/670/EEC, Regulation (EC) 1592/2002 and Directive 2004/36/EC, arts 7 and 21 [2008] OJ L 79/1; on OPS see also Commission Regulation 965/2012/EU of 5 October 2012 laying down technical requirements and administrative procedures related to air operations pursuant to Regulation (EC) 216/2008 of the European Parliament and of the Council [2012] OJ L 296/1, and following amendments; on FCL see also Commission Regulation 290/2012/EU of 30 March 2012 amending Regulation (EU) 1178/2011 laying down technical requirements and administrative procedures related to civil aviation aircrew pursuant to Regulation (EC) 216/2008 of the European Parliament and of the Council [2012] OJ L 100/1.

[56] See Regulation 1108/2009/EC of the European Parliament and the Council of 21 October 2009 amending Regulation (EC) 216/2008 in the field of aerodromes, air traffic management and air navigation services and repealing Directive 2006/23/EC, art 1 [2009] OJ L 309/51.

[57] Communication from the Commission to the European Parliament, the Council, the European Economic and Social Committee and the Committee of the Regions, *An Aviation Strategy for Europe*, COM(2015)598 (7 December 2015) 9–10.

[58] Proposal for a Regulation of the European Parliament and of the Council of 7 December 2015 on common rules in the field of civil aviation and establishing a European Union Aviation Safety Agency, and repealing Regulation (EC) 216/2008 of the European Parliament and of the Council, COM(2015)613.

[59] COM(2015)613, art 6.

[60] Ibid arts 45–47.

operations,[61] cyber-security,[62] research and innovation programmes,[63] and international cooperation.[64]

(i) Adjudication

As far as administrative adjudication is concerned, the EASA retains significant certification functions. The EASA assesses the conformity of aviation products and organisation with the requirements ensuring safety and environmental protection as provided in the relevant EU legislation. The 2015 legislative proposal introduced the specific legal basis empowering the Commission to adopt delegated acts concerning the substantive requirements and conditions for certification.[65] In addition, in emergency situations, the EASA can take specific actions on the certified entities and manage urgency in a flexible and timely way. It decides about granting exemptions to the holders of the certificates in the event of unforeseen urgent operational circumstances or operational needs of a limited duration under the specified conditions that the level of safety is not affected, the exemption does not exceed two months and it is not renewable, and the decision is notified to the Commission.[66]

Certification tasks are exercised either as tasks delegated from the Member States or on a subsidiary basis. In the first case, the EASA acts on behalf of the Member States: the issue, amendment, suspension and revocation of airworthiness and environmental certifications respond to the delegation relationship.[67] The 2015 legislative proposal extended the possibility to transfer responsibilities from Member States to the Agency for the certification, oversight and enforcement of organisations, operators, personnel, aircraft, flight simulation training devices or aerodromes.[68] In the case of certification of entities and activities located outside the Member States and providing services in the EU, as well as in the case of organisations providing pan-European ATM/ANS services, the EASA acts in its own name on a subsidiary basis.[69] The dimension of the activity and the substantial lack of control of the individual states over the performed activities require the intervention of a supranational body which retains competence beyond the national level. This approach is confirmed in the case of authorisations of commercial flights operated by third-country operators within or outside the EU, where

[61] Ibid art 75.
[62] Ibid art 76.
[63] Ibid art 74.
[64] Ibid art 77.
[65] Ibid art 117.
[66] Regulation 216/2008/EC, arts 14 and 18(d). COM(2015)613 split this provision into art 59 covering urgent measures and art 60 dealing with flexibility measures.
[67] Regulation 216/2008/EC, art 20.
[68] COM(2015)613, art 53. In addition, art 55 designs an emergency oversight mechanism, which allows the Commission to temporarily transfer certification, oversight and enforcement tasks to the EASA, where a Member State shows 'a serious and persisting inability' in its performance.
[69] Regulation 216/2008/EC, arts 21, 22a, 22b.

the EASA issues and renews these authorisations, unless a Member State carries out the functions and tasks of the state operator in respect of these operators.[70] In this case, in fact, an individual state can control the activity in question and the supranational intervention is not justified. In addition, the 2015 legislative proposal introduces the possibility for organisations operating multinationally, such as Airbus, to request the Agency to act as the competent authority responsible for the certification, oversight and enforcement of its organisation.[71] This would create a 'one-stop-shop' facilitating industry and attracting in the certification and oversight process under the competence of the EASA.[72]

In the performance of its certification tasks, the EASA enjoys significant inspection and investigation powers to access relevant records and to enter relevant premises in cooperation with the Member States.[73] The 2015 legislative proposal has further strengthened this cooperation. A mechanism for pooling and sharing of inspectors and other personnel with expertise relevant for the exercise of the certification and oversight tasks has been established, to be implemented by delegated acts of the Commission. This creates a unit of European aviation inspectors that perform their oversight and certification activities under the control, instructions and responsibility of the Agency or the national competent authority that requested their assistance.[74] When carrying out these certification activities, the EASA and the Member States' national aviation authorities can allocate specific certification tasks to the expert bodies that comply with the requirements of Annex V to the Basic Regulation (the so-called 'qualified entities'), which have to act under their control and responsibility and cannot directly issue the certificates.[75] The certification task can be exercised only by national agencies and the EASA, but experts can be involved in the certification process with the aim of covering technical skills that might be outside the administrative organisation. The 2015 legislative proposal clarified the principle of accreditation of qualified entities either by the Agency or by a national competent authority, or jointly by two or more national competent authorities, or by the Agency and one or more national competent authorities, and the mutual recognition of accreditations. It also conferred on these accrediting institutions the right to grant to the accredited qualified entities the privilege to issue, revoke and suspend certificates on behalf of the Agency or national competent authority.[76]

Certificates are subject to mutual recognition within the EU; however, the European Commission, on its own initiative or at the request of the EASA or a

[70] Ibid art 23.

[71] COM(2015)613, art 54.

[72] See F Coman-Kund, 'The Future EASA Regulation: Enhancing the Union's Aviation Safety System through "Agencification"?' *EU TARN Blog* (26 October 2017), available at http://eutarn.blogactiv.eu/2017/10/26/the-future-easa-regulation-enhancing-the-unions-aviation-safety-system-through-agencification/.

[73] Regulation 216/2008/EC, art 55.

[74] COM(2015)613, art 52.

[75] Regulation 216/2008/EC, arts 3(f) and 13.

[76] COM(2015)613, arts 58 and 71.

Member State, may initiate a comitology procedure to review the conformity of a particular certificate with the basic regulation and its implementing rules.[77] This is an administrative review which can address both the legality and the matter of the certificate. In the case of non-compliance or ineffective compliance with the requirements provided in the Basic Regulation, however, the Commission cannot take direct action, but it must require the issuer of the certificate to take the appropriate corrective action and the necessary safeguard measures, such as the limitation or suspension of the certificate. As long as the Commission has sufficient evidence that such action has been taken, it reinstates the mutual recognition of that particular certificate.

(ii) Participation in Formal Rule-Making

The EASA retains administrative powers that contribute to designing safety rules in the domain of air transport. The EASA participates in the formal rule-making function by issuing opinions to the Commission in the preparation of its legislative proposals to be presented to the European Parliament and the Council and in the adoption of the implementing rules. The 2015 legislative proposal aims to strengthen the the EASA's contribution, requiring its upon-request assistance also for the preparation of the delegated acts specifying the requirements and the conditions for the application of the regulation.[78] The nature of this assistance is more than consultative support, as the EASA submits to the Commission the draft regulation.[79] In addition, where the drafts comprise technical rules, and particularly if related to construction, design and operational aspects, the Commission may not change their content without prior coordination with the Agency.[80] Formally and substantially, the EASA retains a specific power in the rule-making process: its opinions represent technical assessments which only qualified administrations can issue and any political decision to be passed needs to be motivated on reasonable grounds. By retaining the concerned regulatory function, however, the European Commission does not delegate the responsibility to adopt binding standards to agencies.

Moreover, if a safety problem in a Member State challenges the application of the existing regulation and its exemptions, the EASA issues recommendations addressed to the Commission as to whether the basic regulation and its implementing rules should be amended and specific safety measures should be withdrawn or maintained.[81] The goal is to ensure a certain level of flexibility in the application of the relevant regulation aimed at addressing safety issues more effectively.

[77] Regulation 216/2008/EC, art 11.
[78] COM(2015)613, art 65(1).
[79] See Regulation 216/2008/EC, arts 18(a) and 19(1).
[80] Ibid art 17(2)(b).
[81] Ibid arts 14(2), 18(b).

However, in order to do this, the EASA is asked to evaluate on a technical basis the effectiveness of law in the regulation of facts and in the achievement of a high level of safety. Even if formally this is only a recommendatory power, in practice this is a peculiar kind of regulatory power that allows the EASA to monitor and review the content of EU regulation on technical grounds. The formal process of rule-making cannot be formally and substantially developed without these opinions and recommendations to the Commission.

(iii) Standardisation Practices

Alongside this participation in the formal rule-making, the EASA retains a distinctive power to adopt soft law instruments that aim to standardise the enforcement of EU regulation in the most uniform and effective way. Within the framework of the basic regulation and the European Commission's implementing regulations, the EASA can directly and independently issue acts that implement the principles and the essential requirements contained in the relevant EU legislation.

More specifically, the EASA issues three different kinds of acts which commit Member States to the implementation of EU regulation: certification specification (CS), acceptable means of compliance (AMC) and guidance materials (GM).[82] Among these instruments, only the latter have pure recommendatory content, since they are just a non-binding collection of best practices used to support the interpretation of the implementing regulations. The other two instruments have a factual capability to bind Member States' authorities and organisations to the standards set by the Agency.

Certification specifications provide Member States' competent authorities with a series of product requirements which shape the means and enhance the achievement of the goals covered by the hard EU law;[83] AMCs are measures which cannot create obligations on Member States and organisations, but commit their competent authorities. Since the legislature wanted such material to provide for legal certainty and to contribute to uniform implementation, regulated persons complying with AMC must be recognised as complying with the law. Member States' competent authorities and organisations can, however, deviate from these instruments (since formally these are not binding) but need to demonstrate to the EASA, respectively to the overseeing competent authority, that they are using other means which have equivalent effects on the EASA's standards and can likewise achieve the goals set out in the hard law regulation. This means that even if AMCs are not mandatory, these offer a presumption of compliance with the rule

[82] Ibid arts 18(c) and 19(2).

[83] Certification specifications basically cover prescriptive requirements related to the design of aircraft, performance requirements about how tasks need to be performed efficiently (eg emergency evacuation rules), and probable requirements which according to a risk-based approach to safety need to be complied with in order to demonstrate the safety of the operations.

and in some cases the implementing rules already foresee the process that needs to be followed.[84]

CSs are used in the type-certification process for which the EASA is the competent authority, that is airworthiness and environmental certification.[85] Although the applicant for a type certification may demonstrate compliance with the EU regulation in another way, the compliance with the intent of the standard is a means to demonstrate compliance with the EU regulation itself.[86] CSs are also used in the aerodrome design, aircrew, air operations and ATM/ANS.

In order to ensure the standardisation effect and monitor the implementation of the basic regulation and its implementing rules, the EASA conducts standardisation inspections aimed at checking the compliance of national authorities and undertakings with the goals set out in the EU regulation.[87] During these inspections, the EASA checks the compliance with EU regulation through the compliance either with its own soft law rules or (at least) alternatives used by competent authorities and organisations. In this framework, soft regulation therefore becomes a means to demonstrate and assess the compliance with the basic regulation and its implementing rules.

The exercise of this administrative (even soft) rule-making power is subject to the obligation of the EASA to report the results of its standardisation inspections to the Commission.[88] Moreover, even if at the request of the Agency, only the Commission retains (part of the) powers to impose fines and periodic penalties on certificate holders who do not comply with the Basic Regulation and its implementing rules.[89]

B. Competence of the European Supervisory Authorities in the Financial Markets

The outbreak of the financial crisis in 2008 and the ensuing sovereign debt crisis made the stabilisation of financial markets and financial sector reforms a priority for the EU. Financial regulation has become one of the most prominent areas of

[84] See Commission Regulation 290/2012/EU, with regard to the authority requirements for aircrew (ARA.GEN.120, Annex VI) and to the organisation requirements for aircrew (ORA.GEN.120, Annex VII).

[85] Regulation 216/2008/EC, art 20.

[86] See Commission Regulation 748/2012/EU of 3 August 2012 laying down implementing rules for the airworthiness and environmental certification of aircraft and related products, parts and appliances, as well as for the certification of design and production organizations, Annex I, Part-21, paras 21.A.16A–21.A.17 [2012] OJ L 224/1.

[87] See Regulation 216/2008/EC, art 24; Commission Regulation 736/2006/EC of 16 May 2006 on working methods of the European Aviation Safety Agency for conducting standardisation inspections [2006] OJ L 129/10. See also COM(2015)613, art 73.

[88] Regulation 216/2008/EC, arts 18(e) and 24(1).

[89] According to the multilevel construction of the SES, the sanction power is fragmented between the Commission and the Member States. See ibid arts 25 and 68.

European integration. More specifically, the EU response to the economic crisis has brought about the growth of EU regulation in the internal financial market.

In order to make the EU market stable and able to resist financial risks, the EU established a European System of Financial Supervision (ESFS) and focused on the role of EU agencies in order to achieve an effective regulation of financial markets. Alongside the establishment of the European Systemic Risk Board (ESRB), entrusted with macro-supervision tasks,[90] three EU agencies have been established and they have been allocated significant regulatory competences which cover the area of micro-prudential supervision.

The three EU agencies in question, collectively labelled as European Supervisory Authorities (ESAs), are the European Banking Authority (EBA), the European Securities and Markets Authority (ESMA) and the European Insurance and Occupational Pensions Authority (EIOPA). They respectively cover the regulation of banking, securities and markets, and insurance and pensions with the aim of ensuring a consistent and coherent mechanism of financial supervision at the EU level. In doing so, they have been allocated a range of supervision responsibilities and tasks that aim to reduce the risk and severity of possible future financial crises.

(i) Adjudication as Subsidiary Supervision

When looking at administrative adjudication powers, ESAs' intervention as supervisors is mainly subsidiary in nature, as they intervene to ensure the effective implementation of EU law only when the competent supervisory authorities in the Member States do not do so. To this end, ESAs have three main sets of subsidiary powers: the power to act against the breach of EU law by the competent national authorities;[91] the power to facilitate and coordinate actions of competent national authorities in emergency situations;[92] and the power to settle disagreements between competent national authorities regarding the procedure or the content of measures.[93] In order to perform these subsidiary tasks, ESAs are

[90] Regulation 1092/2010/EU of the European Parliament and the Council of 24 November 2010 on European Union macro-prudential oversight of the financial system and establishing a European Systemic Risk Board [2010] OJ L 331.

[91] Regulation 1093/2010/EU of the European Parliament and of the Council of 24 November 2010 establishing a European Supervisory Authority (European Banking Authority), amending Decision 716/2009/EC and repealing Commission Decision 2009/78/EC, art 17 [2010] OJ L 331/12; Regulation 1094/2010/EU of the European Parliament and of the Council of 24 November 2010 establishing a European Supervisory Authority (European Insurance and Occupational Pensions Authority), amending Decision 716/2009/EC and repealing Commission Decision 2009/79/EC, art 17 [2010] OJ L 331/48; Regulation 1095/2010/EU of the European Parliament and of the Council of 24 November 2010 establishing a European Supervisory Authority (European Securities and Markets Authority), amending Decision 716/2009/EC and repealing Commission Decision 2009/77/EC, art 17 [2010] OJ L 331/84 ('Founding Regulations').

[92] Founding Regulations, art 18.

[93] Ibid art 19. It is, however, required that sector-specific regulation envisages the case of dispute settlements. For instance, Directive 2010/78/EU amended art 22 of Directive 2003/71/EC introducing the power of the ESMA to settle disputes related to the prospectus to be published when securities are offered to the public or admitted to trading. See P Schammo, 'EU Day-to-Day Supervision or

allocated administrative powers of adjudication, so that they can make individual decisions requiring the competent national authorities to take the necessary action in accordance with EU law and, if necessary, they can also substitute the competent national authorities' decisions and make decisions directly applicable to financial institutions. More precisely, if the competent national authority does not comply either with the competent ESA's recommendation or with the Commission's formal opinion and the required acts are directly applicable to financial institutions, the ESA in question may adopt individual decisions addressed to financial institutions, directly requiring them to take necessary action to comply with the obligations under EU law.[94] Similarly, when the Council declares an emergency situation, the competent ESA may adopt individual decisions requiring the competent national authorities to take the necessary action, and if the latter do not comply and the required acts are directly applicable to financial institutions, the competent ESA may directly require private market operators to act.[95] Moreover, when settling disputes between competent national authorities, if they cannot reach an agreement in the conciliation phase, the competent ESA may make a decision requiring them to take specific action or refrain from action with binding effects.[96] If the national competent authority does not comply with such a decision, again the ESA may directly oblige financial institutions to comply with EU law.[97]

Adjudication powers need to be exercised only on the subsidiarity grounds of the multilevel legal order: if the lower level (that is, the competent authorities of the Member States) do not comply and implement EU law and regulation on the financial markets, the upper level (that is, the ESAs placed at the EU level) *may* intervene by substituting the lower level. The autonomy of Member States is therefore preserved as far as it is compatible with the EU framework aimed at assuring the financial stability of the EU.[98] Interestingly enough, the ESAs are not obliged

Intervention-based Supervision: Which Way Forward for the European System of Financial Supervision?' (2012) 32 *Oxford Journal of Legal Studies* 771, 789. The need for an explicit legal provision makes today's mediation powers very limited. In the case of the EBA this has been pointed out by the European Court of Auditors, *European Banking Supervision Taking Shape: EBA and its Changing Context*, Special Report 5/2014 (2014) 28, which also stressed that in order to settle disputes, the EBA had mostly resorted to informal mediation strategies.

[94] Founding Regulations, art 17(6).

[95] Ibid art 18(3) and (4).

[96] Ibid art 19(3).

[97] Ibid.

[98] Only two limitations apply. First of all, according to recital 32 of the Founding Regulations, if EU legislation confers discretion on national competent authorities, decisions taken by the competent ESA cannot replace the exercise in compliance with EU law of that discretion. This provision has been reflected in Regulation 806/2014/EU of the European Parliament and of the Council of 15 July 2014 establishing uniform rules and a uniform procedure for the resolution of credit institutions and certain investment firms in the framework of a Single Resolution Mechanism and a Single Resolution Fund and amending Regulation (EU) 1093/2010, art 95 [2014] OJ L 225 ('SRM Regulation'). Secondly, according to art 38 of the Founding Regulations, if an ESA intervenes in emergency situations or settles disputes and the fiscal responsibilities of the Member States are affected, the ESA's decision may be reviewed upon request of the affected Member State and the Council may decide to terminate it.

to intervene in their supervision capacity, so the decision about how to deal with 'rebellious' national authorities is left to their technical discretion. In the case of settlement of disagreements, the interpretation matters and the illegitimacy of the procedure or content of national measures does not appear to be a necessary element at stake. This leaves to ESAs a genuine capability to mediate and control the implementation of EU law, as well as to define the correct interpretation of EU law in this area.[99] It is not by chance that the ESAs have not exercised these sets of powers yet. They preferred to pursue the supervisory convergence goal by using non-binding mediation, persuasion and reputational instruments which are less burdensome on the addressed national competent authorities.[100]

(ii) Adjudication as Direct Supervision

Direct supervision includes a set of diverse powers of direct action in specific cases provided for by law. Direct supervision might be exercised on an ordinary basis or in risk/emergency situations. In the first case, direct supervision is a competence generally allocated to the relevant ESAs, but still as an exception to the general rule of subsidiary supervision. This is the case of the ESMA, which has been appointed as the single supervisor for credit rating agencies[101] and for trade repositories.[102] This means that in combination with these subsidiary supervision tasks, the ESMA has also been vested with further responsibilities. It exercises the exclusive day-to-day power to authorise, to further control the activities of credit rating agencies and trade repositories, and even to impose administrative fines on them. Although the Commission must adopt further rules of procedure, after an investigation, the ESMA can impose fines and periodic penalty payments on credit rating agencies and trade repositories.[103] This system allows the centralisation of functions on the ESMA in selected cases which is complementary to the general subsidiary supervision of the ESAs in financial markets, as it directly underpins the functions in the face of critical factual circumstances.

[99] P Weismann, 'The European Financial Market Supervisory Authorities and Their Powers to Issue Binding Decisions' (2012) 27 *Journal of International Banking Law and Regulation* 495, 500, who compares the function of settlement of disagreements with the preliminary reference to the Court of Justice.

[100] One reason for the failure to fully use supervisory powers can be found in the structure of the governance of the ESAs. As their board of supervisors is composed of representatives of the national competent authorities, the adoption of restrictive measures addressed to the same national authorities is not easy. See *Report from the Commission to the European Parliament and the Council on the Operation of the European Supervisory Authorities (ESAs) and the European System of Financial Supervision (ESFS)*, COM(2014)509 final (8 August 2014) 7.

[101] See Regulation 513/2011/EU of the European Parliament and the Council of 11 May 2011 amending Regulation (EC) 1060/2009 on credit rating agencies [2011] OJ L 145/30.

[102] See Regulation 648/2012/EU of the European Parliament and of the Council of 4 July 2012 on OTC derivatives, central counterparties and trade repositories, art 55 ff [2012] OJ L 201/1.

[103] Regulation 1060/2009/EC, arts 23e, 36a–36e [2009] OJ L 302/1 as amended by Regulation 513/2011/EU and Regulation 648/2012/EU, arts 64–67.

In the second case, the ESAs have been allocated a distinctive power that is not common to any other agencies in the EU. When particular factual conditions require the prompt intervention of a supranational expert regulator, the ESAs are entrusted with specific powers to take direct action. This is a special power to intervene in non-ordinary circumstances. When substantive sector-specific legislation allows ESAs to act as a regulator or in case of an emergency situation declared by the Council, the ESAs may temporarily prohibit or restrict certain financial activities that threaten the orderly functioning and integrity of financial markets or the stability of the whole or part of the EU financial system.[104] In these well-circumscribed cases, the EU legislature itself has considered the EU supranational level the most appropriate to directly manage the critical situation and has therefore entrusted ESAs with direct hard law powers. Formally, this is a supervision power that might be brought back to the area of adjudication. In practice, however, it may have strong regulatory impact when affecting the access to the market of a number of activities that might endanger market stability. This is a kind of contingently founded regulation that finds its limits in the risk/emergency situation at stake and in the need to reinstate the smooth functioning of the market. The nature of this hard law power is prescriptive: it has the formal feature of adjudication, but it embeds a normative content, so that it might consist either of a general act with rules temporarily limited to specific activities or of an individual decision addressed to a particular party for its specific activity. Building upon Giannini's study of the Italian decisions based on emergency or urgent situations (*ordinanze contingibili ed urgenti*), I would qualify these ESAs' direct supervision powers as risk-based or emergency-based decisions which outline normative acts accomplishing a case of *jus singulare*.[105]

(iii) Participation in Formal Rule-Making

Alongside this set of adjudicatory functions, the ESAs participate in the formal rule-making by assisting the European Commission in the performance of its regulatory responsibilities. The main contribution of the ESAs is aimed at providing a set of rules by drafting the binding technical standards formally issued by the Commission, as delegated under Article 290 of the Treaty on the Functioning of the European Union (TFEU) (the regulatory technical standards) and as implementing acts under Article 291 TFEU (the implementing technical

[104] Founding Regulations, art 9 (5). Under the current review of ESAs, the European Commission is studying the possibility to convert art 9(5) into a self-standing empowerment, so that ESAs would not need any more sector-specific regulation to provide them with the power in question, but could directly exercise it in any sector of competence. See COM (2014) 509, 8–9.

[105] MS Giannini, 'Potere di ordinanza e atti necessitati' in MS Giannini, *Scritti 1939–1948* (Giuffrè, 2002) 957. See also MS Giannini, 'Le ordinanze dispositive della proprietà privata (art. 7 L. 20 marzo 1865, n. 2248, All. E)' in MS Giannini, *Scritti 1949–1954* (Giuffrè, 2003) 206 and 215.

standards) aimed at establishing single rule-books harmonising prudential rules for financial markets.[106] According to the black letter provisions of the Founding Regulations, these are technical rules which are not to involve strategic decisions or policy choices, but only technical issues.[107] The ESAs have the initiative in the rule-making process and only in exceptional circumstances may the Commission adopt technical standards without a draft from the relevant Authority.[108]

If the Commission decides not to endorse a draft technical standard or to endorse it in part or with amendments, it must give reasons and send back the draft to the competent Authority.[109] The competent Authority may amend and then resubmit the draft as a formal opinion to the Commission and the Commission may adopt the amendments considered consistent with its remarks or reject the technical standard.

In addition, recital 23 of the ESAs' Founding Regulations emphasises that the amendment of draft regulatory standards is feasible 'only in very restricted and extraordinary circumstances, since the Authority is the actor in close contact with and knowing best the daily functioning of financial markets'. Draft regulatory technical standards, therefore:

> would be subject to amendment if they were incompatible with Union law, did not respect the principle of proportionality or ran counter to the fundamental principles of the internal market for financial services as reflected in the *acquis* of Union financial services legislation.

On top of that, in the case of non-endorsement or amendment of draft regulatory technical standards, 'where appropriate' a kind of conciliation procedure may take place before the competent committee of the European Parliament or the Council: one of these institutions may invite the responsible Commissioner, together with the Chairperson of the Authority, 'to present and explain their differences' in an 'ad hoc meeting'.[110] As Busuioc emphasised, this is an exceptional procedure which changes the procedure for the adoption of delegated acts as envisaged in the Treaties.[111] By elevating the discussion from the executive to the legislative branch,

[106] Founding Regulations, arts 10–14, on the regulatory technical standards, and art 15, on implementing technical standards.

[107] As pointed out by AG Jääskinen in the withdrawn case on the cap on bankers' bonuses, the impossibility to take policy decisions confirms the limits set by the *Meroni* doctrine, but does not prevent sector-specific legislation from extending the EBA's powers beyond the limits of art 10 of the Founding Regulations. See C-507/13 *United Kingdom v European Parliament and Council* ECLI:EU:C:2014:2394, Opinion of AG Jääskinen, para 58.

[108] Founding Regulations, arts 10(1) and (3) and 15(1) and (3).

[109] Founding Regulations, recitals 23 and 24 also emphasise that the Commission may amend draft regulatory technical standards 'only in very restricted and extraordinary circumstances'; otherwise it should 'rely, as a rule' on them because of the technical expertise of the competent ESA. In this regard see also P Schammo, 'The European Securities and Markets Authority: Lifting the Veil on the Allocation of Powers' (2011) 48 *Common Market Law Review* 1879, 1883.

[110] Founding Regulations, art 14(2).

[111] M Busuioc, 'Rule-making by the European Financial Supervisory Authorities: Walking a Tight Rope' (2013) 19 *European Law Journal* 111, 116–17.

the conciliatory intervention of the European Parliament or the Council aims to preserve the centrality of the ESAs in the adoption of binding technical standards despite its formal status of EU agency in comparison to the Commission.

(iv) Standardisation Practices

The ESAs participate in the definition of financial markets' rules with a further set of legal instruments which contribute in different ways to the performance of regulatory functions. Alongside their participation in the formal rule-making of the Commission, the ESAs retain powers of standardisation for practices and requirements that they exercise independently with a strong regulatory impact on the European financial markets. With this broad set of regulatory responsibilities, the pure issue of technical opinions to support EU institutions becomes a quite marginal activity, which goes under the label of 'other tasks' allocated to the ESAs.[112]

When acting independently, the ESAs can issue guidelines and recommendations to competent national authorities and financial institutions with the aim of establishing consistent, efficient and effective supervisory practices and ensuring the common, uniform and consistent application of EU law.[113] Guidelines and recommendations are not legally binding.[114] However, it should be emphasised that they produce a standardisation effect. As the implementation of guidelines and recommendations is highly recommended, a 'comply or explain' formula operates by making the addressees responsible for their non-compliance: the addressees have to explain why they do not intend to comply with the ESAs' guidelines and recommendations. This means that if a non-compliant national competent authority does not give reasons for non-compliance with soft law, it will act in breach of EU law. The duty to give reasons represents the legally binding effect of the 'comply or explain' formula in the implementation of soft law. Compliance is fundamental for the establishment of a single rule-book about supervisory convergent practices in the EU financial markets and non-compliance should therefore be limited and possibly avoided in light of the supervisory convergence goal. The 'comply or explain' formula pursues the isolation of non-compliant authorities through a reputational mechanism of publication of the rebels' list, which may only be supplemented on a case-by-case basis by the publication of the reasons for non-compliance. Moreover, the ESAs must give an account of the compliance

[112] Founding Regulations, art 34.

[113] Ibid, art 16. According to ibid art 30(3), guidelines and recommendations may be issued also on the basis of peer reviews of the activities performed by the competent national authorities aimed at reaching the supervisory convergence.

[114] In addition, the choice between these instruments does not seem to involve significant differences in the legal regime. According to Chiti, guidelines convey 'a formalised point of view', whereas recommendations represent 'a more direct invitation to take a certain behaviour'; see E Chiti, 'In the Aftermath of the Crisis: The EU Administrative System Between Impediments and Momentum' (2015) 17 *Cambridge Yearbook of European Legal Studies* 311, 325.

status to the European Parliament, the Council and the European Commission and must outline how they intend to ensure compliance in the future in order to achieve the supervisory convergence. This is what van Gestel and van Golen identified as 'the big stick behind the door', 'the threat that the EU legislature will impose binding measures in case of continued non-compliance'.[115] Yet, no coercive measure is provided for non-compliance and the institutional dialogue between the ESAs and the 'rebellious' national authorities is not sufficiently structured.[116]

IV. TOWARDS A DECENTRALISED MODEL FOR REGULATION

The variety of tasks and responsibilities allocated to the EASA and to the ESAs shows that decentralised agencies can perform a number of administrative functions by exercising a set of administrative powers. Binding decision-making, indispensable participation in the Commission's rule-making and autonomous standardisation practices are instruments which can proactively contribute to regulation. The examples of the EASA and the ESAs show that rules and practices have been steadily acquiring comparable dignity in structuring the level playing field in sector-specific domains of EU regulation. Alongside the contribution to formal rule-making, standardisation practices shape the regulatory framework. Even if not legally binding, the ESAs' guidelines and recommendations constitute an integral part of EU financial regulation that cannot be reasonably disregarded by the Member States and financial institutions. The same applies to the EASA, whose safety standards create the minimum safety requirements for all the Member States.

Adjudication activities also contribute to shaping EU sector-specific regulation from a privileged position, as they define the necessary requirements that market operators have to satisfy. The conferral of certification tasks on the EASA centralises in the Agency the supervision on the safety requirements for market access. Similarly, the empowerment of the ESAs to temporarily prohibit or restrict certain financial activities under specific conditions normatively affects market access.

The emerging concept of regulation is therefore a broad one. EU agencies operate to adjust the regulatory behaviour of the Member States and the conducts of the private parties to the public interest protected under EU law and regulation.[117] However, their intervention in the national jurisdiction and in the private sphere

[115] R van Gestel and T van Golen, 'Enforcement by the New European Supervisory Agencies: Quis Custodiet Ipsos Custodes?' in K Purnhagen and O Rott (eds), *Varieties of European Economic Law and Regulation, Liber Amicorum for Hans Micklitz* (Springer, 2014) 757, 766–67.

[116] See Chiti, 'In the Aftermath of the Crisis' (n 114) 325–26.

[117] On the notion of regulation see A La Spina and G Majone, *Lo Stato regolatore* (Il Mulino, 2000) 24–28, who emphasise that regulation means pursuing the relevant public interest through conditional rules that modify private alternatives. The regulatory activity therefore consists of the definition and the implementation of those conditional rules.

is not pursued through the traditional instruments at the disposal of the national administrations, but through a set of softer enforcement instruments which span from standardisation practices to some selected adjudication of powers. From a legal standpoint, the reason lies in the need to accommodate the functional development of agencification with the compatibility of EU agencies' tasks with the *Meroni* doctrine. Whereas EU agencies do not play an exclusively advisory role or their activity is not discretionary at all, the issue of unlawful delegation arises. This is problematic as it might involve a diffusion of responsibilities beyond the Treaties' framework and alter the institutional balance designed in the Treaties. Different regulatory techniques have been developed to reconcile these opposite demands and somehow keep the principle of conferral under control. The following sub-sections analyse the instruments at the disposal of the EASA and ESAs with a view to pointing out their regulatory content. The goal is to show that these instruments make EU agencies the centre of regulation, but their nuanced nature and their limited reach outline only a quasi-regulatory model whose contour is far from being clear and unambiguous.

A. Limits and Potential of Decentralised Adjudication

Adjudication plays a regulatory role inasmuch as it contributes to the early understanding of the compatibility of private activities with public policies, on the one hand, and to remove unlawful conduct, on the other hand. The EASA and the ESAs are empowered to take individual decisions that are binding on the addressees. Evidence of the continuity between adjudication and rule-making in the regulatory process is offered by the so-called flexibility clause that applies to the immediate reaction to safety problems in aviation.[118] If a Member State identifies such a problem, it should notify the EASA, the Commission and the other Member States. Upon notification, the EASA should address the problem by taking appropriate individual decisions. However, if the problem cannot be effectively addressed, the EASA issues a recommendation to the Commission as to whether to amend regulation and its implementing rules and to withdraw or maintain the notified measures. Depending on the nature and the reach of the safety problem at stake, individual decisions may embed additional regulatory content. This mechanism has been clarified in the 2015 legislative proposal, and the EASA has been conferred centralised control and direct intervention power in urgent safety situations in substitution for the Member State where it considers that it can appropriately address the safety problem.[119]

Yet EU agencies' adjudication powers vary and are quite fragmented. The EASA and the ESAs have some powers to dispose the legal conditions aimed at allowing

[118] Regulation 216/2008/EC, art 14(1) and (2).
[119] COM(2015)613, art 59(3).

individual private parties to adjust to public regulation. The EASA's certification activity sets the threshold of safety which is necessary to enter the EU aviation market, whereas the ESAs' (subsidiary and direct) supervisory powers ensure the stability and the effective functioning of financial markets. Only in exceptional circumstances are sanction powers allocated to them. Only the ESMA, in its capacity as single supervisor for credit rating agencies and trade repositories, has these powers. The reason for this differentiation most probably lies in the mentioned conflicts between Member States and the EU about the allocation of regulatory authority. When comparing the allocation of sanction powers between the EASA and ESMA, it is clear that after an inspection/investigation, in the former case the Commission is empowered to impose fines and periodic penalty payments, whereas in the latter the Authority itself retains the power. The Commission clearly loses power in favour of an EU agency. Nonetheless, in some cases, such as in the establishment of ACER, the Commission has used the legal argument of the *Meroni* doctrine to prevent the allocation of sanction powers to EU agencies.[120] It is therefore relevant to understand if and how the allocation of adjudication powers, including sanction powers, is compatible with the *Meroni* doctrine.

In order to keep adjudication powers within the limits of the *Meroni* doctrine, specific conditions should apply to their exercise. According to the 2008 Communication from the European Commission, the boundaries for the exercise of this competency are defined by the nature of activity and by the nature of the power: individual decisions can be adopted only 'in specific areas where a defined technical expertise is required, under clearly and precisely defined conditions and without genuine discretionary power' and no 'general regulatory measures' can be adopted.[121] Previously, in the 2002 Communication, in line with the 2001 White Paper on European governance, the Commission clarified the nature of the power that EU decision-making agencies can exercise by holding that they are authorised to:

> intervene only in areas where a single public interest predominates and in areas where the agencies are not called upon to arbitrate on conflicting public interests, exercise any powers of political appraisal or conduct any complex economic assessments.[122]

These definitions aim to set general limits to EU agencies' decision-making power, but they require interpretation as to its exact nature and reach. When mentioning technical expertise to qualify the nature of the activity, the Commission actually holds that EU agencies cannot act ultra vires, beyond their material area of competence. In fact, with regard to EU agencies, sector-specific expertise qualifies their competence as such. In addition, the identification of the nature of the power as genuinely discretion-free aims to cope with the possible issues of the

[120] See Chamon, *EU Agencies* (n 24) 38–39.
[121] COM(2008)135, para 2.7.
[122] COM(2002)718, 8. See also European Commission, *European Governance: A White Paper*, COM(2001)428 (12 October 2001) 19–20.

non-delegation doctrine, but it does not satisfactorily outline the rationale of EU agencies' powers.

The first reason for dissatisfaction is that the reference to the predominant single public interest in the 2002 Communication is not conclusive. The mandate of every agency, being it national or EU, identifies the competency which is generally oriented to the protection of a main public interest. The EASA is entrusted with the protection of aviation safety and safety appears to be the main public interest that it is to pursue.[123] The ESAs operate for the stability and effectiveness of the financial system[124] and this is the broad and main public interest they have to pursue in their respective areas of competence. However, this does not exclude the balance of competing (public and private) rights in the search for the best way to pursue the predominant public interest. In order to limit agencies' intervention, it is not the predominance of a single public interest as such that is decisive, but the fact that agencies operate in a normative setting where legislation has previously defined the hierarchy of the values to protect the goals and limits of administrative action. The reference to the 'single public interest' should be interpreted as the attempt to avoid that EU agencies rather than the EU legislature set the normative framework of priorities. This is clarified by the statement that they cannot arbitrate on conflicting public interests, because they are not in the constitutional position to decide which public interest should take precedence.

The second reason for dissatisfaction is that the Commission follows the wording of the *Meroni* doctrine without explaining its meaning. The 2002 Communication excluded political appraisal and complex economic assessments from EU agencies' decision-making, while the 2008 Communication excluded the exercise of genuine discretionary power. Although the intention to preclude EU agencies from political choices is evident, what this entails is not clear. The characteristics of the power left to agencies are not identified. In other words, the administrative nature of their powers is not qualified. In addition, both Communications specify that the decision-making powers of EU agencies must be distinguished from those of the Commission, but their aim is to protect the principle of conferral, rather than portray any substantive difference. Both Communications in fact clarify that insofar as the Commission acts as 'guardian of Community law'[125] and its executive powers concern political choices in the internal market, its competence needs to be safeguarded against any interference of EU agencies. This distinction of competence, however, does not inform the nature of the powers that EU agencies can legitimately exercise. The concept of discretionary powers is not exhausted by political choices. The executive powers of the Commission do not necessarily exhaust the (administrative) discretion that EU agencies may legitimately exercise.

[123] See Regulation 216/2008/EC, arts 2(1) and 17(1).
[124] Founding Regulations, art 1(5).
[125] COM(2008)135, para 2.7.

EU agencies can actually take complex technical decisions, as clearly emerged in *Schräder v CPVO*.[126] The General Court considered the Community Plant Variety Office (CPVO) to be entitled to take an administrative decision which was 'the result of complex appraisals in other scientific domains, such as botany or genetics'.[127] According to the Court, the appraisal of 'the distinctive character of a plant variety' in light of the criteria set in the relevant regulation has 'scientific and technical complexity' and 'requires special expertise and technical knowledge'.[128] As Advocate General Léger has pointed out in the *Rica Foods* case, 'discretion of a "political" nature ... corresponds to the political responsibilities which a Community provision confers upon an institution' and as such it is to be distinguished from 'discretion of a "technical" nature', which pertains to the administrative domain and 'is justified by the complexity of the technical, economic and legal situations'.[129]

As in *Meroni*, the clear and precise conditions for the exercise of administrative powers are key to understanding the legitimacy of taking complex decisions pertaining to technical matters. Like regulatory priorities, these conditions are defined in the relevant legislation. In order to set the limit and the potential of decentralised adjudication, these conditions need to be spelled out. The following sub-section illustrates the main principles that make decentralised decision-making legitimate.

(i) Clear and Precise Conditions for Legitimate Adjudication

When looking at the decision-making powers of the EASA and the ESAs, a common framework of necessary conditions emerge. These conditions concern both substantive and procedural issues.

First, decision-making powers can be exercised (upon request or on initiative) either on a subsidiary basis or directly, or upon delegation from the Member States. Subsidiarity appears to be the general rule, whereas the other two options are still exceptional. In all these cases, cooperation is key for adjudication as it allows the control of the relevant agencies that do not act ultra vires, but always in collaboration with national authorities and EU institutions for the better achievement of EU integration goals.

The subsidiary allocation of the decision-making power is based on the regular cooperation between national authorities and EU agencies. Only if the task is better carried out at the supranational level, the power to take the relevant decisions is actually exercised by the competent EU agency. For instance, the EASA

[126] T-187/06 *Schräder v CPVO* [2008] ECR II-3151, paras 59–64.

[127] Ibid para 62.

[128] Ibid paras 63–64.

[129] Case C-40/03P *Rica Foods (Free Zone) NV v Commission* [2005] ECR I-6811, Opinion of AG Léger, paras 45–46. Note that the Advocate General referred to the discretion of EU institutions (and not of EU agencies) when respectively acting as political authorities and as administrative authorities.

can issue authorisations to third country commercial flights to operate in the EU unless the Member States carry out the functions and tasks of the state of operator.[130] In the case of the ESAs, their core supervisory powers are exercised on a subsidiary basis: they can intervene only if competent national authorities do not take action. EU institutions may also be involved in the procedure: if national authorities do not comply with their obligations under EU law, the Commission may intervene upon request of the relevant ESA;[131] whereas the Council should preliminarily declare an emergency situation in order for the relevant ESA to take the relevant decisions.[132] Under specific circumstances, subsidiarity may comprise further substitution powers that design a system of administrative integration. The ESAs have the power to substitute for national authorities and adopt individual decisions addressed to financial operators. Although national authorities remain competent, their subsequent divergent decisions are not applicable.[133] In the management of urgent safety problems, the EASA is entrusted with the power to adopt appropriate decisions in substitution for national authorities. Risks change the ordinary distribution of competence and lift the decision-making function at the supranational level.

Delegation of tasks and responsibilities from the Member States to EU agencies is a way to outsource tasks under the national jurisdiction with the aim of achieving more effectiveness. The EASA can be delegated from single Member States to issue airworthiness and environmental certifications.[134] The ESAs can be delegated from the competent national authorities to exercise national tasks and responsibilities as agreed in specific arrangements which may limit the scope of delegation to the effective supervision of cross-border financial institutions or groups.[135]

When competence is centralised at the EU level by EU regulation, the evaluation of the opportunity to transfer the function is made by the EU legislature rather than the single Member States. This is clear in the case of the ESMA's power to supervise credit rating agencies and trade repositories, as well as in the case of the EASA's power to issue and renew certificates of pilot training organisations, aero-medical centres, ATM/ANS organisations and air traffic controller organisations located outside the territory of the Member States or providing pan-European services.[136]

The second condition for legitimate EU agencies' decision-making is that the relevant EU legislation will establish the criteria and the conditions for the

[130] Regulation 216/2008/EC, art 23(1)(b).

[131] Founding Regulations, art 17(4)–(5). According to Weismann, this provision does not affect the capability of the Commission to initiate infringement proceedings under Art 258 TFEU; see Weismann, 'The European Financial Market Supervisory Authorities' (n 99) 497.

[132] Founding Regulations, art 18(2).

[133] See Weismann, 'The European Financial Market Supervisory Authorities' (n 99) 496.

[134] Regulation 216/2008/EC, art 20(1).

[135] Founding Regulations art 28(1).

[136] Regulation 216/2008/EC, arts 21(1)(b), 22a(b), (c), 22b(b).

exercise of such power. The *ESMA Short Selling* case is paramount. The *jus singulare* competence of direct supervision to prohibit or impose conditions on the entry by natural or legal persons into a short sale conferred on the ESMA should be exercised only if a concrete risk to the financial stability is at stake and no competent national authority has intervened.[137] The ESMA should take into account a number of cumulative factors delineated in the short selling regulation so that the ESMA's intervention does not create further risks in the financial markets (eg the risk of regulatory arbitrage, or the risk of a reduction of liquidity, or the creation of further uncertainty in the market). Moreover, these measures should be temporary and regularly reviewed.[138] In the *ESMA Short Selling* case, the Court of Justice held that intervention criteria and consultation requirements are essential conditions for the EU agencies' exercise of adjudication.

As further condition for legitimate adjudication, EU legislation identifies the fundamental due process principles that should inspire the decision-making process and that should be implemented by the EU agency.[139] If notice, procedural time limit, transparency, the right to be heard, the duty to give reasons, and the right to appeal are the general principles broadly recalled in the legislation, it is then up to the EU agency to establish procedures specifying how these rights and conditions should be applied. Alongside judicial review for EU agencies' decisions, EU legislation also provides administrative review of EU agencies' decisions through the establishment of independent board of appeals within the EU agencies.[140] Procedural arrangements and judicial/administrative review are extremely significant when ensuring the oversight of the exercise of adjudication powers.

B. Participation in Formal Rule-Making: A Hidden Rule-Maker?

As illustrated, the EASA and the ESAs participate in the European Commission's rule-making procedures. The way agencies' expertise is assumed to the rule-making procedure is interesting because it confers on the relevant EU agencies significant powers to master the procedure, whereas it maintains the control (and the responsibility) of the rule-making to the European Commission.

The first significant innovation in this direction is that EASA and the ESAs draft the regulations for the Commission. The EASA participates in both legislative and executive rule-making, whereas the ESAs contribute only to the non-legislative rule-making of the Commission in the elaboration of binding technical standards. The different 'waves' that characterise the establishment of these EU agencies

137 Regulation 236/2012/EU, art 28 (1)–(3). According to recital (11), the ESMA's decision should also prevail on previous measures adopted by national authorities.

138 Ibid art 28(10).

139 Regulation 216/2008/EC, art 53; Founding Regulations, art 39.

140 Regulation 216/2008/EC, arts 42 and 44; Founding Regulations, art 60.

make them the difference as regards their position within the formal rule-making of the Commission. The assistance that the EASA provides to the Commission can be explained as a reinforced acquisition of technical expertise to the rule-making process. Where technical rules are concerned, the Commission has therefore to justify its disagreement and coordinate with the Agency. The duty to give reasons is the legal recognition of the contribution that technical expertise may make in the rule-making process. It does not alter substantively the relations between the Commission and the Agency; it only places a procedural burden on the Commission when the competence of the Agency becomes essential to the rule-making process.

At a different stage of agencification and in the context of a crisis-driven reform, the relations between the ESAs and the Commission in the rule-making process have been severely altered in favour of these agencies. The way the ESAs participate in the Commission's executive rule-making moves the factual ownership of the procedure from the Commission to the EU agencies. Procedural arrangements emphasise the unique role of the ESAs in the rule-making process: the ESAs retain the power of initiating the procedure, the Commission has to justify disagreement and in exceptional cases also a sort of conciliation may take place before the legislative branch. Even if formally responsible for the adoption of technical standards according to the procedures set out in Articles 290 and 291 TFEU, the Commission has the function to control the compatibility of the ESAs' drafts with EU law, the general principles and the functioning of the internal market.

The original power of EU agencies to advise the relevant institutions is therefore strengthened and pushed to the limits: assistance to the Commission does not aim to acquire technical expertise for the regulatory process, but it is structured to provide the general technical framework for regulation. De facto, the ESAs appear to be the actual rule-makers of binding technical standards. This procedural framework originates in the need to compromise the major relevance of technical expertise in the regulatory process with the issues of the (in)compatibility of the delegation of regulatory powers to EU agencies. In fact, the endorsement of these acts by the Commission is the formal disclaimer that allows the circumvention of the *Meroni* doctrine. This complication of the rule-making procedure shows that these agencies have a special position in the regulatory process.

Participation in the formal rule-making of the Commission appears to be more than consultative in nature: even if with significant legal variations, both the EASA and the ESAs have a central role in the rule-making as their contribution is key to the regulatory process. The EU legislature seems to endorse a specific model of regulation where the contribution of decentralised agencies is irreplaceable. The legislative framework seems to admit that the general competence of the Commission cannot cope with the technicality of highly specialised regulatory domains on its own. This is a phenomenon that is not new to national administrations where the externalisation of technical skills produced a dependency of generalist administrative bodies on third parties, whether other public administrations or private parties.[141] This has also led to a more general decentralisation of the regulatory process, conceived as a method of administration to acquire expertise in the general rule-making process. However, the EU presents a peculiar situation. As long as the non-delegation doctrine prevents the outsourcing of direct regulatory functions to EU agencies, the relevant expertise that they retain should be internalised in the rule-making process and should acquire a specific weight.

C. Soft Law Nature of Standardisation

The EASA and the ESAs exercise standardisation powers through specific acts of soft law. As Senden has effectively clarified, soft law concerns 'rules of conduct that are laid down in instruments which have not been attributed legally binding force, but nevertheless may have certain (indirect) legal effects, and that are aimed at and may produce practical effects'.[142] Although Senden's study focused on the phenomenon of soft law and its use by the European Commission and the Council under the first pillar, the EASA's and ESAs' soft instruments can be also read in light of this definition of soft law.

It is clear that these instruments actually establish rules of conduct or practical directions which aim to complement EU legislation with a view to harmonise its enforcement. Fulfilment of these rules of conduct is therefore required in order to achieve effective harmonisation. As Craig has pointed out with regard to the EASA's certification specifications, these are 'codes … that are in effect complex, highly detailed regulatory provisions regarded as binding by the industry, even though they do not have the force of law'.[143] This means that in practice soft law instruments produce legal effects.

As these standardisation practices are formally non-binding, legal effects are not 'inherent' to the act, but they are indirectly produced 'by way of the operation of other legal "mechanisms"'.[144] According to the Court of Justice, as it is always possible to find alternative means to achieve the goals set in the legislation, soft law cannot be considered binding. However, the CJEU recognises that this does not mean that soft law cannot produce incidental or indirect legal effects.[145] Even though it is not even de facto binding, soft law can limit action of the relevant

[141] In the law and economics literature, the principle of 'make or buy' explains this phenomenon; for an application of the principle to regulatory agencies in the United States see SA Shapiro, 'Outsourcing Government Regulation' (2003) 53 *Duke Law Journal* 389, 390–95.

[142] L Senden, *Soft Law in European Community Law* (Hart Publishing, 2004) 112. See also F Snyder, 'The Effectiveness of European Community Law: Institutions, Processes, Tools and Techniques' (1993) *Modern Law Review* 19, 32; F Snyder, 'Soft Law and Institutional Practice in the European Community' in S Martin (ed), *The Construction of Europe, Essays in Honour of Emile Noël* (Kluwer, 1994) 197, 198.

[143] Craig, *EU Administrative Law* (n 32) 150.

[144] Senden, *Soft Law in European Community Law* (n 142) 235 and 246.

[145] C-360/09 *Pfleiderer* [2011] ECR I-5161, para 21; C-526/14 *Kotnik and others* ECLI:EU:C:2016:570, paras 38–40.

institutions by introducing some practical commitments on the involved parties. According to the EU case law, it is able to bind the administrative practice (the discretionary action) of the institution that issues the soft law acts.[146] In addition, soft law instruments are understood as legal acts that must be taken into account by their addressees, but that have no legal force to impose themselves.[147] This approach covers the distinction that emerges from the Treaties between 'legally binding' acts and acts that are 'intended to produce legal effects *vis-à-vis* third parties' against which judicial review should also be ensured.[148]

The legal effects in question are indirectly produced by the content of the rule of conduct itself or by the applicable law. In the interpretation of Terpan, either the obligation identified by the norm that is its source or content, or the enforcement of the norm, is hard: if both are hard, then the norm is hard law; if both are soft, then the norm is 'mere politics'.[149]

It can be the very substance of the act that makes it 'incidentally' binding.[150] In the case of EU agencies, the technical content of their standards contributes to enhancing their incidentally binding force. When technical rules of conduct are assumed in soft law acts, it is difficult for the addressed parties to deviate from such rules. This is particularly evident in the case of the EASA's CSs: the detailed safety requirements set for products and performances might not be binding as such, but deviation risks endangering the safety of flight operations.

[146] C-226/11 *Expedia Inc* [2012] ECLI:EU:C:2012:795, para 28.

[147] C-322/88 *Grimaldi* [1989] ECR 4407, paras 18–19.

[148] Respectively see Arts 288 and 263(1) TFEU. The latter has codified the judicial protection against any act that produces substantive legal effects despite its legal qualification, as had already been held by the CJEU in 294/93 *Les Verts* [1986] ECR 1339, para 24.

[149] F Terpan, 'Soft Law in the European Union: The Changing Nature of EU Law' (2015) *European Law Journal* 68, 72–74. This approach finds confirmation in the Italian legislation on public procurement. In the implementation of the 2014 EU legislative package on public procurement and concession contracts (Directive 2014/23/EU of the European Parliament and of the Council of 26 February 2014 on the award of concession contracts [2014] OJ L 94/1; Directive 2014/24/EU of the European Parliament and of the Council of 26 February 2014 on public procurement and repealing Directive 2004/18/EC [2014] OJ L 94/65; and Directive 2014/25/EU of the European Parliament and of the Council of 26 February 2014 on procurement by entities operating in the water, energy, transport and postal services sectors and repealing Directive 2004/17/EC [2014] OJ L 94/243), Law 28 January 2016, no 11 (*legge delega*), art 1(1)(t) and Legislative Decree 18 April 2016, no 50 (*Codice dei contratti*), art 213(2) conferred on the national anticorruption authority (ANAC) the power to adopt directives (*atti di indirizzo*), such as recommendations and guidelines, aimed to promote best practices, information sharing and efficiency in the award of public contracts. This provision distinguishes between binding acts and non-binding acts. In its Opinion on the legislative draft, the Italian Supreme Administrative Court, Consiglio di Stato, clarified this distinction on the grounds of the specificity of their content as provided by the legislation. Where the provisions conferring the power on ANAC were precise (eg criteria and requirements for the appointment as member of the selection committee), ANAC's acts would be binding. Conversely, where the provisions were generic and their content was not predetermined, they would not be binding. See Consiglio di Stato, Special Commission, 1 April 2016, no 855, 39. In the literature see F Cintioli, 'Il sindacato del giudice amministrativo sulle linee guida, sui pareri c.d. precontenzioso e sulle raccomandazioni di ANAC' (2017) *Diritto processuale amministrativo* 381, 383.

[150] See Senden, *Soft Law in European Community Law* (n 142) 248–58.

The applicable law can also make soft law instruments able to produce legal effects. This happens through the general principles of EU law or through the imposition of procedural burdens on the rule of conduct. As Stefan has observed with regard to the Commission guidelines in the area of competition law and state aid, the CJEU's case law recognised the legal effects of these soft law instruments on the Commission (and its exercise of discretion) as the publication of these acts was able to create legitimate expectations for third parties.[151] The application of the principles of legal certainty, legitimate expectations and equal treatment might therefore be the source of indirectly binding effects of soft law.

The procedure through which a rule of conduct is assumed to the sphere of the addressee can also be relevant to understanding the indirectly binding nature of the rule itself. According to Advocate General Kokott in the Opinion in the *Expedia Inc.* case, the duty to take into account soft law should also involve a duty to give reasons. Although the CJEU did not rule on this aspect, the Advocate General pointed out that Member States' authorities and courts should have the duty to give reasons for any divergence with the Commission's assessments of *de minimis* restrictions of competition as set out in the soft law notice, reasons that 'can be judicially reviewed'.[152] The conclusion of Advocate General Kokott makes sense when considering the ESAs' guidelines and recommendations and the EASA's AMCs. In both these cases, the duty to give reasons accompanies the deviation from the rule of conduct. The 'comply or explain' mechanism that operates in the implementation of the ESAs' guidelines makes deviation dependent upon disclosure and this generates reputational mechanisms of compliance.[153] Möllers has called this regulatory approach 'hoft law' to emphasise how soft law instruments produce practical effects like hard law.[154] In addition, in the case of AMCs, the duty to give reasons is strengthened by the further duty to demonstrate that alternative means reach the same level of safety. Substantive equivalence is the further condition for compliance.

[151] See O Stefan, 'Hybridity Before the Court: A Hard Look at Soft Law in the EU Competition and State Aid Case Law' (2012) 37 *European Law Review* 49, 62–64; O Stefan, 'European Union Soft Law: New Developments Concerning the Divide Between Legally Binding Force and Legal Effects' (2012) *Modern Law Review* 879, 889. The reference is particularly to C-189/02 *Dansk Rørindustri* [2005] ECR I-5425, para 211; C-75/05 and C-80/05P *Kronofrance* [2008] ECR I-6619, para 60; C-226/11 *Expedia Inc* (n 146) para 28.

[152] Case C-226/11 *Expedia Inc* [2012] ECLI:EU:C:2012:795, Opinion of AG Kokott, para 39. The CJEU did not follow the Advocate General and simply held that the notice was not binding on the competition authorities and the courts of the Member States (C-226/11 *Expedia Inc* (n 146) paras 24, 27, 29–31).

[153] See R van Gestel, 'Primacy of the European Legislature? Delegated Rule-Making and the Decline of the "Transmission Belt" Theory' (2014) 1 *Theory and Practice of Legislation* 1, 11.

[154] TJ Möllers, 'Sources of Law in European Securities Regulation: Effective Regulation, Soft Law and Legal Taxonomy from Lamfalussy to de Larosière' (2010) 11 *European Business Organization Law Review* 379, 400.

(i) Standardisation Effect

The indirect legal effects that EU agencies' soft law acts produce is that of standardisation: they create the conditions for the uniform implementation of EU legislation. Standardisation supports and supplements EU secondary law by concretely implementing legislative provisions or by facilitating their interpretation. By nature, therefore, EU agencies' standardised practices cover what Senden calls the 'post-law function' of soft law; that is, 'providing guidance as to the interpretation and application of existing Community law'.[155] As she pointed out, this implies not only the restatement of legislative provisions, but also the development of further rules which are not necessarily inherent in the legal framework.[156] In addition, they may also serve as 'steering instruments' aimed at fostering cooperation and harmonisation between Member States in a non-binding fashion.[157]

In order not to be ultra vires, soft law cannot create new rights and obligations on third parties.[158] However, as Scott has pointed out, if the existing law is vague, 'it will frequently be impossible to make a clear determination of where the boundaries of the existing obligation begin and end', with the consequence that interpretation can practically produce significant effects.[159] EU agencies might happen to further develop the legislation by interpreting it in light of the EU policy goals and by adjusting the pursuit of these goals to the regulatory context. This view is confirmed by a decision of Joint Board of Appeal of the ESAs, holding that even if not legally binding, guidelines 'address the matter from a practical perspective, and assist in the interpretation of the scope of the [legislative] provisions'.[160] By reading article 22 of Directive 2006/48/EC on robust governance arrangements for credit institutions in conjunction with the EBA 2012 guidelines on the assessment of the suitability of members of the management body and key functions holders, the Joint Board of Appeal found admissible a complaint under article 17 of the EBA's Founding Regulations concerning the suitability of the management of a branch of a bank and envisaged that non-compliance with interpretative guidelines might be able to cause a breach of EU law.[161] As Moloney observed with

[155] Senden, *Soft Law in European Community Law* (n 142) 118.

[156] Ibid 120.

[157] Ibid 119.

[158] C-366/88 *France v Commission* [1990] ECR I-3671, paras 23–25.

[159] J Scott, 'In Legal Limbo: Post-Legislative Guidance as a Challenge for European Administrative Law' (2011) 48 *Common Market Law Review* 329, 342; see also Stefan, 'European Union Soft Law' (n 151) 882.

[160] *SV Capital OÜ v EBA* [2013] Ref. EBA C 2013 002, Decision of the Board of Appeal of the European Supervisory Authorities, BoA 2013-008, para 56.

[161] This approach has been confirmed by *SV Capital OÜ v EBA* [2014] Ref. BoA 2014-C1-02, Board of Appeal of the ESAs, BoA 2014-C1-02, para 79. BoA particularly derives the validity of its approach from the fact that by repealing art 22 of Directive 2006/48/EC, art 74 of Directive 2013/36/EU has now explicitly recognised the competence of the EBA to issue guidelines on governance arrangements for credit institutions. In the literature see Moloney, *EU Securities and Financial Markets Regulation* (n 22) 930–31, who recognised in this case evidence of 'the "hard" quality of ESA guidelines'.

regard to the ESMA, soft law instruments 'build a 'soft rulebook' which acquires coercive force through national supervisory practices'.[162]

Guidelines have also been shown to be able to anticipate the entry into force of the relevant legislation and play what Senden labelled as a 'para-law function'.[163] In the sector of insurances and pensions, the EIOPA has used guidelines as a means to substantive regulatory purposes. In October 2013, it issued a set of guidelines on own risk and solvency assessment[164] that worked as an instrument to prepare national contexts for the transposition of the Solvency II Directive.[165] Before that, the entry into force of such a Directive had been procrastinated for years (because of the fragmentation of insurance markets), while the negotiation of further amendments in the so-called Omnibus Directive reforming the after-crisis European architecture was expected to bring further delays.[166] By issuing guidelines in key areas of the Solvency II Directive, the EIOPA ensured that the implementation of the common regulatory framework could effectively take place and preserved the momentum where uncertainty might have persisted regarding agreement over the Directive's reform, which was in fact reached in November 2013.

The EIOPA adopted a similarly proactive approach with the implementation of the product oversight and governance (POG) requirements under the Insurance Distribution Directive.[167] As the national enforcement of the Directive was expected by 2018, the EIOPA issued preparatory guidelines.[168] The case is interesting because in doing this, the EIOPA also anticipated the adoption of Commission delegated acts aimed to specify the principles of POG.[169] Only in 2017 did

162 Moloney, *EU Securities and Financial Markets Regulation* (n 22) 933.

163 Senden, *Soft Law in European Community Law* (n 142) 119–20.

164 Guidelines on System of Governance, EIOPA-CP-13/08; Guidelines on Forward Looking Assessment of Own Risks (based on the ORSA Principles), EIOPA-CP-13/09; Guidelines on Submission of Information to National Competent Authorities, EIOPA-CP-13/010; Guidelines on Pre-Application for Internal Models, EIOPA-CP-13/011. The guidelines followed the Opinion of EIOPA of 20 December 2012 on interim measures regarding Solvency II, which makes the proactive role of the Agency in the improving of the functioning of the internal market explicit. See also Gideon Benari's interview with Carlos Montalvo, Executive Director of EIOPA, of 9 March 2014, available at www.solvencyiiwire.com/getting-ready-solvency-ii/139462.

165 The transposition of Directive 2009/138/EC of the European Parliament and the Council of 25 November 2009 on the taking-up and pursuit of the business of insurance and reinsurance (recast) [2009] OJ L 335 ('Solvency II Directive') has been postponed by Directive 2013/58/EU of the European Parliament and the Council of 11 December 2013 amending Directive 2009/138/EC [2013] OJ L 341/1 as regards the date for its transposition and the date of its application, and the date of repeal of certain Directives ('Solvency I Directive').

166 Directive 2014/51/EU of the European Parliament and the Council of 16 April 2014 amending Directives 2003/71/EC and 2009/138/EC and Regulations (EC) 1060/2009, (EU) 1094/2010 and (EU) 1095/2010 in respect of the powers of the European Supervisory Authority (European Insurance and Occupational Pensions Authority) and the European Supervisory Authority (European Securities and Markets Authority).

167 Directive 2016/97/EU of the European Parliament and of the Council of 20 January 2016 on insurance distribution (recast), art 25 [2016] OJ L 26.

168 Preparatory Guidelines on Product Oversight and Governance Arrangements by Insurance Undertakings and Insurance Distributors, EIOPA-BoS-16-071.

169 Directive 2016/97/EU, art 25(2).

the Commission start to elaborate such regulation and the EIOPA was requested to issue its technical advice.[170] The EIOPA guidelines played a para-law function that stretched the inherent purpose of this kind of act. Although guidelines aim to ensure consistent implementation and cooperation between Member States, and foster common supervisory practices, the EIOPA has been using them as interim measures aimed at anticipating the subsequent implementation by the Member States and the delegated powers of the Commission. Strictly speaking, the application of EU law through the guidelines preceded the legal transposition of the Directive in question by Member States and intruded on the Commission's powers. It may be argued that to a certain extent the EIOPA exceeded its competence by extending the scope of its guidelines.

Similarly, the 2012 ESMA guidelines on automated trading addressed high-frequency algorithmic trading (HFT),[171] which was regulated only later under the 2014 MiFID II and MiFIR reforms.[172] As Moloney pointed out, these guidelines applied the MiFID I rule-book to new risks, but they were carefully designed as an application of this legal framework, 'and not a soft law extension', and the ESMA emphasised that they operated within this legal framework and were not binding.[173] The legal (and logical) inversion between soft law and hard law in these cases has been allowed by the flexibility of the instrument in question; that is, by its soft law nature. Nonetheless, this proactive approach to the implementation of the insurance internal market and to the control of specific risks emphasises the regulatory impact of soft law. Despite its non-coercive nature, soft law can produce some practical legal effects that might be able to compete with the *Meroni* doctrine.

V. FINAL REMARKS

The study of the EASA and the ESAs reveals a complex set of powers that these agencies may exercise that go beyond any pure advisory or assistance functions. These case studies challenge the powers of information and cooperation traditionally allocated to EU agencies by developing a different model of cooperation with EU institutions and the Member States. These agencies proactively contribute to regulation by disposing of insightful mechanisms to implement sector-specific legislation. Reinforced participation into formal rule-making, standardisation

[170] Technical Advice on Possible Delegated Acts Concerning the Insurance Distribution Directive, EIOPA-17/048.

[171] ESMA Guidelines 2012/122 of 24 February 2012, Systems and Controls in an Automated Trading Environment for Trading Platforms, Investment Firms and Competent Authorities.

[172] Directive 2014/65/EU of the European Parliament and of the Council of 15 May 2014 on markets in financial instruments and amending Directive 2002/92/EC and Directive 2011/61/EU, art 2(1)(d)(iii) [2014] OJ L 173/349; and Regulation 600/2014/EU of the European Parliament and of the Council of 15 May 2014 on markets in financial instruments and amending Regulation (EU) 648/2012 [2014] OJ L 173/84.

[173] See Moloney, *EU Securities and Financial Markets Regulation* (n 22) 932–33.

practices and adjudication activities make these EU agencies express an original model of decentralised regulation that the EU seems to have embraced in a highly technical domain with cross-border impact.

This model aims to compromise the legal commitment to the non-delegation doctrine with the political/economic need for expert regulators, not centralised in the Commission, but still operating at a supranational level. On the one hand, the subsidiarity approach typical of the EU multilevel organisation is challenged by the need to (de)centralise responsibilities and tasks as it ensures harmonisation and coordination beyond the limited reach of national jurisdictions. On the other hand, a latent tension permeates EU agencies' powers and catches them between their potential as independent technical regulators/supervisors that can rule and build trust in the sector under their competence, and the non-delegation constraints of the EU polity.

It is not by chance that the 2012 Common Approach has introduced an 'alert/warning system' to be activated by the Commission if it has 'serious reasons for concern' that an EU agency may act beyond its mandate, may violate EU law or may be 'in manifest contradiction with EU policy objectives'.[174] If the EU agency does not accommodate the Commission's request, the latter informs the European Parliament and the Council with the aim of settling the institutional conflict. Vos has suggested that this provision might be susceptible to introducing a form of 'ministerial responsibility for agencies' acts' in relation to EU Commissioners.[175] Far from being crystal-clear, better understanding of the nature of such responsibility would be key to unravelling the principle of EU agencies' autonomy and the reach of their powers.

According to Schammo, the current system of ESAs represents, on the one hand 'a form of conditional intervention' which fits within the EU multilevel legal order and the constitutional boundaries of non-delegation better than a centralised EU supervisory system and, on the other hand, 'an intermediate step between an approach based on soft powers or informal standards, and one based on "hard" exclusive EU supervisory powers'.[176] The outcome is a hybrid model of quasi-regulatory powers that corrosively erode the traditional model of indirect administration in favour of further administrative integration. This requires the reconsideration of the substantive role of EU agencies in the EU polity. The subtle functioning of the analysed quasi-regulatory instruments generates some legal uncertainty about the legitimacy, effects and justiciability of EU agencies' powers. As Chiti has recognised:

> the result is a tension between two opposite forces, one driving towards the reinforcement of the powers of EU satellite administrations and the clarification of their discretionary

[174] Common Approach, para 59.

[175] See Vos, 'European Agencies and the Composite EU Executive' (n 24) 32–33.

[176] On the conditional-intervention model of ESAs, see Schammo, 'EU Day-to-Day Supervision or Intervention-based Supervision' (n 93) 791.

nature, the other obstructing the effective exercise of these powers and presenting them as purely technical.[177]

In order to avoid a soft killing of the non-delegation doctrine and creeping changes to the EU institutional framework, the actual nature of the phenomenon in question needs to be ascertained. Legal uncertainty needs to be reduced. A deeper understanding of the nature of these quasi-regulatory powers is key, as it increases the EU agencies' decision-making capacity and may concretely affect the functional division of powers between EU institutions. In fact, as the *ESMA Short Selling* case has to some extent suggested, the pragmatic approach of the CJEU to the sources of law does not rule out the possibility that EU agencies might exercise some normative powers, which may potentially interfere either with the legislative power itself or with the delegated powers of the Commission. The understanding of the nature and the limits of EU agencies' powers is therefore a conceptual premise for the articulation of a legal discourse on their normative competence or incompetence. Only on these grounds should the tenability of EU agencies' powers be understood. Chapter 3 will therefore investigate the nature of the powers conferred on EU agencies with the aim of figuring out their contribution to the EU administrative regulation beyond the black letter provisions of the Treaties.

[177] Chiti, 'In the Aftermath of the Crisis' (n 114) 313.

3

Administrative Governance Beyond the Treaties: The Challenge of Administrative Powers

I. INTRODUCTION

QUASI-REGULATORY RESPONSIBILITIES of EU agencies open new prospects for the development of administrative powers beyond the state in the framework of EU law. They challenge the traditional model of EU administrative law, caught between indirect administration by the Member States and direct administration by EU institutions. In the absence of clear provisions in the Treaties about the nature, the reach and the limits to EU agencies' action, the principles, the rules and the practices of EU administrative law are called on to fill the existing gaps and contribute to shedding light on the development of quasi-regulatory powers beyond the black letter provisions of the Treaties.

The key question is what model of legality do we want to pursue at the EU level? So far, the *Meroni* doctrine has been the mantra pushing away the legal need for such a discourse; however, the increasing relevance of EU agencies' powers and the openness of the Court of Justice of the European Union (CJEU) to their recognition in light of the Lisbon Treaty make such a discourse theoretically unavoidable. The key issue is the nature of the powers that can be allocated to EU agencies. Only by understanding this, is it possible to provide an adequate accountability framework that contains such powers and prevents them from escaping the system of the Treaties. This would contribute to situating the organisational model of EU agencies within the EU executive and to figuring out its compatibility with the structural principle of institutional balance.

EU administrative law has been kept clear from the discussion on the discretionary nature of administrative power on the grounds that EU agencies can only exercise technical powers, as opposed to political powers. This approach does not grasp the reality of administration. It does not reflect law in practice and ends up stretching the concept of technical powers by including under their umbrella further evaluation powers that go beyond technical assessments, but do not reach the level of political choices.

This Chapter aims to investigate the nature of the quasi-regulatory powers allocated to EU agencies and to understand the triggering *agencification* process as a specific instrument of EU administrative governance. To understand the substance of EU agencies' powers, two instruments assist: the notion of administrative discretion, as a threshold concept emerging from the commonalities in the legal traditions of the Member States; and the existing models of administrative governance at the EU level as a benchmark of comparison for the action of EU agencies.

The Chapter is organised as follows. First, it analyses the concept of discretion under EU law and outlines its limits (section II). Being caught by the dichotomy between political discretion and technical powers under EU law, EU administrative law does not characterise effectively the specificity and the reach of EU agencies' powers. By building upon the national understandings of administrative discretion, section III identifies this concept as the distinctive characteristic of administrative power. Section IV challenges the consolidated approach of EU administrative law which has not yet consistently characterised discretion beyond the political sphere. It shows that EU agencies' action requires some degree of administrative discretion both in adjudication and standardisation. On these grounds, the Chapter aims to reconcile the exercise of administrative discretion with the non-delegation doctrine (section V).

To evaluate the compatibility of administrative discretion with the system of the Treaties, the Chapter compares the problematic development of EU agencies' quasi-regulatory powers with other cases of administrative governance where discretion is exercised beyond the black letter provisions of the Treaties (section VI). The focus is on two cases of administrative regulation that are not directly envisaged in the Treaties: the allocation of standardisation powers with a strong regulatory impact to private standardisation bodies not recognised at all in the Treaties under the so-called 'New Approach' to harmonisation; and the allocation to the European Central Bank (ECB) of supervisory tasks under the Single Supervisory Mechanism (SSM), which create a system of administrative governance not explicitly covered in the Treaties. Section VII concludes.

II. CONCEPT OF DISCRETION UNDER EU LAW

Discretion is a polysemous concept under EU law. Pertaining to the different understandings developed under diverse national legal orders, discretion has been generically identified by the CJEU as the power of choice allocated to a certain authority under specific circumstances by a higher-ranking source of law or authority.[1] Broadly speaking, the Court of Justice has identified in discretion the limit to judicial review. It is thus the degree of discretion recognised in

[1] See R Caranta, 'On Discretion' in S Prechal and B van Roermund (eds), *The Coherence of EU Law: The Search for Unity in Divergent Concepts* (Oxford University Press, 2008) 185.

an authority that shapes the reach of judicial review.[2] This approach, however, does not allow the characterisation of different types of discretion that authorities with different powers might exercise. As Mendes has pointed out, this 'negative' approach does not sufficiently emphasise how value judgments enshrined in legal norms should guide and limit discretion 'beyond the judicial paradigm' and it prevents placing the relation between discretion and law at the core of EU law.[3] This has also prevented EU administrative law from characterising the specific nature of administrative discretion.

Administrative discretion, in fact, concerns the power of choice guided and limited by the laws. In pursuit of a specific public interest, the rule of law limits the possibility of public administration to choose between different options that cement the legislative goals and defines the legality of their action. If this concept is clearly developed in the Member States and reflects their distinct legal traditions, at the EU level it is still underdeveloped.

The ambiguous characterisation of discretion in EU case law makes the identification of the nature of an activity less evident. Under EU law, discretion has not been strongly conceptualised, so its characterisation is broader and less sophisticated than in the Member States. One reason lies in the need of the courts to cover the diverse legal traditions of the Member States. The principle of indirect administration requires some flexibility and ambiguity to make all the Member States able to implement EU law. Another reason pertains to the peculiar polity and goals pursued by the European Union, where the need to leave some margin of manoeuvre to EU institutions for an effective development of EU policies has been confronted with the counter-need to ensure the legitimacy and the accountability of EU action.[4] However, direct administration by bodies other than EU institutions has been suffering from the lack of a clearly defined concept of administrative discretion as a key to the identification of the nature and the reach of their powers.

As far as EU agencies are concerned, the ambiguity of the *Meroni* doctrine about the notion of political discretion highlights the difficulties of distinguishing the different operational domains of administrative discretion in the EU case law. Although after almost 60 years, the CJEU has concluded that the European Securities and Markets Authority (ESMA) as an EU agency can exercise

[2] Ibid 185; see also J Mendes, 'Bounded Discretion in EU Law: A Limited Judicial Paradigm in a Changing EU' (2017) *Modern Law Review* 443, 461; J Mendes, 'Law and Administrative Discretion in the EU: Value of Comparative Perspective', paper presented at the Comparative Administrative Conference, Yale, April 2016, 19–21, available at <www.law.yale.edu/system/files/area/conference/compadmin/compadmin16_mendes_law.pdf.

[3] See Mendes, 'Bounded Discretion in EU Law' (n 2) 461–63; Mendes, 'Law and Administrative Discretion in the EU' (n 2) 24–26.

[4] See P Craig, *UK, EU and Global Administrative Law* (Cambridge University Press, 2015) 385–88, who emphasises 'the Janus dimension of judicial review' as it serves both the accountability of power as well as its efficacy. On the evolution of EU case law caught between these different purposes see also P Craig, 'Law, Fact and Discretion in the UK, EU and the USA' in *La chaire, Mutations de l'Action Publique et du Droit public*, 21–23, 30, available at www.sciencespo.fr/chaire-madp/sites/sciencespo.fr.chaire-madp/files/paul_craig.pdf.

administrative powers yet still fit within the *Meroni* definition of 'clearly defined executive powers'[5] of a technical nature, the content and the limits of such administrative powers under EU law are still far from being unequivocally categorised and it is difficult to predict how EU courts will review such discretion.[6]

By elaborating on the distinction between political evaluations and technical assessments,[7] legal scholarship has contributed to understanding the concept of discretion in the case law of the EU courts. Hofmann, Rowe and Türk narrowed the concept of discretion to the extent that it reflects the *Meroni* distinction between political powers of 'wide' discretion and administrative execution. They consider discretion only as the powers covered by the category of policy decisions, whereas 'the satisfaction of the statutory requisites of an administrative decision' is understood as 'bound decision-making'.[8]

In the framework of the dichotomy between political discretion and technical powers, other interpretations have further characterised the discretionary content of administrative action. Craig has distinguished the discretion to set priorities from both the 'classical discretion' clearly specifying the conditions for actions and the discretion requiring the characterisation of the conditions for action being broadly framed through undetermined legal concepts.[9] By typifying discretion through the analysis of the allocation of liability under EU law, Caranta has distinguished policy decisions from complex factual evaluations requiring technical choices under a defined hierarchy of public interests and complex and/or unclear legal rules which leave room to different interpretations in good faith.[10] In Hofmann, Rowe and Türk's reading, instead, complex factual evaluations and the interpretation of unclear statutory terms do not envisage any kind of discretion as they do not 'decide about the substance of a certain policy, also with a view to future situations' and cannot be addressed 'as matters of specific "complexity" both with respect to' legislative and administrative acts, intended 'as a shorthand for the requirement of undertaking a decision balancing up a combination of

[5] C-270/12 *United Kingdom v Parliament and Council* ECLI:EU:C:2014.18, paras 44–54.

[6] See Caranta, 'On Discretion' (n 1) 187; Mendes, 'Law and Administrative Discretion in the EU' (n 2) 22.

[7] See Mendes, 'Law and Administrative Discretion in the EU' (n 2) 3.

[8] HCH Hofmann, GC Rowe and AH Türk, *Administrative Law and Policy of the European Union* (Oxford University Press, 2011) 499.

[9] P Craig, *EU Administrative Law*, 2nd edn (Oxford University Press, 2012) 404–5 and 409–15. The author identifies the discretion to set priorities in 98/78 *Racke* [1979] ECR 69; classical discretion in 57/72 *Westzucker* [1973] ECR 321; and discretion under broadly framed conditions in 730/79 *Philip Morris Holland BV v Commission* [1980] ECR 2671.

[10] Caranta, 'On Discretion' (n 1) 195–207. The author identifies the case for political discretion in 83/76, 94/76, 4/77, 15/77 and 40/77 *HNL v Council and Commission* [1978] ECR 1209, but he questions the setting of the permissible limits of potentially harmful ingredients in cosmetic products in C-352/98P *Bergaderm* [2000] ECR I-5291 and the assessment of factors that should fit the criterion of the most economically competitive offer in the award in the procurement of works in T-4/01 *Renco* [2003] ECR II-00171, as political discretion instead of complex factual evaluations. The author also identifies the case for interpretation of complex and/or unclear legal rules in C-392/93 *British Telecommunications* [1996] ECR I-1631 and C-224/01 *Köbler* [2003] ECR I-10239.

various factors, of evaluations and prognoses of future factual developments, and of interests and rights'.[11]

Although in different terms, Craig's and Caranta's taxonomies both identify discretion as political, if characterised by priority setting and the definition of the criteria for decision-making in light of the objectives fixed in the Treaties. Both the taxonomies distinguish this kind of discretion from the evaluations that can be taken within the already given set of objectives, priorities and criteria.

Legal scholarship, however, has not decisively elaborated on the latter and has not yet deeply focused on the discretionary content of these evaluations. So far, the compatibility of administrative action with the Treaties has been tested against the technicality of administrative action, as this action does not (or only marginally) involve a balance of interests and therefore might qualify as executive action. This has not allowed the development of the category of administrative discretion, which has either been improperly included within the concept of wide discretion as political in nature, or usefully hidden behind technical tasks. As Mendes pointed out, 'to maintain the aura of legality that the reallocation of authority within the EU has, possibly, compromised', in the *ESMA Short Selling* case the CJEU emphasised the dichotomy between complex technical decisions and policy choices and 'solidified the gap between the authority that the EU institutions and bodies effectively have and the competences they have been formally attributed'.[12]

EU law has identified administrative activities through their supposed technical nature, rather than through the hierarchy of the sources of law, as national administrative laws did. The result is that the distinction between legislative and administrative acts is not founded on a legal basis, but on the allegedly factual dichotomy between political and technical issues. If this dichotomy was supposed to clarify responsibilities, it has instead blurred them. Very effectively, Schneider has observed:

> legislative discretion is highly different from purely administrative discretion, which has the function to allow the administration to adopt context-adequate decisions of no actual political importance. These are two poles of a sliding scale on which we will find diverging grades of discretion.[13]

Schneider advocates for the EU to adopt the legal foundation of a specific administrative decision-making space. The increasing growth of EU agencies' competences makes the legal identification of this space unavoidable. EU agencies' action needs to be confronted with a firmer conception of legality that goes beyond the dichotomy between political and technical tasks.

[11] Hofmann, Rowe and Türk, *Administrative Law and Policy of the European Union* (n 8) 494–495. Note that under this approach the *Bergaderm* case qualifies as a policy decision addressing complexity 'with respect to administrative decision-making'.

[12] Mendes, 'Bounded Discretion in EU Law' (n 2) 448.

[13] J-P Schneider, 'A Common Framework for Decentralized EU Agencies and the *Meroni* Doctrine' (2009) 61 *Administrative Law Review* 29, 38.

III. DISTINCTIVE SIGNIFICANCE OF ADMINISTRATIVE DISCRETION

Perceiving administrative action as technical action, EU law has not reflected the legal reach of (the degrees of) discretion that EU agencies may perform. As illustrated in Chapter 1, in the *ESMA Short Selling* case, the CJEU recognised that the Agency had a legitimate margin of non-political discretion, but it failed to specifically conceptualise the legal nature of these powers, as EU law has not yet clearly conceptualised the legal foundations of administrative powers.

Although the understandings of administrative discretion substantially vary at national level, nonetheless national traditions can provide further principles and practices that can help us to understand the precise nature of EU agencies' powers. Adequately transposed in the supranational context, national taxonomies of administrative powers can help to frame the distinctive limits to EU agencies' action by disclosing the ability of administrative agencies to make specific types of choices beyond the reductive dichotomy between political and technical action.

Under national administrative laws, administrative discretion is the typical power of public administration. Despite the specificity of national approaches, it clearly represents the margin of choice that is necessarily limited by the law and possibly by specialised scientific or technical knowledge. Italian administrative law scholarship has contributed to characterising this margin of choice as the concrete balance of public and private interests. Giannini convincingly outlined the concept of administrative discretion as 'il potere di apprezzare in un margine determinato l'opportunità di soluzioni possibili rispetto alla norma amministrativa da attuare';[14] that is, the margin of appreciation of possible options in light of the legal rule that needs to be implemented.

The difference between the margin of appreciation of the legislature and that of administration is the rule of law itself. Unlike the legislature, an administrative agency is bound by the law and cannot set the priorities and the criteria against which the different interests at stake should be compared and balanced. The range of administrative discretion varies according to the level of detail in the law. This may leave to administration a significant power to balance the main public interest at stake with secondary competing public and private interests, and confers on administrative agency the capability to identify their best composition and adopt the best decision in context.[15] This means that administration cements the value judgements expressed in law by adjusting and evaluating them in context. More specifically, it decides how to concretely pursue the public interest assigned by the law through the administrative procedure. If the law provides all the relevant

[14] MS Giannini, *Il potere discrezionale della pubblica amministrazione* (Giuffrè, 1993) 52.

[15] Ibid; BG Mattarella, 'Discrezionalità amministrativa' in S Cassese (ed), *Dizionario di Diritto Pubblico* (Giuffrè, 2006) vol III, 1993; BG Mattarella, 'L'attività' in S Cassese (ed), *Trattato di diritto amministrativo* (Giuffrè, 2000) vol I, 629; FG Scoca, 'La discrezionalità nel pensiero di Giannini e nella dottrina successiva' (2000) *Rivista trimestrale di diritto pubblico* 1045.

details and conditions for action, no room for administrative discretion is left and administrative power is completely tied by the law.

This notion has emerged in the different national traditions through the judicial review of administrative powers. Accumulated case law has shaped the limits to the exercise of these powers and outlined the jurisdictional boundaries of administrative action. The main issue has been the identification of the substantive limits to the exercise of discretion beyond the control of the legality of administrative measures.

French administrative law has particularly contributed to the definition of the substantive limits to the authoritative exercise of administrative powers through the judicial control of the *détournment de pouvoir.*[16] In the *recours pour l'excès de pouvoir*, this ground of review operates as a substantive control that administrative power has not been concretely used in contrast with the functions assigned by the law. By preventing the use of discretionary power in such a way that exceeds or distorts the goals pursued by the law, this scrutiny goes beyond the enquiry on the formal existence of the power. It rests on the analysis of the subjective intentions that diverted the administration from the pursuit of the public interest.[17] The difficulty of this search has contributed to diluting the control of the abuse of administrative power in the more objective scrutiny of the unreasonableness of administrative acts. This has particularly consisted of the control over the *erreur manifeste d'appréciation* in the legal qualification of facts that set up the exercise of administrative powers.[18] The enquiry about the proportionality of administrative action has accompanied the control over the *erreur de qualification juridique des faits* and the reasons for the decision as means to balance costs and advantages of action (*bilan coût-avantages*).[19] By elaborating on the French notion

[16] See Y Gaudemet, *Droit Administratif*, 21st edn (LGDJ, 2015) 152 ff; J M Woehrling, 'Le contrôle jurisdictionnel du pouvoir discrétionnaire en France' (1999) 52 *La Revue Administrative* 75.

[17] See H Welter, *Le contrôle juridictionnel de la moralité administrative: étude de doctrine et de jurisprudence* (Sirey, 1929); R Vidal, 'L'évolution du détournement de pouvoir dans la jurisprudence administrative' (1952) *Revue du Droit Public* 275; J Lemasurier, 'La preuve dans le détournement de pouvoir' (1959) *Revue du Droit Public* 36; G Camus, 'Réflexions sur le détournement de procédure' (1966) *Revue du Droit Public* 65; L Fernandez-Maublanc, 'Le prétendu déclin du détournement de pouvoir' in *Études offertes à Jean-Marie Auby* (Dalloz, 1992) 239; Gaudamet, *Droit Administratif* (n 16).

[18] See *Lagrange*, Conseil d'État, 15 February 1961, which connected the *détournement de pouvoir* to further flaws, such as *faits matériellement inexacts, une erreur de droit, une erreur manifeste d'appréciation.* See B Kornprobst, 'L'erreur manifeste' (1965) *Recueil Dalloz* 121; JY Vincent, 'L'erreur manifeste d'appréciation' (1971) *Revue Administrative* 407; B Lagasse, *L'erreur manifeste d'appréciation en droit administratif* (Bruylant, 1986); J Rouvière, 'Réflexions sur l'erreur manifeste' in *Rapport public* (Conseil d'État, 1988) 65; JP Bourgois, *L'erreur manifeste d'appréciation: la décision administrative, le juge et la force de l'évidence* (L'Espace Juridique, 1988); R Chapus, *Droit administratif général* (Montchrestien, 1988) 782.

[19] See *Benjamin*, Conseil d'État, 19 May 1933. However, the first consistent application of the proportionality principle is in the matter of confiscation (*Ville Nouvelle Est*, Conseil d'État, 28 May 1971; *Sté Civile Sainte-Marie de l'Assomption*, Conseil d'État, 20 October 1972; *Grassin*, Conseil d'État, 26 October 1973; *Grimaldi*, Conseil d'État, 4 October 1974; *Gorlier*, Conseil d'État, 24 January 1975) and exemptions to urban planning (*Ville de Limoges*, Conseil d'État, 18 July 1973). See H Amiel, 'L'examen particulier des circonstances: contribution à l'étude du contrôle du pouvoir discrétionnaire

of *détournment de pouvoir*, Italian administrative justice has initially addressed the abuse of administrative discretion through scrutiny on the excess of power (*eccesso di potere*) based on the identification of a series of symptoms of its misuse (*figure sintomatiche*) that may convey a deviation of the powers from its original purpose.[20] However, this approach has been steadily substituted by the control over the breach of general principles. The conformity of administrative action to general principles has become (also under the influence of EU law) the means to ascertain the correct exercise of administrative discretion,[21] with proportionality consistently playing a leading role.[22]

In the common law tradition, the United Kingdom has also tested the arbitrariness of administrative action on the intrinsic coherence of the decision-making process, beyond its formal compliance with black letter law. By building upon the category of ultra vires related to the non-existence of the power to adopt an administrative measure,[23] the limits of administrative discretion have been found in the *Wednesbury* principle of unreasonableness, which covered both the formal legality of the measure and the substantive rationality of the exercised power.[24] Only in the *GCHQ* case did the Diplock categories of invalidity identify in irrationality the specific ground of review of discretion and distinguished it from errors committed on the grounds of illegality.[25] Among these categories, Lord Diplock identified the potential of proportionality review as a remedy to control

par le juge administratif français dans la jurisprudence récente' (1979) *Revue de Droit Prospectif* 25; M Fromont, 'Le principe de proportionnalité' (1995) *AJDA* 156; A Sandulli, 'Eccesso di potere e controllo di proporzionalità. Profili comparati' (1995) *Rivista Trimestrale di Diritto Pubblico* 329, 347–48; J Ziller, 'Le principe de proportionnalité' (1996) *AJDA* 185.

[20] See *Vastarini-Cresi*, Consiglio di Stato, sez IV, 7 January 1852, no 3; *Ruffoni*, Consiglio di Stato, sez IV, 28 January 1892, no 32. In the literature see GD Romagnosi, *Principi fondamentali di diritto amministrativo onde tesserne le istituzioni*, 3rd edn (Guasti, 1835) 138; FG Scoca, 'Profili sostanziali del merito amministrativo' (1981) *Nuova Rassegna* 1376, 1380; G Sacchi Morsiani, 'Eccesso di potere amministrativo' in *Novissimo Digesto Italiano* (Utet, 1982) vol 3, 219, 220–21; F Modugno and M Manetti, 'Eccesso di potere amministrativo' (1989) 12 *Enciclopedia Giuridica* 2; BG Mattarella, 'Il provvedimento' in S Cassese (ed), *Trattato di diritto amministrativo* (Giuffrè, 2000) vol I, 705; R Villata and M Ramajoli, *Il provvedimento amministrativo*, 2nd edn (Giuffrè, 2017) 339.

[21] Legislative Decree 2 July 2010, no 104, art 1, on administrative process; Law 7 August 1990, no 241, art 1(1), on administrative procedure.

[22] See A Albanese, 'Il ruolo del principio di proporzionalità nel rapporto fra amministrazione e amministrati' (2016) 37 *Istituzioni del Federalismo* 697. See C Marzuoli, 'Eccesso di potere' (2016) *Enciclopedia Treccani online*, available at www.treccani.it/enciclopedia/eccesso-di-potere_%28Diritto-on-line%29/.

[23] See *Anisminic Ltd v Foreign Compensation Commission* [1969] 2 AC 147, which considered the error of law as the absence of administrative competence leading to the recognition of the measure as ultra vires.

[24] *Associated Provincial Picture Houses Ltd v Wednesbury Corporation* [1948] 1 KB 223. See P Craig, *Administrative Law* (Sweet & Maxwell, 2008) 615–16. Although the principle of reasonableness emerged in the case *Rooke* (1598) 5 Co Rep 99b, it became the yardstick of the legality of the decision-making process in *Roberts v Hopwood* [1925] AC 578, where the decision of the Poplar Borough Council to pay workers above the market rate was considered unreasonable. In *Home Office v Dorset Yacht Co Ltd* [1970] AC 1004, the principle acquired autonomous recognition in the sphere of public law.

[25] *Council of Civil Service Unions v Minister for the Civil Service* [1985] AC 374.

the use of discretion.[26] The compliance of administrative action with the substantive objectives of the law emerges as the key aspect of administrative legality. Judicial review of administrative action has been positively constructed as adherence to the principles and the rules provided by the law. The limits to administrative discretion lie in the rule of law—the principle of legality—and symmetrically in (the intensity of) judicial review.

Italian scholarship has theoretically distinguished administrative discretion from technical evaluations, traditionally and improperly labelled as technical discretion. Technical evaluations cover the administrative decision based on a specialised field of scientific/technical knowledge. Administrative action is required (by law) to focus only on (even complex) facts and no balance of interest is involved.[27] Scientific and technical considerations must lead administrative decisions. However, this does not mean that technical decisions are uncontroversial, as they may rely on disputable evaluation criteria provided for by the relevant field of scientific knowledge. Their questionability does not amount to an opportunity judgement, because the criteria of evaluation are not interest-based, but are technically/scientifically-based. The more certain the science, the closer the administrative decision to a technical verification (*accertamento tecnico*).[28] In addition, when different but equivalent technical options are available, the identification of the most suitable one should be based on a value judgement, which should be legitimate under the rule of law.[29]

Although moving from a stricter notion of discretion, German administrative law has reached similar conclusions about technical evaluations. In the German understanding the concept of discretion (*Ermessen*) is opposed to the undetermined legal concepts (*unbestimmte Rechtsbegriffe*) and the conditions for action (*Tatbestand*).[30] Discretion is the power conferred by the law to make a choice aimed

[26] The principle of proportionality has been accepted in UK law as a principle deriving from EU law, but its application has been controversial as it implies an intense control over the administrative action. Its autonomy from the principle of unreasonableness, therefore, encountered difficulties. Only in the leading case *R v Secretary of State for the Home Department ex parte Brind* [1991] 1 AC 696, the House of Lords eventually recognised proportionality as an autonomous ground of review, but it still refused to recognise its application in UK law. See P Craig, 'Unreasonableness and Proportionality in UK Law' in E Ellis (ed), *The Principle of Proportionality in the Laws of Europe* (Hart Publishing, 1999) 85, 88–89; Lord LH Hoffmann, 'The Influence of the European Principle of Proportionality upon UK Law' in E Ellis (ed), *The Principle of Proportionality in the Laws of Europe* (Hart Publishing, 1999) 107, 112–13.

[27] See D de Pretis, *Valutazione amministrativa e discrezionalità tecnica* (Cedam, 1995) 231 ff, who identifies technical evaluations as non-discretionary assessments in between administrative discretion and tied by legal action.

[28] The Italian administrative judge has characterised technical verification as a pure recognition of the relevant elements, in contrast with technical evaluations which require both recognition and evaluation; see Consiglio di Stato, sez IV, 12 December 1996, no 1299.

[29] See V Bachelet, *L'attività tecnica della pubblica amministrazione* (Giuffrè, 1967) 103 ff; F Ledda, 'Potere, tecnica e sindacato giudiziario' (1983) *Diritto Processuale Amministrativo* 371; C Marzuoli, *Potere amministrativo e valutazioni tecniche* (Giuffrè, 1985) 211–14, who infers that technical evaluations attain to the merit of the decision and therefore they are included in the power reserved to the administration (220–30) and their content cannot be substituted by the evaluation of the judge (215–20).

[30] See Mendes, 'Bounded Discretion in EU Law' (n 2) 454.

at defining the content of an act, whereas in the other two cases the indeterminacy is not aimed at conferring the power to make a choice on the administration, but it is unintended and it simply allows the administration to fit the legislative will into the circumstances of the case.[31] Since the 1950s, German scholarship has, however, weakened this qualification. When the decision-making requires value judgements that are not univocal and may lead to different legal consequences (*Rechtsfolge*), the legislature might want to reserve some margin of appreciation to the administration (*Beurteilungsspielraum*).[32] Although this German scholarship has recommended that the potentially controversial nature of these value judgements would necessarily prevent the judicial substitution of the administrative evaluation without interfering with the principle of separation of powers, German courts reserve powers to administrative agencies only in specific cases.[33]

Judicial review of technical evaluations differs from the review of administrative discretion to the extent that scientific and technical facts can be ascertained. The unreliable nature of the administrative assessment can be inferred from the flaws of the administrative decision or from the incorrect application of technical rules. Judicial review can therefore cover the external reasonableness of the measure, as well as the substantive adequacy of the evaluation strongly based on proportionality review. Italian administrative justice has adopted an intermediate approach and construed judicial review as the control over the factual grounds of technical evaluations with regard to reasonableness, proportionality and soundness of the applied knowledge, without admitting the possibility of judicial substitution.[34]

[31] See W Jellinek, *Gesetz, Gesetzesanwendung und Zweckmäßigkeitserwägung* (Mohr Siebeck, 1913); on Jellinek's approach see also de Pretis, *Valutazione amministrativa e discrezionalità tecnica* (n 27) 47–56. See also E Schmidt-Assmann, *La Teoría General del Derecho Administrativo como Sistema* (Marcial Pons, 2003) 220; M Bullinger, 'Le pouvoir discrétionnaire de l'administration publique fédérale d'Allemagne' (1988) 4 *Revue Francaise de Droit Administratif* 684.

[32] See O Bachof, 'Beurteilungsspielraum, Ermessen und unbestimmter Rechtsbegriff im Verwaltungsrecht' (1955) *Juristenzeitung* 97; O Bachof, *Verfassungsrecht, Verwaltungsrecht, Verfahrensrecht in der Rechtsprechung des Bundesverwaltungsgerichts* (Mohr Siebeck, 1964) vol I; CH Ule, 'Zur Anwendung unbestimmter Rechtsbegriffe im Verwaltungsrecht' in O Bachof et al (eds), *Forschungen und Berichte aus dem Öffentlichen Recht, Gedächtnisschrift für Walter Jellinek* (Isar Verlag, 1955); CH Ule, *Verwaltungsprozeßrecht. Ein Studienbuch* (Beck, 1978). More specifically, Bachof links the margin of appreciation (*Beurteilungsspielraum*) to the intended indeterminacy of the undetermined legal concept, whereas Ule considers that indeterminacy produces a plurality of legitimate options (*Vetretbarkeit*) which differ only on the ground of a value judgement. See also de Pretis, *Valutazione amministrativa e discrezionalità tecnica* (n 27) 59–117.

[33] In the judicial review of undetermined legal concepts, German case law admitted that the administration has a reserved margin of appreciation only in exceptional cases where the subjective nature of the value judgement is manifest or the specific administrative organisation makes the substitution inappropriate. The only exception to this general approach is *I. Senat*, BVerwG 16 December 1971, on the ban of dangerous books for children.

[34] See Consiglio di Stato, sez VI, 2 March 2004, no 926 and Consiglio di Stato, sez IV, 21 March 2008, no 2404. The higher administrative court reversed its previous conflicting jurisprudence divided between the 'weak review' based on the external reasonableness of the decision (Consiglio di Stato, sez VI, 6 October 2001, no 5287; Consiglio di Stato, sez VI, 23 April 2002, no 2199), and a 'strong review' admitting the judicial substitution of the technical evaluation. However, this strong review was conducted on the basis of previous interpretation of the case law (Consiglio di Stato, sez IV,

Whatever approach any legal order may embrace, technical evaluation challenges the judicial review of administrative action in different directions. On the one hand, the judicial scrutiny over the correct application of scientific/technical knowledge is key to ensuring the substantive review of technical evaluations. This control requires technical advice as a crucial component of the judicial practice.[35] On the other hand, judicial scrutiny falls back on the controversial nature of scientific and technical knowledge and on the difficulty of distinguishing it from the appreciation of the interests that may be relevant in complex technical evaluations.

This non-exhaustive outline suffices to characterise administrative discretion as a threshold concept of administrative action and points to the need to identify effective judicial practices to make administrative tasks susceptible to being controlled. The national characterisations of administrative discretion have a paradigm of substantive legality in common that frames the evaluation and choice of public administrations. Setting aside the extremely relevant contexts for development of national administrative powers, this paradigm limits and controls the allocation of powers and it can be usefully applied at the EU level to understand the discretionary nature of administrative activity. It cannot be ignored that national administrative law is deeply rooted in a specific conception of the state as an authoritative entity legitimised by the democratic principle. Nonetheless, the substantive legal paradigm for administrative action might be transposed at the EU level to understand the legal issues that arise from the allocation of powers to EU agencies.

IV. EU AGENCIES AND ADMINISTRATIVE DISCRETION

As illustrated in Chapter 2, decentralised EU agencies may exercise their competence through quasi-regulatory instruments. Although assuming different legal forms, they substantially shape sector-specific regulation and develop a peculiar system of direct administration. These powers of EU agencies are distinct from the political responsibility, as well as from pure enforcement tasks under the Weberian model of the 'transmission belt' administration.[36] They fall in between, as they require evaluations within a defined normative setting. EU case law considers them as technical assessments that might involve the evaluation of the different technical options. However, these powers do not completely exclude any concrete

9 April 1999, no 601) or of common sense (Consiglio di Stato, sez VI, 23 February 2004, no 685). See A Travi, 'Il giudice amministrativo e le questioni tecnico-scientifiche: formule nuove e vecchie soluzioni' (2004) *Diritto Pubblico* 439, 445–49.

[35] Italian administrative justice has been reluctant to use technical advice and has left to the administration the jurisdiction over questionable issues. See Travi, 'Il giudice amministrativo e le questioni tecnico-scientifiche' (n 34) 447–48 and 454–56.

[36] On the 'transmission belt theory' of administrative law see R Stewart, 'The Reformation of American Administrative law' (1975) 88 *Harvard Law Review* 1667, 1676–77.

balance of interests within the normative framework of priorities and values set at the legislative level.[37] While technical evaluations are predominant, considerations of expediency might accompany them. Factual assessments may support administrative choices.

The following sub-sections aim to demonstrate that some discretionary content is embedded in the implementation powers of EU agencies. Adjudication and standardisation practices particularly show that EU agencies have a margin of choice that cannot be reduced to the application of technical knowledge. A concrete evaluation of value judgments and interests is a constituent element of the decision-making process that cannot be substantively reduced to purely technical operation.

A. Adjudication and Discretion

Adjudication powers are mostly understood as the technical enforcement of EU law and policies. This approach has shielded these powers from the *Meroni* doctrine and has legitimised their allocation to EU agencies as purely technical decision-making. This traditional interpretation, however, does not cover the reality of EU agencies' administrative adjudication. In the words of Moloney:

> supervision can (and typically does) involve discretionary decisions as to how rules are applied and can (and, increasingly in the crisis-era environment, is expected to have) normative effects on market behaviour, potentially breaching the Meroni prohibition.[38]

When the law confers on EU agencies the power to choose how to give effect to EU policies, the legal effects of their decisions may combine technical evaluations with some discretionary content. This option recalls the *rechsfolgeermessen* of German administrative law for the concretisation of undetermined legal concepts. This is the case of the European Supervisory Authorities (ESAs)' adjudication powers.

The exercise of the subsidiary powers either against the breach of EU law, in emergency situations or for the settlement of disagreement, as well as the direct supervisory powers of the ESMA, are subject to the appreciation of the relevant ESAs, which take the decision to act on the grounds of opportunity judgements. In addition, the powers on short selling allow the ESMA to also choose the legal instruments through which it will intervene in the case: by requiring the notification to a competent authority of net short positions in relation to a specific financial instrument or class of financial instruments; by disclosing to the public details of any such position; by prohibiting certain transactions or by imposing conditions on them.[39] The variety of decisions shows different ways of pursuing

[37] See also Mendes, 'Law and Administrative Discretion in the EU' (n 2) 28–32.

[38] N Moloney, *EU Securities and Financial Markets Regulation*, 3rd edn (Oxford University Press, 2014) 994–95.

[39] Regulation 236/2012/EU, art 28(1)(a) and (b) [2012] OJ L 86/1. See Mendes, 'Law and Administrative Discretion in the EU' (n 2) 16.

the public interest in the orderly functioning and the integrity of financial markets and in the stability of the whole or part of the financial system in the EU. This has different legal effects on the interested financial entities operating on short selling markets.

Even decision-making may cover some discretionary assessment in light of the objectives, priorities and criteria set out in the regulation requiring their action, as well as in light of the specific expertise. EU courts have recognised the existence of such discretion as a constituent component of complex technical assessments. In the *Schräder v CPVO* cases, EU courts held that the Community Plant Variety Office (CPVO)'s complex botanic decisions are characterised by a broad margin of discretion.[40] Likewise, in relation to the power of the European Aviation Safety Agency (EASA) to approve flight conditions for the Robinson R66 helicopter, the General Court pointed out that the EASA's decision constituted a complex technical assessment that enjoyed discretion to determine whether the aircraft was capable of safe flight.[41] In the appeal case, the Court of Justice emphasised the existence of such discretion, blurring the dichotomy between political discretion and technical powers provided in *Meroni*. The Court, in fact, recognised that the approval of flight conditions 'falls within a complex assessment for which a wide discretion must be acknowledged to EASA'.[42] This approach is inconsistent with the language of the *Meroni* doctrine, but the rulings indirectly identify the administrative nature of such discretion. The CJEU sets the reach and the limits of the EASA's discretion in 'the conditions and restrictions specified by the applicable regulations'.[43] This provides further evidence of the existence of administrative discretion, as a distinctive power to evaluate within the predetermined normative setting of relevant objectives, priorities and criteria.

Complex technical assessments may to some extent require a balance of interests and even their technical conclusions may be controversial. The recent decision of the Agency for the Cooperation of Energy Regulators (ACER) on the determination of electricity capacity calculation regions exemplifies the controversial nature of some administrative decisions. Under Commission Regulation 2015/1222/EU on capacity allocation and congestion management ('CACM Regulation'), the failure of national regulatory authorities to reach an agreement on the Transmission System Operators' (TSOs) proposal on the definition of the geographic areas for cross-border capacity allocation and congestion management required the subsidiary intervention of ACER.[44] Austrian regulatory authority

[40] T-187/06 *Ralf Schräder v Community Plant Variety Office (CPVO)* [2008] ECR II-3151, para 73, confirmed on appeal C-38/09P *Ralf Schräder v Community Plant Variety Office (CPVO)* [2010] ECR I-03209; T-133/08, T-134/08, T-177/08 and T-242/09 *Ralf Schräder v Community Plant Variety Office (CPVO)* ECLI:EU:T:2012:430, para 154, as confirmed on appeal C-546/12 *Ralf Schräder v Community Plant Variety Office (CPVO)* ECLI:EU:C:2015:332, para 56.

[41] T-102/13 *Heli-Flight GmbH & Co KG v EASA* ECLI:EU:T:2014:1064, para 74.

[42] C-61/15 P *Heli-Flight GmbH & Co KG v EASA* ECLI:EU:C:2016:59, paras 101–2.

[43] Ibid para 102.

[44] Commission Regulation 2015/1222/EU of 24 July 2015 establishing a guideline on capacity allocation and congestion management, art 9(11) [2015] OJ L 197/24.

(E-Control) particularly opposed the establishment of a bidding zone border for TSOs between Germany/Luxemburg and Austria as the splitting of this wholesale market was expected to increase electricity prices. ACER upheld the TSOs' proposal to set such a border to ensure efficient congestion management and overall market efficiency.[45] In practice, the absence of the border electricity exchanges in the region would be favoured at the expense of major structural congestions on the neighbouring borders and distort competition and market integration. This decision required a technical balance of the Austrian interest in the efficiency of its national market (the secondary interest in administrative law terms) in light of the objectives and the criteria set out in the CACM Regulation (the primary interest). Receiving E-Control and others' appeal, the ACER Board of Appeal considered the ACER decision as legitimate because ACER correctly exercised its administrative powers and legitimately disregarded E-Control's amendment request.[46] The grounds of review suggest that the Board of Appeal recognised the discretionary content of ACER's decision, as well as the controversial nature of technical decisions. First, it emphasised that 'the discretionary power granted to the Agency in respect of the Contested Decision is not unlimited. It is circumscribed by various conditions and criteria which limit Agency's discretion'.[47] ACER correctly evaluated the case in light of the conditions and the criteria in the CACM Regulation. Secondly, the Board of Appeal held that 'the Agency should be granted a certain *margin of appreciation* of methodological nature to precise the concrete requirements to be met to assess that there is a situation of structural congestion'.[48] In the evaluation of a complex economic and technical issue, ACER therefore did not make a manifest error of assessment of the case and the appellants did not provide sufficient evidence about congestion at the German-Austrian border. In addition, the appellants did not prove the breach of proportionality principle in the evaluation of the congestion management requirements.[49] Controversial technical decisions engage a proportionate margin of appreciation that swings between technical evaluations and discretionary choices within the limits set in the legislation.

B. Standardisation Practices and Discretion

Standardisation practices are characterised as purely based on technical evaluations and, apparently, discretion is only left to national administrations that may decide (not) to comply with the standards defined by the relevant EU agency.

[45] ACER Decision 6/2016 of 17 November 2016 on the electricity transmission system operators' proposal for the determination of capacity calculation regions, paras 58–60.

[46] Decision of the Board of Appeal of the Agency for the Cooperation of Energy Regulators ('ACER BoA') of 17 March 2017.

[47] Ibid para 69.

[48] Ibid para 108.

[49] Ibid 114.

However, the reality of these practices is that they involve a marginal balance of the different interests at stake, while requiring national administration to comply with unusual administrative instruments based on reputational mechanisms, rather than on legal coercion.

The standardisation of the most suitable technical solutions through soft law requires an evaluation of the different public and private interests that shape a sector-specific policy. As in the case of adjudication, standardisation practices require evaluations that may involve a margin of appreciation. How to implement a specific policy objective is not a neutral question. Different technical solutions may accommodate different (public and private) interests and require different efforts of compliance.

The organisational structure of EU agencies also affects the evaluation process. First, the composition of EU agencies' boards structures the process of evaluation. Where boards reflect a nation-based composition, this cannot be non-influential on the decision-making practice.[50] Boards where the Member States have no individual representation and a rotation system applies, such as the European Food and Safety Authority (EFSA), are conceived as predominately scientific bodies instrumental to scientific discussion among the relevant actors,[51] rather than institutionalised bodies for interest-based cooperation. Although the voting members of the ESAs' Boards of Supervisors are bound to the independence requirement,[52] they are head representatives of the national public authorities responsible for the sector regulation in each Member State.[53] The Board of Supervisors elects within itself six representatives who should form the Management Board.[54] In the absence of an explicit independence requirement, the EASA has a Management Board composed of one representative of each Member State and one representative of the Commission, selected on the basis of their recognised experience and commitment in the field of civil aviation, their managerial capabilities and their expertise.[55] Interviewing a member of the EASA Management Board in 2011, Scholten noticed that representatives from the Member States

[50] See J Saurer, 'The Accountability of Supranational Administration: The Case of European Union Agencies' (2009) 24 *American University International Law Review* 429, 475, who stressed that 'the extent to which Member States representatives actually act as agents of their nations, rather than as agents of the European Community, is not always clear'. See also M Busuioc, *European Agencies: Law and Practices of Accountability* (Oxford University Press, 2013) 17, who pointed out that the emphasis on the autonomy of EU agencies contrasts with the 'strong position' occupied by the Member States.

[51] E Chiti, 'An Important Part of the EU's Institutional Machinery: Features, Problems and Perspectives of European Agencies' (2009) 46 *Common Market Law Review* 1395, 1396.

[52] Founding Regulation, art 42.

[53] Ibid art 40. The Board of Supervisors includes also representatives with no voting rights, which are one representative of the Commission, one representative of the ESRB and for the EBA and the ESMA also one representative of the European Central Bank, as well as one representative of each of the other two ESAs.

[54] Founding Regulation, art 45.

[55] Regulation 216/2008/EC, art 34. According to Saurer, the members of the EASA's Management Board are subject to directives of national governments; see Saurer, 'The Accountability of Supranational Administration' (n 50) 476.

perceive their membership as necessary for political and legal reasons.[56] On the one hand, they can be asked to give account before national parliaments and, on the other hand, they can control that the EASA exercises its powers in conformity with the Member States' international commitments under the International Civil Aviation Organization (ICAO) regime.

As Giannini put it, the identification of the primary interest pursued by a public administration relies on its organisation, and namely on the structure and the assignment of its offices.[57] In the case of EU agencies, the institutionally patchy composition of the decision-making bodies complicates the concrete identification of the primary interest to protect. The national structure of their boards affects the ways in which the main public interest identified by EU secondary law is identified and pursued. The implementation of quasi-regulatory tasks must deal with the composition of the represented national interests in the decision-making process. At least, boards should consider different approaches and regulatory methods and accommodate them in light of EU objectives. At most, they might deal with conflicts of interest generated by the 'double-hattedness' of the membership.[58] Cooperative schemes such as the networks of national regulators apply, with the difference being that cooperation is embedded within a single structure of governance, the supranational EU agency.[59] Cooperation and conflicts therefore flow into the content of the legal action or inaction of EU agencies. The presence of representatives of the Member States on the management boards of EU agencies may help to find more sustainable regulatory solutions that take into account the diversification of national contexts. However, empirical research has not provided conclusive findings on the effects of this organisation. Buess has noted that the more independent and powerful EU agencies are, the less accountable they are to national institutions.[60] This means that while this organisation complicates the identification of the public interest to pursue, it does not provide effective de jure or de facto vertical accountability mechanisms connecting members of the management boards and the corresponding national institutions.

Secondly, EU agencies establish stakeholders' bodies as their own organs that may be consulted on regulatory issues. The ESAs have sector-specific stakeholder groups that must be consulted on regulatory technical standards and implementing technical standards, but can also have a say on guidelines and recommendations

[56] M Scholten, *The Political Accountability of EU and US Independent Regulatory Agencies* (Brill Nijhoff, 2014) 89–90.

[57] MS Giannini, *Lezioni di diritto amministrativo* (Giuffrè, 1950) 90.

[58] S Lavrijssen and A Ottow, 'Independent Supervisory Authorities: A Fragile Concept' (2012) 39 *Legal Issues of Economic Integration* 419, 439; Busuioc, *European Agencies* (n 50) 17.

[59] According to Schneider, 'although formally they are legal bodies under EU law, they are nevertheless an example of an integrated administrative organization' which pools together representatives and officials from the Member States and the Commission. See Schneider, 'A Common Framework for Decentralized EU Agencies and the *Meroni* Doctrine' (n 13) 30.

[60] M Buess, 'European Union Agencies and their Management Boards: An Assessment of Accountability and Demoi-Cratic Legitimacy' (2015) 22 *Journal of European Public Policy* 94, 101–7.

to the extent that these do not concern individual financial institutions.[61] Similarly, the EASA has established an advisory body of interested parties which must be consulted on specific issues under the competence of the management board, but at its discretion also on all the other issues.[62] In particular, the advisory body intervenes (with non-binding opinions) in the adoption of the procedure for the development of opinions, certification specifications, acceptable means of compliance and guidance material. This procedure reserves to the advisory body the intervention in the adoption of these acts.[63] This means that the institutionalised interests of the relevant stakeholders participate in standard-setting by identifying secondary interests that need to be protected in the regulatory process.

This organisational structure shows that some discretion in the identification of the most suitable technical standards might apply. The choice between different technical options for the definition of a rule of conduct might also be based on an appreciation and a marginal balance of public interests of national administrations and the private interests of the relevant stakeholders. At least, they may try to influence the choice of technical standards with technical arguments, which nonetheless may serve interests related to the other membership.

V. ADMINISTRATIVE DISCRETION AND THE NON-DELEGATION DOCTRINE

This overview shows that the consolidated conception of EU agencies' competence has under-estimated some aspects of their powers, particularly the discretionary content of their administrative action. Some scholars have emphasised that such discretion is political in nature: decisions alleged to be technical may in reality hide political questions. Mendes particularly identified 'grey areas of what may be considered a technically complex assessment and what may involve a policy choice'.[64] Others have stressed that 'the mere fact that a decision is technical does not mean that it is not political'.[65] EU agencies' discretion clearly has a political dimension as long as it involves value judgements and some balance of interests, but it should be distinguished from the policy choices characterised by the setting of objectives, priorities and criteria for action.

To enforce the *Meroni* doctrine, so far EU administrative law has repressed the political nature of EU agencies' action. On the one hand, this has created the false myth of its neutrality to the public and private interests; on the other hand,

[61] Founding Regulation, art 37.

[62] Regulation 216/2008/EC, art 33(4).

[63] See EASA Management Board Decision 01-2012, arts 5, 7, 10 and 15, amending and replacing Decision 08-2007 concerning the procedure to be applied by the Agency for the issuing of Opinions, Certification Specifications and Guidance Material ('Rulemaking Procedure').

[64] Mendes, 'Bounded Discretion in EU Law' (n 2) 460.

[65] H Kühnert, P Böhler and S Polster, 'A Tale of Delegation and Power: ACER and the Dichotomy of the Non-Delegation Doctrine and the Creation of a Genuine Internal Market in Electricity' (2017) 1 *European Competition and Regulatory Law Review* 47, 48.

it has contributed to stretching the technical content of agencies' decisions, so as to also cover the evaluation of their expediency. The *Meroni* doctrine has fed this fear of discretion. By circumscribing EU agencies' powers to technical tasks, the *Meroni* doctrine has aimed to protect the democratic principle. However, it failed to reconnect the very nature of administrative power to this key principle. The absence of effective accountability mechanisms that can consistently frame the exercise of administrative discretion has favoured the consolidation of the *Meroni* approach.

As Chiti has observed,[66] when dealing with administrative power, EU administrative law has focused on how to functionalise it to the implementation of EU law, but it has not been concerned with the establishment of a conceptual framework aimed at understanding the exercise of administrative powers in conformity with the rule of law and democracy. The reason for this failure lies in the disconnection of EU administrative law from its political roots and in its reduction to a functional means of integration. As soon as EU administrative law recognises the relevance and the role of administrative discretion, a coherent accountability system for decentralised supranational administrative action needs to be implemented.

I argue that the nature of EU agencies' activity needs to be understood beyond the dichotomy between political and technical powers, and the discretionary content of EU agencies' powers may reconcile with the non-delegation doctrine under specific conditions. In the 'spirit' of the *Meroni* case, the shift of the political choices and responsibilities conferred upon EU institutions in favour of other bodies is contrary to the non-delegation principle. As illustrated, administrative discretion is different in nature. According to the interpretation of Advocate General Jääskinen in the *ESMA Short Selling* case, in the *Meroni* case the Court was concerned about the absence of any judicial review of agencies' acts and aimed to prevent the delegation of powers so broad that they became arbitrary.[67] In every national jurisdiction, administrative discretion does not amount to an exercise of arbitrariness from public administrations, but it rather concerns the legitimate exercise of authority. Such legitimacy is ensured by the law and the system of judicial review of administrative acts.

As demonstrated in Chapter 1, as long as the concept of 'clearly defined executive powers' does not necessarily cover the content of the exercised powers but only outlines its boundaries, administrative discretion may fit into it. The ambiguity of the concept allows extensive interpretation, so that the competence should be firmly circumscribed, but not the modalities of implementation of that competence. As in national jurisdictions, the 'strict review in the light of objective criteria' ensures the legitimacy of agencies' acts and, more particularly, their compliance with the rule of law interpreted in the double sense consistently recognised by

[66] E Chiti, 'Is EU Administrative Law Failing in Some of Its Crucial Tasks?' (2016) 22 *European Law Journal* 576, 587–91.

[67] C-270/12 *United Kingdom v Parliament and Council* (n 5), Opinion of AG Jääskinen, para 64.

Italian administrative law scholarship: the concretisation of the value judgements/primary interest pursued by the relevant law (*legalità indirizzo*) and the observance of the limits to action laid down by the law (*legalità garanzia*). As Moloney has pointed out, the key issue is 'how much discretion along a spectrum is valid and whether the margin of discretion is overly wide where policy choices are, to some extent, engaged'.[68] Moloney complains of the use of conditionality requirements on EU agencies' action as an antidote to the breach of the *Meroni* doctrine arising from the uncertainty of the operational framework, 'rather than the dictates of operational effectiveness'.[69]

If the specific nature and domain of administrative discretion was recognised in the EU case law, the focus of non-delegation would become the accountability of administrative powers intended as the pool of legal guarantees and institutional controls that ensure their sustainability in the EU legal order, rather than the search for the technical nature of EU agencies' action and the denial of any margin of appreciation. Compatibility with the system of the Treaties would therefore be grounded on the structured justification for their exercise, rather than on the assessment of their neutrality to the competition of rights and interests. We should look for the specificities of administrative powers beyond the artificial dichotomy between political and technical competence. A developed system of checks-and-balances curbing the intrinsically political dimension of administrative action would follow. The recognition of the main gaps in the current framework is therefore key for the development of effective instruments that can circumscribe administrative discretion.

VI. EU AGENCIES AND FRAMEWORKS FOR ADMINISTRATIVE GOVERNANCE

The recognition of the unsatisfactory taxonomy of administrative power in the EU and the proposal of a different approach require stronger characterisation of implementation activities that EU agencies may pursue. To evaluate the compatibility of administrative discretion at the core of the administrative function with the non-delegation doctrine as non-interference within the powers of the EU institutions, the legitimacy of EU agencies' administrative powers needs to be analysed in the broader context of EU administrative governance.

As Chiti emphasised, the growth of EU agencies' tasks and (administrative) responsibilities is an organisational phenomenon that concerns the externalisation and the differentiation of the executive function.[70] However, the diffusion of administrative powers does not concern only EU agencies, but may empower the most different bodies and create different systems of administrative governance

[68] Moloney, *EU Securities and Financial Markets Regulation* (n 38) 995.

[69] Ibid 995.

[70] E Chiti, 'In the Aftermath of the Crisis: The EU Administrative System between Impediments and Momentum' (2015) 17 *Cambridge Yearbook of European Legal Studies* 311, 316–17.

not explicitly envisaged in the Treaties. Yet, the allocation of administrative responsibilities to EU agencies appears to be just a further option for policy implementation in the domain of the EU legislature and the Member States.[71]

Implementation powers cover different enforcement tasks, spanning from adjudication to rule-making. As seen in Chapter 2, EU agencies may retain harmonisation and supervisory functions. In order to understand the peculiarity of EU agencies' implementation powers, they can be usefully compared and contrasted with other significant cases of harmonisation and supervision that create relevant regimes of EU governance, which may also affect the institutional balance of powers emerging from the system of the Treaties. This comparison targets the private standardisation bodies under the so-called 'New Approach' to harmonisation and the supervisory tasks allocated to the European Central Bank (ECB) under the Single Supervisory Mechanism (SSM). By outlining the differences that exist between these different experiences, the specificity of pursuing administrative governance through EU agencies emerges. On the one hand, the case of European standardisation bodies highlights that harmonisation goals may be pursued even by bodies not recognised at all in the Treaties, so that mechanisms of public-private governance may emerge beyond the black letter provisions of the Treaties. On the other hand, the case of the ECB shows that the allocation of strong implementing powers must remain within the framework of the Treaties and be compatible with the principle of conferral (and for EU agencies, also with the *Meroni* doctrine). By putting EU agencies' powers in this context, the strength and the weakness of the decentralised system of EU agencies' administration may emerge.

A. European Governance of Standards

The removal of technical barriers to trade in the internal market has been a complex legal and technical issue that resulted in a set of different instruments aimed at smoothing the trade in goods. By introducing a European standardisation system, the so-called 'New Approach' to harmonisation has given an effective boost to the functioning of the internal market so far blocked by the political negotiations on standard-setting. The new harmonisation method aimed to tackle the previous delays in the adoption of harmonisation Directives derived from the need for unanimity on the technical specifications and the ineffective application of mutual trust in the national implementation of such Directives.[72] In the 1985

[71] R Dehousse, 'Misfits: EU Law and the Transformation of European Governance' in C Joerges and R Dehousse (eds), *Good Governance in Europe's Integrated Market* (Oxford University Press, 2002) 207, 221; M Everson and E Vos, *European Agencies: What about the Institutional Balance?*, Maastricht Working Papers 4/2014 (2014), 16.

[72] See E Previdi, 'The Organisation of Public and Private Responsibilities in European Risk Regulation: An Institutional Gap Between Them' in C Joerges, KH Ladeur and E Vos (eds), *Integrating Scientific Expertise into Regulatory Decision-Making: National Traditions and European Innovations* (Nomos Verlagsgesellschaft, 1997) 225.

White Paper on completing the internal market, the Commission proposed to give back to expert bodies the concrete definition of product standards and to keep the definition of the 'essential requirements' of health and safety at law-making level.[73] The 2012 reform aimed to extend this regulatory regime to services.[74]

The 'New Approach' aimed to ensure the autonomy of the standardisation process as a phenomenon of private governance by reducing the political negotiation on the recognition of their legal effects.[75] By reducing the political opinion on the 'essential requirements' to be generally agreed before the start of the substantive standardisation process, the technical debate has been left to expert operators.

By structurally detaching technical issues from the political level, the referral of standard-setting powers to the private standardisation bodies has accelerated the harmonisation process and ensured its flexibility.[76] The task of defining the technical specifications of products in conformity with the legislative 'essential requirements' is performed by European standardisation bodies established under national laws as independent not-for-profit organisations contributing to transposing international standards in Europe. These bodies are constituted as 'peak associations'[77] of the national standardisation bodies and the relevant stakeholders. Upon mandate of the Commission, Comité Europeen de Normalisation (CEN), Comité Europeen de Normalisation Electronique (CENELEC) and European Telecommunication Standards Institute (ETSI) ensure the safety of products in the internal market.[78] They thus operate on the grounds of general guidelines

[73] See Communication from the Commission to the European Council, *Completing the Internal Market*, COM(1985)310 (14 June 1985), para 68. This approach was elaborated from the experience of the 1973 Low Voltage Directive (see Council Directive 73/23/EEC of 19 February 1973 on the harmonisation of the laws of Member States relating to electrical equipment designed for use within certain voltage limits [1973] OJ L 77/29) and was thus approved by Council Resolution of 7 May 1985 on a new approach to technical harmonisation and standards [1985] OJ C 136/1. To enhance coherence, the 'New Approach' was revised by Decision 768/2008/EC of the European Parliament and of the Council of 9 July 2008 on a common framework for the marketing of products, and repealing Council Decision 93/465/EEC [2008] OJ L 218/82 and Regulation 765/2008/EC of the European Parliament and of the Council of 9 July 2008 setting out the requirements for accreditation and market surveillance relating to the marketing of products and repealing Regulation (EEC) 339/93 [2008] OJ L 218/30. The standardisation regime was thus reformed by Regulation 1025/2012/EU of the European Parliament and of the Council of 25 October 2012 on European standardisation, amending Council Directives 89/686/EEC and 93/15/EEC and Directives 94/9/EC, 94/25/EC, 95/16/EC, 97/23/EC, 98/34/EC, 2004/22/EC, 2007/23/EC, 2009/23/EC and 2009/105/EC of the European Parliament and of the Council and repealing Council Decision 87/95/EEC and Decision 1673/2006/EC of the European Parliament and of the Council [2012] OJ L 316/12.

[74] Regulation 1125/2012/EU, recitals 10–12 and art 1 [2012] OJ L 331.

[75] This approach is complemented by notification to the Commission and the designated standards institutions of the standards programmes drawn up by the national institutions; see Council Directive 83/189/EEC of 28 March 1983 laying down a procedure for the provision of information in the field of technical standards and regulations [1983] OJ L 109/8.

[76] See J Pelkmans, 'The New Approach to Technical Harmonization and Standardization' (1987) 25 *Journal of Common Market Studies* 249, 257–61.

[77] See M Egan, 'Regulatory Strategies, Delegation and European Market Integration' (1998) 5 *Journal of European Policy* 485, 492.

[78] Since 2006 the Commission has published annual Action Plans for European Standardisation to enhance the use of standards and strengthen the participation of the interested parties. See Communication from the Commission to the European Parliament and the Council of

for cooperation with the Commission[79] and in consultation with the Standing Committee assisting the Commission.[80]

Subsequently, the Commission publishes the reference to these harmonised standards in the *Official Journal*[81] and Member States must transpose and enforce these standards at national level, including market surveillance, to ensure that non-conforming products are withdrawn from the market. Product manufacturers, however, are not obliged to apply them. If they decide to apply European standards, the presumption of conformity with the essential requirements operates and products enjoy free movement. The marking of European conformity (the so-called CE marking) on products adds up to a declaration of presumed conformity with the relevant European standard, but as such it is not a guarantee of the quality of the product nor does it indicate a prior approval of the product.[82] If manufacturers avail of other non-European standards, they must demonstrate before the designated national standardisation body that these other standards conform with the 'essential requirements' through a system of tests and certificates (the so-called EC-type certification examination) which leads to the acquisition of the CE mark.[83]

In this framework, manufacturer liability remains a key principle in the assurance of product safety,[84] so that compliance with standards does not exclude objective liability for products traded on the internal market. This ensures both reparation for injury and distributive justice.[85] Standardisation bodies remain contractually liable for the service they may have provided. However, standardisation has long remained the fortress of organised network interests, whose 'clubhouse' has been breached only by the public intervention for the completion of the internal market.[86] The justiciability of the legal effects that standards produce

18 October 2004 on the role of European standardisation in the framework of European policies and legislation, COM(2004)674.

[79] See General Guidelines for Cooperation between CEN, Cenelec and ETSI and the European Commission and the European Free Trade Association of 28 March 2003 [2003] OJ C 91/7, which replaced the first cooperation agreement adopted on 13 November 1984 and published as CEN/Cenelec Memorandum No 4, Part 1.

[80] Regulation 1125/2012/EU, arts 22 and 23. See also Council Resolution of 7 May 1985, para IX.

[81] Regulation 1125/2012/EU, art 10(6). See also Council Resolution of 7 May 1985, para V.

[82] Decision 768/2008/EC, art 5.

[83] Ibid, art 6 and Annex. This method has been particularly used to encourage innovation in the production of toys; see Directive 2009/48/EC of the European Parliament and of the Council of 18 June 2009 on the safety of toys, art 20 [2009] OJ L 170/1, replacing Council Directive 88/378/EEC of 3 May 1988 on the approximation of the laws of the Member States concerning the safety of toys [1988] OJ L 187.

[84] Council Directive 85/374/EEC of 25 July 1985 on liability for defective products [1985] OJ L 210/29.

[85] See S Rose-Ackerman, 'Product Safety Regulation and the Law of Torts' in J Hunziker and T Jones (eds), *Product Liability and Innovation: Managing Risk in an Uncertain Environment* (National Academy Press, 1994) 151, 153–57; G Brüggemeier, *Common Principles of Tort Law: A Pre-Statement of Law* (BIICL, 2004) 3 and 22.

[86] See R van Gestel and HW Micklitz, 'European Integration through Standardization: How Judicial Review is Breaking Down the Club House of Private Standardization Bodies' (2013) *Common Market Law Review* 145, 150.

through the presumption of conformity has therefore started to be debated in conjunction with the emergence of the public interests involved in standard-setting. The 2012 reform of the New Approach and the recent case law of the Court of Justice favoured the phenomenon of 'juridification' of standards.[87]

The 2012 reform strengthened the possibility to contest the conformity of the proposed standards with the essential requirements through the formal objection of the Member States and the European Parliament to the publication of the reference standard in the *Official Journal*.[88] This safeguard procedure has assumed the de facto function of 'an extra layer of administrative verification of the technical content of standards'.[89] The 2012 restyle, however, has indirectly contributed to the justiciability of standards. As Schepel has pointed out, by changing the safeguard procedure into a decision of the Commission about the publication and the withdrawal of the references to harmonised standards in the *Official Journal*, the 2012 reform has introduced a decision that is amenable to judicial review.[90] In *GGP Italy v European Commission*, the General Court has confirmed that 'the decisions relating to the publication of harmonised standards are legal acts against which an action for annulment may be brought'.[91]

The Court of Justice has further opened the possibility to challenge standards in courts by increasing its opportunities to control the legal effects of standards. In the *Fra.Bo* case, it sanctioned an unlawful restriction on free movement of goods under Article 34 TFEU, the (even de facto) conferral by national legislation of legal effects on (non-harmonised) standards, and certification activities of a private law body that have the effect of restricting market access.[92] According to the Court, therefore, where standards may produce legal effects, they may be deemed justiciable. Schepel has hypothesised that insofar as the Court of Justice has extended the application of Article 34 TFEU also to EU institutions in *Alliance for Natural Health*, harmonised standards and the regulatory arrangement of the New Approach may also become amenable to judicial review under the free movement clause.[93]

[87] H Schepel, 'The New Approach to the New Approach: The Juridification of Harmonized Standards in EU Law' (2013) 20 *Maastricht Journal of European and Comparative Law* 521.

[88] Regulation 1125/2012/EU, art 11. Previously, the safeguarding procedure was covered by Council Resolution of 7 May 1985, para VII and specific directives ensured the participation of Member States and the Commission in the standard-setting process. The 2012 reform extends the right to object to standards to the European Parliament, but removes the right of the Commission as it now has the power to decide on the case. See also 815/79 *Cremonini and Vrankovich* [1980] ECR 3583, paras 10–11 and C-112/97 *Commission v Italy* [1999] ECR I-01821, para 56.

[89] H Schepel, *The Constitution of Private Governance: Product Standards in the Regulation of Integrating Markets* (Hart Publishing, 2005) 238.

[90] See Schepel, 'The New Approach to the New Approach' (n 87) 529–31.

[91] T-474/15 *Global Garden Products Italy SpA (GGP Italy) v European Commission* ECLI:EU:T:2017:36, para 60.

[92] C-171/11 *Fra.Bo* ECLI:EU:C:2012:453, paras 31–32.

[93] See Schepel, 'The New Approach to the New Approach' (n 87) 527–28. See also C-154/04 and C-155/04 *Alliance for Natural Health* [2005] ECR I-6451, para 49.

In the *James Elliott Construction* case, the CJEU also admitted its jurisdiction to give a preliminary ruling on the conformity of European standards insofar as they are part of EU law by virtue of the presumption of conformity.[94] By emphasising the public contribution to standard-setting, the Court recognised the responsibility of the Commission in the adoption of standards. The Court stressed that the relevant aspects of procedure are in the legal oversight of the Commission: the mandate, the publication and the obligations of the standardisation bodies to submit their work programmes, any proposal for addition of aspects not contained in the mandate and their annual reports to the Commission.[95] Justiciability follows as a corollary of this public approach to standardisation.

In the 2017 resolution on European standardisation, the European Parliament has, however, set back this position, repositioning standards under a private governance approach.[96] Although claiming more control and accountability mechanisms, it has contended that standards belong to the realm of EU law, 'since legislation and policies regarding the level of consumer, health, safety, environment and data protection and the level of social inclusion are determined by the legislator' and not by standards which remain:

> a voluntary, market-driven tool providing technical requirements and guidance the use of which facilitates compliance of goods and services with European legislation and supports European policies when they are developed in an accountable, transparent and inclusive way.[97]

Aiming to preserve their autonomy, CEN and CENELEC also welcomed the European Parliament's approach.[98]

According to Van Cleynenbreugel and Demoulin, the European Parliament's approach is a clear rejection of the justiciability clause set out in the *James Elliott Construction* case, yet is in line with the judicial concern for a reform of the current standardisation governance in light of the principles of openness, accessibility and transparency.[99] Embracing the private governance approach to standardisation, the European Parliament recognised the need to reform the system of governance, enhancing its own democratic oversight[100] and the transparency of the standardisation process.[101] Sharing the objective to modernise EU

[94] C-613/14 *James Elliott Construction Ltd v Irish Asphalt Ltd* ECLI:EU:C:2016:821, paras 40 and 47.

[95] Ibid paras 36–39 and 45.

[96] European Parliament Resolution of 4 July 2017 on European standards for the twenty-first century, 2016/2274(INI).

[97] Ibid, para 4.

[98] See CEN CENELEC Brief News, 'European Parliament approves the Report on European Standards of MEP Marlene Mizzi', <www.cencenelec.eu/news/brief_news/pages/tn-2017-025.aspx.

[99] P Van Cleynenbreugel and I Demoulin, 'The EP's "European Standards" Resolution in the Wake of *James Elliott Construction*: Carving Ever More Holes in the Pandora's Box?', *European Law Blog* (25 September 2017) available at http://europeanlawblog.eu/2017/09/25/the-eps-european-standards-resolution-in-the-wake-of-james-elliott-construction-carving-ever-more-holes-in-pandoras-box.

[100] Resolution 2016/2274(INI), paras 46 and 51.

[101] Ibid paras 45, 69 and 80.

standardisation policy,[102] the Commission has welcomed the recommendations of the European Parliament and the reinforcement of inter-institutional dialogue on standardisation.[103] This sort of debate between EU institutions about the nature of standardisation shows the complexity of the legal issues embedded in this model of governance and the difficulty for institutions to disentangle its regulatory effects.

(i) *Ambiguous Regime of Public-Private Governance under EU Law*

Beyond the formal detachment between the political and technical phases in the process of standardisation, the New Approach to harmonisation has in practice aimed to balance the EU need to remove technical barriers to internal market trade and the counter-need to ensure the autonomy of standard-setting as a market-driven phenomenon.[104] In so doing, it has deeply unpacked and diluted the regulatory function through different levels of governance. On the one hand, standard-setting has become an issue of administrative cooperation followed by national administrative enforcement; on the other hand, industry can lead the standard-setting process and private manufacturers are free to choose the best means to comply with the principles established by EU legislation. Schepel has observed the diffusion and re-allocation of powers in the series of relationships that this system of public-private governance has developed: in the vertical dimension, the power of standard-setting shifts from the national level towards the supranational one; but in a horizontal dimension, the effective capability to define the standards shift from public institutions towards private standardisation bodies. In a diagonal relationship, however, national public authorities can block the European standards bodies through the safeguard procedure, while private operators can decide not to apply European standards.[105] The result is a 'new' system of governance that aims to solve the problems of full legislative harmonisation by reinstating the centrality of private regulation as much as possible.

The legal understanding of this system of governance has easily encroached on the issue of its compatibility with the Treaties. The level of safety in the EU is established through a mechanism that is not covered in the Treaties. The phenomenon

[102] Communication from the Commission to the European Parliament, the Council, the European Economic and Social Committee and the Committee of the Regions, *European Standards for the 21st Century (so-called Standardisation Package)*, COM(2016)358 (1 June 2016); Joint Initiative on Standardisation, *Responding to a Changing Marketplace*, GROW.DDG1.B.3 (12 July 2016).

[103] Communication from the Commission to the European Parliament, the Council, the European Economic and Social Committee and the Committee of the Regions, *The Annual Union Work Programme for European Standardisation for 2018*, COM(2017)453 (25 August 2017) 2–3.

[104] See C Joerges, H Schepel and E Vos, *The Law's Problems with the Involvement of Non-Governmental Actors in Europe's Legislative Process: The Case of Standardisation under the 'New Approach'*, EUI Working Paper Law no 99/9 (1999), 9.

[105] Schepel, *The Constitution of Private Governance* (n 89) 143.

of public-private governance has not received any clear, unified qualification under the Treaties. In addition, standard-setting is a process of selection among interests competing on the market and the presumption of conformity under EU law has significant distributive effects.[106] This has opened the legal interpretation to competing understandings of the 'New Approach' legal regime, alternatively as a system subject to EU public law or as a phenomenon of private governance. These diverging interpretations lead to different legal regimes with regard to the nature and the limits of the standardisation activities.

Legal scholarship has emphasised the problem of compatibility with the democratic principle that holds in the EU legal order. In this reading, European standardisation bodies create a two-fold problem. First, they are not public institutions under EU law and they are not bound by the Treaties. The referral of the standard-setting powers by the Commission to these bodies has therefore raised questions on non-delegation under the *Meroni* doctrine. Secondly, the internal structure of standardisation bodies has not been considered compatible with the public relevance of their activity. The standard-setting has been criticised for the lack of transparency and the risk of capture of private standardisation bodies by the industry's interests. The need to ensure the participation of all the affected interests, including consumers, and to strengthen the accountability of standardisation bodies have been pinpointed as key reforms for the legitimate functioning of the system.[107] The 2012 reform has aimed to strengthen public participation as a means to remedy legitimacy gaps and ensure good governance.[108]

With regard to the non-delegation issue, the legal debate could not help but consider the imposition of public requirements on the standard-setting process; the possibly vague terms of the 'essential requirements'; the strong public interest implications of standard-setting; the legally binding nature of standards on Member States; and their de facto imposition on the market as constitutional hurdles in the compatibility of standardisation with EU law.[109] The voluntary implementation of standards by private parties and the standardisation mandates conferred by the Commission on CEN and CENELEC have been used (especially by the Commission) as arguments that formally lessened the criticalities of *Meroni*, so that no transfer of public powers could have occurred and standards

[106] See Egan, 'Regulatory Strategies, Delegation and European Market Integration' (n 77) 494–95.

[107] N Burrow and H Hiram, 'Legal Articulation of Policy in the EC' in T Daintith (ed), *Implementing EC Law in the UK: Structures for Indirect Rule* (Wiley, 1995) 29, 44; C Daelemans, 'The Legitimacy and Quality of European Standards: The Legitimation of Delegation of Powers and Standard-Setting Procedures' in Joerges, Ladeur and Vos, *Integrating Scientific Expertise into Regulatory Decision-Making* (Nomos Verlagsgesellschaft, 1997) 257, 270–71.

[108] Regulation 1125/2012/EU, arts 3–7, art 16 and Annex III, which strengthen the transparency of standard-setting and ensure the participation of the European Associations of Consumers (ANEC), environmental interests (ECOS), trade unions (ETUC) and SMEs in the proceedings by granting them EU financing.

[109] See Hofmann, Rowe and Türk, *Administrative Law and Policy of the European Union* (n 8) 599.

could remain under the responsibility of the European standardisation bodies.[110] However, in its 1990 Green Paper the Commission addressed the delegation's concern by unsuccessfully proposing to institute an Agency supervising the functioning of standardisation.[111] So far, the legal debate on delegation has been trapped in the passive acceptance of the existence of non-democratic standard-setters on the grounds of its output legitimacy; that is, the effective success of the system to remove technical barriers to trade.[112] However, the incumbent juridification of standards may lead to the revitalisation of the *Meroni* concerns. In the *James Elliott Construction* case, Advocate General Campos Sanchez-Bordona identified in the New Approach 'a case of "controlled" delegation in favour of a private standardisation body' and mentioned in an *obiter dictum* the doubts of some scholarship on the compatibility of the method of referring to harmonised standards with the *Meroni* doctrine.[113] When upholding the existence of the Commission's responsibility in standard-setting, the Court of Justice did not enter into the delicate domain of *Meroni*, but indirectly envisaged its compatibility with the *Meroni* doctrine:

> It must, moreover, be noted that while the development of such a harmonised standard is indeed entrusted to an organisation governed by private law, it is nevertheless a necessary implementation measure which is strictly governed by the essential requirements defined by that directive, initiated, managed and monitored by the Commission, and its legal effects are subject to prior publication by the Commission of its references in the 'C' series of the Official Journal of the European Union.[114]

The characterisation of standard-setting recalls the 'clearly defined executive powers' at least in the mellowed interpretation of the Court in the *ESMA Short Selling* case. Nonetheless, as Volpato correctly pointed out, the appearance of compatibility of the current legal framework with the control of discretion under the

[110] J Falke, 'Achievements and Unresolved Problems of European Standardization: The Ingenuity of Practice and the Queries of Lawyers' in C Joerges, KH Ladeur and E Vos (eds), *Integrating Scientific Expertise into Regulatory Decision-Making: National Traditions and European Innovations* (Nomos Verlagsgesellschaft, 1997) 187, 221–22.

[111] European Commission, *Green Paper on the Development of European Standardization: Action for Faster Technological Integration in Europe*, COM(90)456 (8 October 1990). See also Communication from the Commission to the Council and the European Parliament on the Broader Use of Standardization in Community Policy, COM(95)412 (30 October 1995). The 2011 Impact Assessment conducted by the Commission in a view to prepare the 2012 reform also rejected the policy option of the establishment of an Agency managing the standard-setting process; see Commission Staff Working Paper, *Impact Assessment, Accompanying Document to the Proposal for a Regulation of the European Parliament and the Council on European Standardisation and amending Council Directives 89/686/EEC and 93/15/EEC and Directives 94/9/EC, 94/25/EC, 95/16/EC, 97/23/EC, 98/34/EC, 2004/22/EC, 2007/23/EC, 2009/105/EC and 2009/23/EC*, SEC(2011)671 (1 June 2011), para 6.1.3.

[112] See G de Búrca, 'Institutional Development of the EU: A Constitutional Analysis' in P Craig and G de Búrca (eds), *The Evolution of EU Law* (Oxford University Press, 1999) 55, 79.

[113] C-613/14 *James Elliott Construction Ltd v Irish Asphalt Ltd* ECLI:EU:C:2016:821, Opinion AG Campos Sanchez-Bordona, para 55.

[114] Ibid para 43.

Meroni doctrine does not solve 'the conundrum of legitimacy of the standard-setting organizations' role within the institutional balance of the EU', insofar as the Court has not explicitly disentangled the mentioned key constitutional hurdles.[115]

Some scholarship has convincingly argued that the *Meroni* debate is conceptually biased by the idea that:

> standard-setting is inherently a public activity in need of hierarchical legitimation. The imagery behind it is that the Community in the 'New Approach' sub-contracts the very same activity it carried out itself in the 'old approach'.[116]

Schepel has remarked that the non-delegation issue reveals the 'marvellous paradox underlying the official New Approach doctrine that "law" and "technology" occupy clearly separate spheres': law perceives that standardisation involves normative value judgements and therefore aims to subject it 'to the rigours of constitutional hierarchy or at least to the rigours of the surrogate political process constituted by administrative procedure'.[117] Instead, in his view, by making safety dependent on legal obligations rather than on market mechanisms of consensus, law has occupied the technical sphere. The problem lies in 'the political instrumentalisation of private rulemaking' and the cure in 'the public-regardingness of responsive self-regulation'.[118] The role of the Commission therefore would be to supervise private rule-making with the aim of ensuring the responsiveness of standard-setting to the public interest concerns.[119] In other words, the non-delegation doctrine cannot effectively reconcile the apparently conflicting domains of public law and private standardisation, because there is no hierarchical relationship between the EU institutions and the European standardisation bodies. A different approach to the public dimension of private standard-setting is therefore needed.

If the activity of the European standardisation bodies is performed in the protection of a general interest, but not within a framework of hierarchical delegation of public powers, standard-setting may be understood as a *munus publicum*. Borrowing the terminology of Giannini, the concept of *munus* describes the subjective office of a private party that receives by law the task of taking care of the interest of another legal party, be it a person, a body or an entire community.[120] The ordinary activity of the former party is therefore legally functionalised to the protection of a general interest. The so-called *munus publicum* acts under its own responsibility, but the effects of its activity are relevant for the person, body or community for whom the activity is carried out. A typical case of *munus publicum*

[115] A Volpato, 'The Harmonized Standards before the ECJ: James Elliott Construction' (2017) 54 *Common Market Law Review* 591, 602.

[116] Joerges, Schepel and Vos, 'The Law's Problems with the Involvement of Non-Governmental Actors in Europe's Legislative Process' (n 104) 27.

[117] Schepel, *The Constitution of Private Governance* (n 89) 255.

[118] Ibid 257.

[119] Hofmann, Rowe and Türk, *Administrative Law and Policy of the European Union* (n 8) 600.

[120] See MS Giannini, *Diritto amministrativo*, 3rd edn (Giuffrè, 1993) vol 1, 119 ff. See also A Benedetti, *Certezza pubblica e "certezze private". Poteri pubblici e certificazioni di mercato* (Giuffrè, 2010) 20–21.

is the liberal profession of notaries, who certify (private) acts according to the law. They perform an economic activity that serves the public interest in legal certainty and legality, but they are not part of the public administration as a state organisation endowed with public authority.[121]

European standardisation is a private activity with public relevance, as European standardisation bodies are the private bodies performing the standardisation activity relevant for the functioning of the internal market. Standardisation bodies are created as the social expression of stakeholders, and not by authoritative public powers.[122] The Commission does not confer standardisation powers on them, but it only recognises the public effects of their activity. This recognition takes place through the principle of 'reference to standards' in harmonisation Directives and it triggers the implementation duties of the Member States.

As standardisation is not a purely certifying activity, but involves the appreciation of private and public interests, further supervision by the Commission is required to conform standard-setting to the pursued public goals. As no hierarchical relation exists, the Commission engages in a contractual relationship with the European standardisation bodies. The mandate for setting standards in conformity with the essential requirements of the Directives is an agreement that requires the acceptance of both the parties.[123] Likewise, the general guidelines for cooperation between the Commission and these standardisation bodies provide a contractual framework that aims to maximise the protection of the general interest in question by granting the full support of EU and European Free Trade Association (EFTA) institutions to the functional duties of the European standardisation bodies.

The application of the *Meroni* doctrine seems to be inappropriate, as standardisation powers are not delegated, but are only regulated by EU law. European standardisation bodies are not part of the functional administrative system endowed with public powers to make regulatory choices, but they are an expression of a sectional legal order whereby activity intersects the objectives of the EU legal order. European standard-setting is therefore a phenomenon of public-private regulation that rests on the cooperation of public and private actors. No single legal regime can capture this model of governance, as no such regime is currently provided under the current framework of EU law. This does not imply

[121] Insofar as notaries do not directly exercise public authority, the Court of Justice has applied to them the freedom of establishment and excluded the exception applicable to the activities connected, even occasionally, with the exercise of official authority under Art 51(1) TFEU. C-47/08 *European Commission v Belgium* [2011] ECR I-04105; C-50/08 *European Commission v France* [2011] ECR I-04195; C-51/08 *European Commission v Luxemburg* [2011] ECR I-04231; C-53/08 *European Commission v Austria* [2011] ECR I-04309; C-54/08 *European Commission v Germany* [2011] ECR I-04355; C-61/08 *European Commission v Greece* [2011] ECR I-04399. See F Spagnuolo, 'La nozione europea di poteri pubblici' (2011) *Giornale di Diritto Amministrativo* 1289.

[122] See A Predieri, 'Le norme tecniche nello Stato pluralista e prefederativo' (1996) *Il Diritto dell'Economia* 251, 262 and 281. According to Predieri, the horizontal interpretation of the principle of subsidiarity covers the activities of the standardisation bodies.

[123] Schepel, *The Constitution of Private Governance* (n 89) 240; Hofmann, Rowe and Türk, *Administrative Law and Policy of the European Union* (n 8) 600.

the illegitimacy of standardisation, but shows that significant substantive regulation may be pursued beyond the black letter provisions of the Treaties. The steady justiciability of standard-setting therefore can be understood as an effort by the judiciary to fill the constitutional gap between public-private governance and the EU legal order.

(ii) Specificity of EU Agencies' Harmonisation

EU agencies differ from European standardisation bodies both organisationally and functionally. First, the legal status of EU agencies is recognised in the Treaties. They are administrative bodies established under EU public law. They are a structural part of the administrative apparatus of the EU legal order created by the EU legislature in the exercise of hierarchical power to legislate. Secondly, EU agencies contribute to internal market harmonisation through the autonomous exercise of (various, yet limited) implementing powers conferred upon them under EU law and they do not need any further recognition of the legal effects of their powers by EU law. EU agencies therefore represent a further level in the organisation of regulatory responsibilities.

The nature of EU agencies' powers, however, may not significantly differ from the harmonisation activities of European standardisation bodies. On the one hand, EU agencies may have standardisation functions arranged as soft law instruments; on the other hand, they contribute to harmonisation by injecting technical standards in the rule-making of the Commission and technical inputs in the legislative process. The difference from European standardisation bodies is that by participating in the exercise of EU public powers, their action is strictly subject to the principle of institutional balance and needs to be justified under the *Meroni* doctrine.

Although the constraints on EU agencies' action have been stricter to date, when multiple risks might affect the management of an internal market issue, a mechanism of private governance such as the New Approach would not be effective. On the one hand, standardisation bodies have no specific skills to 'set all the parameters and the reference values to flesh out the legislative objectives, which by their nature cannot be part of the voluntary area nor set consensually through technical negotiation'.[124] On the other hand, more specificity in the 'essential requirements' would necessarily affect the autonomy of the standard-setting and the rationale of the mechanism itself.[125]

[124] Previdi 'The Organisation of Public and Private Responsibilities in European Risk Regulation' (n 72) 241.

[125] See ibid 239.

Previdi has correctly pointed out that risk regulation cannot be effectively conducted with the 'dual approach' of the New Approach, and that EU agencies represent 'a third level in the organisation of regulatory responsibilities':

> The crucial point will be … to restore the single responsibility of the regulatory authority during all the successive stages of the risk management process, while at the same time ensuring that the technical and scientific co-operation has the essential autonomy to be effective, quick-acting and independent in judgment, for both the health and safety areas.[126]

Although Previdi did not realise the peculiarities of such public-private governance mechanism and unconvincingly proposed to set up a regulatory Agency for the management of standardisation, he sketched out the specificity of EU agencies as an organisational model. Previdi correctly stressed that EU agencies perform 'a function of translating political objectives defined in the legislation into practical regulatory acts' by availing of 'autonomous decisional competencies independent from those of the Member States (thus excluding any decisional procedure of a comitology type!) and responding to the professionalism requirements indispensable for risk regulation'.[127]

By avoiding the stage of political negotiation and by founding their action only on the rule of law, EU agencies operationalise EU policies and inject uniformity and effectiveness in the implementation process. In doing this, they exercise public powers of evaluation that define the content of the pursued public interest and go beyond the reach of a purely technical consensus on a subject matter. Unlike in the case of European standardisation bodies, EU law cannot simply recognise and conform to EU agencies' action through contractual instruments. Conversely, EU law must regulate the exercise of the administrative discretionary powers in order to keep them within the framework of EU public powers.

B. Administrative Governance under the Single Supervisory Mechanism

The Single Supervisory Mechanism (SSM) is one of the most significant reforms that the financial crisis brought about. As a pillar of the European Banking Union (EBU), the SSM has centralised banking supervision at the supranational level, creating new models of administrative integration beyond the black letter provisions of the Treaties.

The EBU aims to interrupt the vicious circle between banks and states in the management of banking crises that led to of the European sovereign debt crisis. To enhance the control over the stability of financial institutions, the EBU relies on three pillars: European supervision on the risks to cross-border banking operations which may be overlooked in the limited jurisdiction of national

[126] Ibid 240.
[127] Ibid 241.

competent authorities; the European deposit insurance scheme pooling risks across banks to better deal with possible crises; and the European resolution of those banks whose business is no longer viable.[128] On the one hand, by conferring on the European Central Bank (ECB) the micro-prudential supervision on significant financial institutions, the SSM aims to prevent financial instability and minimise risks for taxpayers.[129] In addition, harmonised national deposit guarantee schemes aim to create a buffer against risks and are financed by the contributions from the participating banks, and this regime is going to be strengthened by the establishment of a single European Deposit Insurance Scheme (EDIS).[130] On the other hand, the Single Resolution Mechanism (SRM) aims for the controlled resolution of unviable financial institutions and the establishment of the Single Resolution Fund with a view to avoiding severe systemic disruption and reducing the exposure of taxpayers to losses.[131]

From an institutional standpoint, the SSM has re-organised the allocation of supervisory competence between the EU and Member States. It has created a new regulatory framework that confers on the ECB strong powers for the supervision of credit institutions in the participating Member States; that is, in the Eurozone Member States and in the other Member States whose currency is not the Euro and which have established a close cooperation with the SSM. The multiple models of administrative governance that the SSM establishes, synthetise different collaboration schemes between national competent authorities and the ECB.

The SSM is based on the substitution of the ECB to the national competent authorities in the day-to-day supervision of EU-significant credit institutions. The mechanism is somehow hierarchical, but it strongly relies on cooperation. Lo Schiavo has effectively described this hybrid form of governance as a 'top-down cooperative system'.[132] As Tröger pointed out, however, the distribution

[128] On the principles of banking policy, see J Pisani-Ferry, A Sapir, N Véron and GB Wolff, *What Kind of European Banking Union?*, Bruegel Policy Contribution 2012/12 (2012), 4–6.

[129] Council Regulation 1024/2013/EU of 15 October 2013 conferring specific tasks on the European Central Bank concerning policies relating to the prudential supervision of credit institutions [2013] OJ L 287/63.

[130] See Directive 2014/49/EU of 16 April 2014 on deposit guarantee schemes (recast) [2014] OJ L 173. On EDIS see Communication to the European Parliament, the Council, the European Central Bank, the European Economic and Social Committee and the Committee of the Regions on completing the Banking Union, COM(2017)592 (11 October 2017), 11–13.

[131] Regulation 806/2014/EU of 15 July 2014 establishing uniform rules and a uniform procedure for the resolution of credit institutions and certain investment firms in the framework of a Single Resolution Mechanism and a Single Resolution Fund and amending Regulation (EU) 1093/2010 [2014] OJ L 225/1; Council Implementing Regulation 2015/81/EU of 19 December 2014 specifying uniform conditions of application of Regulation (EU) 806/2014 of the European Parliament and of the Council with regard to ex ante contributions to the Single Resolution Fund [2015] OJ L 15.

[132] G Lo Schiavo, 'The Single Supervisory Mechanism: Building the New Top-Down Cooperative Supervisory Governance in Europe' in F Fabbrini, EH Ballin and H Somsen (eds), *What Form of Government for the European Union and the Eurozone?* (Hart Publishing, 2015) 111, 125–26. See also E Wymeersch, *The Single Supervisory Mechanism or "SSM", Part One of the Banking Union*, ECGI Working Paper Series in Law 240/2014 (2014), 32.

of competences gives the general impression that 'the new architecture … is more rooted in the mistrust vis-à-vis (captured) national supervisors than in the ambition to provide an integrative framework that optimises effective transnational supervision'.[133]

When acting in its capacity within the EBU framework, the ECB takes on the tasks of the national competent authorities. Residually, national authorities maintain the day-to-day supervision of the other less significant institutions. In this residual area, the ECB still retains supervisory tasks and a general oversight of the system. According to Lastra, 'recourse to national authorities is a practical necessity, since supervision is a resource and personnel intensive task'.[134]

As the single supervisor, the ECB's control is limited to the significant banks; that is, to the big, systemic and cross-border credit institutions, or to those benefitting from public financial assistance.[135] However, in consultation with national authorities, this category can be extended at the ECB's discretion, to ensure a consistent application of high supervisory standards where necessary.[136] In the *Landeskreditbank v ECB* case, the General Court has described this power to remove direct prudential supervision from national authorities as a prerogative of the ECB, involving broad discretion.[137] Indeed, the reach of the ECB's mandate is left to the appreciation of the ECB itself in the exercise of its exclusive competence.

In *Landeskreditbank v ECB*, the General Court has clarified that the competence of the ECB is exclusive, but needs 'to be implemented within a decentralised framework'.[138] Insofar as the SSM framework does not distribute tasks between the ECB and national authorities, the direct prudential supervision under national jurisdiction is 'a mechanism of assistance to the ECB rather than the exercise of autonomous competence'.[139] The SSM consists of a cooperative mechanism under the exclusive competence of the ECB, rather than as a shared competence between the ECB and national authorities. Both ECB and national authorities cooperate over the day-to-day supervision of credit institutions, but all this occurs under the exclusive competence of the ECB.

[133] TH Tröger, 'The Single Supervisory Mechanism: Panacea or Quack Banking Regulation? Preliminary Assessment of the New Regime for the Prudential Supervision of Banks with ECB Involvement' (2014) 15 *European Business Organization Law Review* 449, 455.

[134] RM Lastra, 'Banking Union and Single Market: Conflict or Companionship?' (2013) 36 *Fordham International Law Journal* 1190, 1207.

[135] Council Regulation 1024/2013/EU, art 6(4).

[136] Ibid art 6(5)(b).

[137] T-122/15 *Landeskreditbank Baden Württemberg—Förderbank v ECB* ECLI:EU:T:2017:337, para 61.

[138] Ibid paras 54 and 63. See E Ferran and V Babis, *The European Single Supervisory Mechanism*, University of Cambridge Legal Studies Research Paper Series 10/2013 (2013), 6 and 9–10; E Ferran, *European Banking Union: Imperfect, But It Can Work*, University of Cambridge Legal Studies Research Paper Series 30/2014 (2014) 6–8.

[139] T-122/15 *Landeskreditbank Baden Württemberg—Förderbank v ECB* (n 137) para 58.

This approach has relevant consequences for the inoperability of the subsidiarity principle where no shared competences apply.[140] It is up to the ECB to carry out a discretional evaluation to delegate direct prudential supervision to national authorities where it 'is less able to ensure achievement of the objectives of the basic regulation' (Council Regulation 1024/2013/EU) with regard to a significant credit institution.[141] This also affects the application of the proportionality principle, as 'the assessment of the proportionality of a measure must be reconciled with compliance with discretion'.[142] Only if it is demonstrated that national supervision is better able to ensure the SSM objectives, the classification of a specific credit institution as a significant entity can be ruled out, no matter if the ECB applies criteria of assessment different than the ones applied for similar decisions in other cases.[143]

The strength of supervision is further enhanced by the powers assisting exclusive supervision, such as the capability to carry out investigations, supervisory reviews including stress tests, on-site inspections, and to impose administrative penalties on those financial institutions that breach intentionally or negligently directly applicable acts of EU law.[144] These powers confer on the ECB the means to effectively control the sustainability of banking activities and enhance financial stability.

Yet the decentralised exercise of the ECB's exclusive competence is complemented by further collaborative schemes with national authorities. As Giglioni has emphasised, the administrative governance of the SSM also covers the model of decentralised integration where national authorities operate within the framework established by EU bodies, and the one of co-administration where national authorities participate in the ECB's decision-making process.[145] Although national authorities supervise the less significant credit institutions, the ECB may issue regulations, guidelines and general instructions concerning the exercise of supervisory tasks at the national level.[146] This model of decentralised integration aims to promote coordination and harmonisation of supervisory practices, not different from the tasks that EU agencies perform in the internal market regulation.

Conversely, co-administration requires a more active role of national authorities, but the ECB maintains its discretionary powers. The authorisation regime exemplifies the supremacy of the ECB's evaluations. The ECB has power to issue and withdraw authorisations to take up the business of all credit institutions in

[140] Ibid para 65.
[141] Ibid para 46.
[142] Ibid para 68.
[143] Ibid paras 81–82.
[144] See Council Regulation 1024/2013/EU, arts 4 (1)(f), 9, 10, 11, 12, 13, 14 and 18.
[145] See F Giglioni, 'The European Banking Union as a New Model of Administrative Integration?' in E Chiti and G Vesperini (eds), *The Administrative Architecture of Financial Integration: Institutional Design, Legal Issues, Perspectives* (Il Mulino, 2015) 123, 127–28.
[146] Council Regulation 1024/2013/EU, art 6(5)(a).

close cooperation with national authorities.[147] The latter verify that credit institutions meet all the relevant conditions for authorisation set out in the relevant national law and propose a draft to the ECB, which may accept the draft decision through tacit consent.[148] The ECB can object to the draft only where the conditions for authorisation set out in EU law are not met and must give reasons for the rejection. Likewise, the ECB may withdraw the authorisation acting either on the proposal of national competent authorities or on its own initiative, but in consultation with national authorities. In the first scenario, the withdrawal is based on national law and the ECB adopts the withdrawal decision 'taking full account of the justification'[149] provided by national authorities. In the second scenario, the withdrawal occurs in the cases set out in the relevant EU law and the ECB must act in consultation with national authorities. Only where the ECB determines that national authorities have not taken 'proper actions necessary to maintain financial stability'[150] is the withdrawal decision immediately applicable.

The authorisation regime should have a limited content of discretion, as the compliance with the relevant requirements does not involve a substantive balance of public interests, but mainly consists of the verification that the financial institution in question holds the required characteristics. However, the combination of the authorisation powers with other discretionary powers to assess the structural adequacy of credit institutions that the ECB retains as single supervisor may significantly enhance the discretionary content of the decision. In fact, the ECB holds further supervisory tasks with stronger discretionary content. For instance, it assesses the acquisition and the disposal of qualifying holdings in credit institutions[151] and it sets further prudential requirements that range from holding own funds in excess of capital requirements and introducing further constraints on own funds, to the imposition of specific liquidity requirements, to the reinforcement of governance and risk management, to recovery plans, and the restriction of business operations.[152] EU legislation does not specifically circumscribe these powers; on the contrary, the allocation of extensive powers to be used by the ECB at its own discretion is aimed at tailoring the supervision and flexibly adapting intervention to the specific evaluation of the particular case. Logically, such discretion cannot be ruled out from the authorisation regime either.

Alongside these traditional models, an innovative model of administrative governance further strengthens the ECB's powers. When carrying out its supervisory tasks, ensuring high standards of supervision, the ECB is empowered to implement EU law and the national legislation transposing EU Directives into

[147] Ibid art 14.
[148] Ibid art 14(3).
[149] Ibid art 14(5).
[150] Ibid art 14(6).
[151] Ibid art 15.
[152] Ibid art 16.

domestic law.[153] In practice, this allows the banking supervision by the ECB also in areas reserved by Directives to national implementation.[154] In addition, in the exercise of the supervisory tasks on credit institutions in the participating Member States and on credit institutions of non-participating Member States that establish branches or provide cross-border services in the participating Member States, and when applying higher requirements for capital buffers as a macro-prudential tool, the ECB may require national authorities to make use of their powers under national law and control their use, where the powers are not conferred directly on the ECB.[155] The reach of this power of instruction still needs to be clarified. Witte proposed a narrow interpretation, as a power to provide further guidance on the national exercise of the other ECB's instructions received.[156] However, a more extensive reach of this power cannot be completely excluded, as the allocation of competences within the SSM seems to point to the intensive supervision. This model of governance ends the traditional distinction of administrative competence between the national and the supranational level. By going beyond cooperative modules, it introduces a further model on the take-over of national jurisdiction by an EU institution.

(i) Supervision Beyond Meroni

The decentralisation of supervisory powers at the ECB has been secured by the existence of a legal basis in the Treaties that opportunely avoided the issue of non-delegation beyond the general principles of conferral and institutional balance. By providing that Council regulations may confer 'specific tasks upon the European Central Bank concerning policies relating to the prudential supervision of credit institutions and other financial institutions with the exception of insurance undertakings', Article 127(6) TFEU has legally covered the extensive reach of the ECB's supervisory powers.

The choice of Article 127(6) TFEU as a legal basis has ensured that the new competence of the ECB had the most explicit coverage in the Treaties. As Witte has emphasised, this would have reduced the chances to successfully challenge the SSM in courts, whereas alternative legal bases would have provided a weaker justification for the allocation of strong supervisory powers: Article 114 TFEU is less specific and Article 352 TFEU requires the absence of other legal bases in the Treaties.[157] Some legal scholarship, however, considered the extensive responsibilities conferred on the ECB under Article 127(6) TFEU to be at odds with the special procedure of this legal basis and its reach limited to 'specific

[153] Ibid art 4(3).

[154] A Witte, 'The Application of National Banking Supervision Law by the ECB: Three Parallel Modes of Executing EU Law?' (2014) 21 *Maastricht Journal of European and Comparative Law* 89, 109.

[155] Council Regulation 1024/2013/EU, art 9.

[156] Witte, 'The Application of National Banking Supervision Law by the ECB' (n 154) 104.

[157] Ibid 92.

tasks ... concerning policies related to prudential supervision of credit institutions and other financial institutions'.[158] Others do not see substantive obstacles to the allocation of extensive supervisory tasks to the ECB under Article 127(6) TFEU.[159]

As an EU institution, the ECB is not constrained by the limits of the *Meroni* doctrine, but it is still subject to the structural principle of institutional balance. Where the conferral of new powers does not encroach on the powers of the other EU institutions, it can even be effectively conferred wide discretionary powers. The decentralisation of prudential supervision in an institution therefore has the advantage of enhancing supranational control without requiring the EU legislature to set meaningful substantial limits to the exercise of the power. Because of their stronger legal constraints, EU agencies would have failed to ensure the same effectiveness of the ECB. As Lo Schiavo pointed out, the EBA would have not had 'real-teeth powers' to lead the SSM.[160]

Although the SSM Regulation predates the CJEU's decision in the *ESMA Short Selling* case, the reach of the ECB's discretion rules out the legal capacity of EU agencies even in the mellowed version of the *Meroni* doctrine. In my view, in the current system of the Treaties, it is the reach of the ECB's powers and not their nature which rules out the possibility to confer the same powers on EU agencies. The ECB's core powers cover the wide discretion sanctioned in the *Meroni* case, because the priorities and criteria of the decision-making are not specified in the EU legislation, but are left to the evaluation of the ECB.

The absence of well-defined boundaries to the exercise of direct supervision is what distinguishes the ECB's powers under the SSM from the ESMA's powers on credit rating agencies and trade repositories. As seen in Chapter 2, the ESMA has extensive powers to register, supervise day-to-day and impose sanctions on credit rating agencies (CRAs)[161] and trade repositories.[162] However, the exercise of these powers is limited by meaningful criteria that narrow their reach and aim to make the function compatible with the non-delegation doctrine. Unlike the ECB's authorisation for credit institutions, the registration of CRAs has a low content of discretion, as the ESMA is required to examine the application 'based on the compliance of the credit rating agency with the conditions set out in this regulation'.[163] The withdrawal of the registration is also limited to specific cases

[158] See G Napolitano, 'La risposta europea alla crisi del debito sovrano: il rafforzamento dell'Unione economica e monetaria. Verso l'Unione bancaria' (2012) 65 *Banca Borsa* 747, 765; M Mancini, 'Dalla vigilanza nazionale armonizzata alla *Banking Union*' (2013) *Quaderni di Ricerca Giuridica* 5, 21–22.

[159] See G Lo Schiavo, 'From National Banking Union to a Centralized Model of Prudential Supervision in Europe?' (2014) 21 *Maastricht Journal of European and Comparative Law* 110, 121; Tröger, 'The Single Supervisory Mechanism' (n 133) 464.

[160] Lo Schiavo, 'The Single Supervisory Mechanism' (n 132) 114. See also C Brescia Morra, 'The Evolution of the Banking Supervision Architecture in Europe' in R Virzo and I Ingrallo (eds), *Evolutions in the Law of International Organizations* (Brill Nijhoff, 2015) 224, 235.

[161] Regulation 1060/2009/EC, as amended by Regulation 513/2011/EU ('CRA II Regulation'), Directive 2011/61/EU, Regulation 462/2013/EU ('CRA III Regulation') and Directive 2014/51/EU.

[162] Regulation 648/2012/EU.

[163] Regulation 1060/2009/EC as amended, arts 16(1) and 17(1). The same principles apply to trade repositories under Regulation 648/2012/EU, art 55.

that generally concern the compliance with the requirements for registration.[164] In this case, the ESMA acts upon the request of national competent authorities and can decide not to withdraw the registration only by providing 'full reasons'.[165] Full investigation powers and on-site inspections are granted to the ESMA, but their exercise is subject to a number of conditions, such as the specification of the matter and purpose of the action, the possible periodic penalty payments in case of infringements, the possible requirement of judicial authority's authorisation for inspections, and the legal remedies.[166] In addition, by defining the complete list of infringements (Annex III) and specific criteria for setting the level of fines (Annex IV), the Regulation strongly limits the ESMA's power to sanction CRAs.[167] As Di Noia and Gargantini emphasised, sanction powers show that 'narrow—albeit not negligible—discretion is left to ESMA'.[168] The ESMA evaluates whether a CRA infringes the Regulation's requirements, but the consequences of such infringement are stated in the Regulation itself.[169]

Although the ECB's supervision is also an activity that is administrative in nature, the absence of meaningful criteria in the exercise of the powers makes it an activity reserved to the responsibility of EU institutions. Quite interestingly, Carmassi, Luchetti and Minossi envisaged the possibility of creating a Single Supervisory Mechanism under the lead of the EBA by building upon its binding mediation powers and amending articles 19–21 of its Founding Regulation.[170] This alternative model of governance would have improved the national supervision by enhancing the powers of the EBA to participate in the Colleges of Supervisors over cross-border groups and by settling disagreements between national supervisory authorities. Nonetheless, the allocation of strong supervisory powers to the ECB has been also exposed to criticism. The organisational principles of the SSM struggle with the institutional structure of the ECB and its position in the EU legal order. SSM Regulation requires the ECB to carry out the prudential supervision tasks 'without prejudice and separately from its tasks relating to monetary policy any other tasks'.[171] To this end, article 26 of the SSM Regulation confers the planning and execution of these tasks on the Supervisory Board, an ECB

[164] Regulation 1060/2009/EC as amended, art 20(1). For trade repositories see Regulation 648/2012/EU, art 71.

[165] Regulation 1060/2009/EC as amended, art 20(2).

[166] Ibid arts 23(a), (b), (c), (d). See RG Alcubilla and JR Del Pozo, *Credit Rating Agencies on the Watch List* (Oxford University Press, 2012) 118–19. The same principles apply to trade repositories under Regulation 648/2012/EU, arts 61–63.

[167] For trade repositories, see ibid arts 65–66.

[168] C Di Noia and M Gargantini, 'Unleashing the European Securities and Markets Authority: Governance and Accountability after the ECJ Decision on Short Selling Regulation (Case 270/12)' (2014) 15 *European Business Organization Law Review* 1, 30–31.

[169] See Alcubilla and Del Pozo, *Credit Rating Agencies on the Watch List* (n 166) 111.

[170] J Carmassi, E Luchetti and S Micossi, *Overcoming Too-Big-to-Fail: A Regulatory Framework to Limit Moral Hazard and Free Riding in the Financial Sector, Report of the CEPS-ASSONIME Task Force on Bank Crisis Resolution* (CEPS, 2010) 74.

[171] Council Regulation 1024/2013/EU, art 25(2).

internal body composed of four representatives of the ECB and one representative of the national competent authorities in each participating Member State. As Wymeersch noted, the Supervisory Board is dominated by national supervisors, and the provision set out in article 19(1) of Regulation 1024/2013/EU that the Board should act 'in the interest of the Union as a whole' may not be sufficient to neutralise national interests.[172]

Although functionally independent, the Supervisory Board structurally hinges upon the governing structure of the ECB. The Governing Council must adopt internal rules setting out in detail its relations with the Supervisory Board, but it is also responsible for the formal adoption of the decisions of the Supervisory Board through a non-objection procedure.[173] However, any alternative solution of conferring on the Supervisory Board organisational independence would have encountered problems in terms of compatibility of its extensive powers with the framework of the Treaties. As Lo Schiavo emphasised, the establishment of a new independent body would have remained in a 'non-Treaty limbo', whereas the separation of tasks in the Governing Council would have required an amendment of the Protocol on the Statute of the European System of Central Banks (ESCB) and of the ECB under Article 48 of the Treaty on European Union (TEU).[174] If the latter option would have required more time, the former would have removed the conferral of discretionary powers from the protection of the *Meroni* doctrine.[175] These legal and political constraints, together with the strong reputation of the ECB, called for the least troublesome and most effective solution.

(ii) Institutional Paradoxes of Administrative Governance

The special supervisory regime of the SSM applies over and above the internal market regulation of banking harmonisation and supervision. Mancini emphasised that the architecture of banking regulation portrays a two-speed Europe, where deeper integration in the Eurozone (and other willing Member States) rests upon the general harmonisation in the internal market.[176] This concentric structure of integration creates some inconsistencies in the institutional design of banking regulation. As Lastra has stressed, 'the existence of two "banking authorities" EBA and ECB is a reflection of the co-existence of the Single Market and the Banking Union. These realities have different jurisdictional domains though some of their needs intersect'.[177]

The relationship between the ECB and the EBA is particularly telling of the difficulties and the legal challenges that the role played by the EBA creates with

[172] Wymeersch, 'The Single Supervisory Mechanism or "SSM"' (n 132) 52.
[173] Regulation 1024/2013/EU, art 26(8) and (12).
[174] Lo Schiavo, 'The Single Supervisory Mechanism' (n 132) 121.
[175] See Wymeersch, 'The Single Supervisory Mechanism or "SSM"' (n 132) 17 and 20–21.
[176] Mancini, 'Dalla vigilanza nazionale armonizzata alla *Banking Union*' (n 158) 5 and 33.
[177] Lastra, 'Banking Union and Single Market: Conflict or Companionship?' (n 134) 1212.

regard to the coherence of the EU institutional architecture. Not by chance, the EBA's Founding Regulation was amended to adjust the structure and the functioning of the EBA in light of the new tasks conferred on the ECB under the SSM.[178] The reform aimed to maintain the effectiveness of the EBA's tasks in the internal market.

The ECB in its capacity as single supervisor is required to act in accordance with EU law. This means that it must comply with the EBA's supervisory and harmonisation acts; it must implement the binding technical standards aimed at harmonising prudential rules in a single rule-book as well as the provisions aimed at developing a European supervisory handbook.[179] As a consequence, when acting within the single supervisory mechanism, the ECB is to be treated in the same way as the national competent authorities with regard to the application of soft law: it will also apply the 'comply or explain' formula for the implementation of the EBA's guidelines and recommendations. Furthermore, the ECB is subject to the EBA's monitoring powers and particularly to peer review, which consists of the assessment of the adequacy of the ECB's resources and governance arrangements; of the degree of convergence the ECB has reached in the application of EU law and supervisory practice; of the effectiveness and the degree of convergence the ECB has reached with regard to the enforcement of EU law provisions and the development of best practices.[180] The ECB's decisions, soft law powers and even its organisational regulations under Article 132 TFEU are to be substantively conditioned by the EBA's soft law action.

As a matter of practice, it seems unfeasible that the EBA may intrude on the ECB's supervision powers under the SSM.[181] As a matter of law, if this makes sense in the functional perspective of the SSM being part of the internal market regulation, nonetheless this raises some questions with regard to the institutional design. The ECB acts in its capacity as single supervisor for a group of Member States, which are subject to the EBA's subsidiary supervision aimed at harmonisation in the internal market; however, this creates a paradox when thinking about the (even mellowed) *Meroni* doctrine: an EU institution such as the ECB will be functionally subject to assessment by an EU agency and to compliance with its acts.[182]

[178] Regulation 1022/2013/EU of the European Parliament and of the Council of 22 October 2013 amending Regulation (EU) 1093/2010 establishing a European Supervisory Authority (European Banking Authority) as regards the conferral of specific tasks on the European Central Bank pursuant to Council Regulation (EU) 1024/2013 [2013] OJ L 287/15.

[179] Regulation 1024/2013/EU, art 4 (3) and recital 32.

[180] EBA Founding Regulation, art 30.

[181] Tröger, 'The Single Supervisory Mechanism' (n 133) 483.

[182] See N Moloney, 'European Banking Union: Assessing Its Risks and Resilience' (2014) 51 *Common Market Law Review* 1609, 1665, who considers that the relationship between the ECB and the EBA 'presents something of a constitutional conundrum in terms of the institutional balance set up under the Treaties'; B Wolfers and T Voland, 'Level the Playing Field: The New Supervision of Credit Institutions by the European Central Bank' (2014) 51 *Common Market Law Review* 1463, 1493; G Ter Kuile, L Wissink and W Bovenschen, 'Tailor-made Accountability Within the Single Supervisory Mechanism' (2015) 52 *Common Market Law Review* 155, 180.

In addition, in some regulatory areas the allocation of responsibilities between the EBA and ECB is not straightforward. The ECB has limited powers to adopt guidelines and recommendations within the framework of technical standards adopted by the Commission and the guidelines and recommendations of the EBA, but it can also adopt regulations for the implementation of its supervisory tasks.[183] As both the EBA and ECB develop supervisory handbooks, conflicts may arise yet which one is to be applied in SSM countries may be unclear; furthermore, as the ECB can develop bilateral cooperation with non-SSM countries, it may question the EBA's supervisory practices and coordination role.[184] This affects the legal certainty of private operators who must comply with the EBA's standards and the ECB's supervision, and who might be confused by the architecture of EU regulators and may misconstrue who is responsible for which rules.[185] However, the ECB is in the position to control and lead the national interpretations of supranational legislation, so that in practice it can become 'a *de facto* more powerful standard setter than the EBA'[186] with significant effects on non-participating Member States (and operators), as well as on the EBA's capacity to pursue internal market integration.

Concerning the organisational structure, the ECB is supposed to cooperate with the EBA, but the EU legal framework only weakly encourages such participation. Alongside reporting and information exchange, the ECB is expected to cooperate in the rule-making of binding technical standards. However, efforts may be frustrated by the fact that, unlike other competent national authorities, the ECB has only a non-voting seat on the EBA's board of supervisors.[187] This arrangement, together with the double majority voting of participating and non-participating Member States on the EBA's decisions, may rebalance the power of the ECB in the internal market regulation.[188] Nonetheless, it complicates the participation of the ECB as the single supervisor in the EBA's decision-making process.

To make the ECB's participation more effective, different cooperative mechanisms will be provided. The EBA may be invited to the ECB Supervisory Board's meetings as an observer when discussing matters for which the EBA is to develop

[183] Regulation 1024/2013/EU, art 4(3).

[184] On these issues see European Court of Auditors, *European Banking Supervision Taking Shape: EBA and its Changing Context*, Special Report 5/2014 (2014) 28, 35.

[185] See also JM Roldán and K Lannoo, *ECB Banking Supervision and Beyond, Report of a CEPS Task Force* (CEPS, 2014) 37, who point out that confusion of the markets about who is in charge may emerge about the division of labour between the ECB and the EBA. The authors also show that duplication in reporting may occur when banks respond to the EBA's stress tests and the ECB's asset quality review, even if the methodology used and the data formats are the same. On the need for clarification of the ECB's and EBA's responsibilities and tasks, see COM(2014)509, 4; European Court of Auditors, 'European Banking Supervision Taking Shape' (n 184) 40.

[186] Tröger, 'The Single Supervisory Mechanism' (n 133) 485.

[187] Regulation 1024/2013/EU, art 4(3). See Mancini, 'Dalla vigilanza nazionale armonizzata alla *Banking Union*' (n 158) 36–37; Roldán and Lannoo, *ECB Banking Supervision and Beyond* (n 185) 38.

[188] See G Lo Schiavo, *The Role of Financial Stability in EU Law and Policy* (Kluwer, 2017) 157.

technical standards or issue guidelines.[189] Clearly, these mechanisms leave to a discretionary evaluation the decision about the expediency of cooperation. Effective cooperation between these authorities is therefore left to the specific weight of the role that the ECB plays in the practice and to the substantive influence that it can exercise as an EU institution, as well as to the capability of all the bodies in question to build fruitful networks of information exchange. This illustrates that the institutional framework matters, and this indirectly confirms the EBA's marginal institutional capability to actively contribute to shaping banking supervision under the SSM.[190]

VII. DISTINCTIVE MODEL OF EU AGENCIES' POWERS

EU agencies' powers represent a different model of administrative governance in the internal market. Unlike standardisation bodies, they institutionalise the system of administration, yet in an administrative space that does not emerge as such from the black letter provisions of the Treaties. EU agencies are autonomous bodies, have legal personality under EU law and act as supranational centres of quasi-regulatory cooperation in the internal market regulation and enforcement. Their powers, however, cannot reach the level of discretion exercised by the ECB under the SSM.

The model of administrative governance that EU agencies portray can be distinguished in terms of competence and become a complementary tool at the disposal of the EU legislature (and the Member States) to foster the decentralised implementation of internal market integration. So long as the principle of institutional balance sets the limits to the competence of EU agencies, their functions cannot interfere with the exercise of EU institutions' powers, although some material overlaps may not be excluded. As discussed in Chapter 1, in the *ESMA Short Selling* case, the Court of Justice has not considered the powers of the Commission in competition with EU agencies' powers. The Court has hinted at a co-existence of different implementation measures under the Treaties and simply accepted EU agencies' acts as distinct instruments from the Commission's delegated acts under Article 290 TFEU and implementing acts under Article 291 TFEU. The Court particularly distinguished the powers of the ESMA on two grounds: first, their inclusion under 'a series of rules designed to endow the competent national authorities and the ESMA with powers of intervention to cope with adverse developments' threatening financial stability and market confidence; and secondly, the 'high degree of professional expertise' of the ESMA that institutionally the Commission cannot hold.[191] The first part of the distinction hints at

[189] Regulation 1024/2013/EU, recital 70. See Moloney, 'European Banking Union' (n 182) 1668.
[190] The issue of the marginalisation of the EBA has been pointed out by Ferran and Babis, *The European Single Supervisory Mechanism* (n 138) 23.
[191] C-270/12 *United Kingdom v Parliament and Council* (n 5) para 85.

the administrative nature of EU agencies' powers, whereas the second part recognises in the decentralised agencies another organisational model of administrative cooperation based on expertise.

Competition between non-legislative sources of law cannot be ascertained through the black letter provisions of the Treaties, as these portray an non-detailed picture of administrative competences. The institutional balance of power should be concretely ascertained in administrative implementation, through the examination of the distinctive significance of EU agencies' powers. The characterisation of administrative discretion as a margin of evaluation within a predetermined framework of priorities and criteria for action represents the core of EU agencies' powers and limits their reach. Only within this bounded area can administrative governance by EU agencies emerge and a co-regulatory space, administrative in nature, be legitimately recognised.

To understand whether EU agencies may legitimately exercise administrative powers with a regulatory impact on internal market integration, this chapter aimed to disentangle the nature of their powers. If we accept a model of legality where EU agencies may exercise quasi-regulatory powers at a non-legislative level, the key legal question becomes how do they exercise their discretionary powers, so that they do not abuse their organisational position in the EU institutional framework and do not take arbitrary decisions that may affect individual rights? As in the Member States, the legitimate exercise of administrative powers requires legal guarantees and institutional controls. The following Chapter will deal with the issue of how EU agencies are kept accountable and the compatibility of their administrative discretion is ensured.

4

Administrative Power Bundled Up: A Tenable EU Agencies' Governance?

I. INTRODUCTION

THE EVIDENCE THAT EU agencies' governance can be contained within the limits of the Treaties and the non-delegation doctrine, may justify in principle the conferral of administrative responsibilities and tasks on them. However, this is not sufficient to ensure that their exercise of administrative powers is compatible with the democratic principle and the rule of law on which the EU legal order is based. In Western democracies and, particularly, in all the EU Member States, the allocation of administrative powers that are to some extent authoritative in nature must be accompanied by the introduction of adequate checks-and-balances to their exercise. These checks-and-balances structure the accountability of administrative bodies: they reconnect administrative powers to the unitary exercise of the executive function as a necessary public power, submit their exercise to the rule of law and make them justiciable. Without these checks-and-balances, administrative powers are arbitrary by design and not useful by implication for the democratic performance of public goals. Institutional mechanisms of control and legal guarantees in the exercise of powers must frame EU agencies' action.

Only in a model of legality where legal ties structure the exercise of administrative discretion, can EU agencies legitimately exercise discretionary powers. Control normatively counter-balances the conferral of administrative responsibilities and tasks. A series of organisational and functional arrangements will keep the exercise of administrative discretion within acceptable boundaries that do not encroach on the democratic principle that informs the EU legal order. As Fisher emphasised, accountability instruments need to be 'disentangled' from the wider context of 'what is and should be the role and nature of European institutions' as a debate over the model of European integration.[1] If the complexity of the single market integration may require the establishment of supranational administrative

[1] E Fisher, 'The European Union in the Age of Accountability' (2004) 24 *Oxford Journal of Legal Studies* 495, 511.

bodies which govern sector-specific areas, how this system of governance is kept accountable becomes a central concern for its compatibility with the model of the Union as a democratic community based on the rule of law.

Organisational and functional arrangements must ensure the constitutional compatibility of EU agencies; that is, their coherence with the system of the EU as designed by the Treaties. On the one hand, EU agencies' organisational set-up needs to support the effective achievement of the implementation goals. Founding regulations claim the independence of EU agencies as the key condition for their impartial functioning. On the other hand, the structure of their decision-making needs to be designed so as to ensure that administrative discretion is functionalised to the pursuit of the legitimate objectives of single market integration and that its exercise provides effective protection for competing rights and interests and, particularly, the justiciability of unfair administrative acts.

Questioning how EU agencies exercise their powers is therefore essential to understand whether their discretionary powers are tenable in the current EU legal framework. As scholarship has emphasised, the establishment of an effective accountability regime is a key condition for the delegation of powers.[2] As seen in Chapter 1, under the *Meroni* doctrine, instruments of political accountability and legal justiciability emerged as necessary conditions for the lawful delegation of powers to EU agencies.[3] Although only sketched, procedural guarantees, supervision of the delegating authority and judicial review emerged as key requirements for lawful delegation under the *Meroni* case. In the Opinion of Advocate General Roemer in *Meroni*, the option to challenge EU agencies' acts in courts was considered a 'decisive element' for the (non-) delegation of powers to EU agencies.[4] The recent *ESMA Short Selling* case confirmed the relevance of judicial control for the legitimate conferral of powers on EU agencies.[5] Building upon the key principle of accountability affirmed in EU case law, I suggest that the question of *if* EU agencies can exercise powers with a regulatory impact, should also be complemented and answered in light of another key question; that is, *how* EU agencies exercise these powers. To ascertain that administrative powers are not an arbitrary privilege conferred on unaccountable bodies, how they are institutionally responsible for their action and comply with the rule of law becomes a fundamental issue of democratic impact.

The principles of impartiality and fairness need to shape EU agencies' organisation and guide their adoption of administrative acts. In fact, these principles prevent discrimination and arbitrariness in the exercise of public powers and

[2] See M Busuioc, *European Agencies: Law and Practices of Accountability* (Oxford University Press, 2013) 53–54; M Scholten, *The Political Accountability of EU and US Independent Regulatory Agencies* (Brill Nijhoff, 2014) 87.

[3] 9/56 and 10/56 *Meroni & Co, Industrie Metallurgiche, SAS v High Authority of the European Coal and Steel Community* [1958] ECR 53, 173.

[4] 9/56 and 10/56 *Meroni v High Authority* (n 3), Opinion of AG Roemer, 194.

[5] C-270/12 *United Kingdom v Council and European Parliament* ECLI:EU:C:2014:18, para 53.

define the Western model of administration pursuing public interests objectively and reasonably. The Lisbon Treaty has endorsed this model of administration and based it on the pillars that govern and legitimise the decisions of contemporary national administrations: independence, transparency and efficiency in the decision-making,[6] both in the organisation and in the procedure, and judicial review of the decisions taken.[7] As part of EU administration, EU agencies must comply with those primary rules that shape administrative action and thus design a specific legal relationship between administration and individual rights.

In this general framework, the oversight of administrative discretion will be appraised through substantive arrangements and formal guarantees that cover organisational and procedural issues of a wider accountability framework. These mechanisms of control are to provide the adequate checks-and-balances to the exercise of administrative discretion and enhance the legitimacy of EU agencies' action in the absence of a clear justification of their competence in the Treaties. Insofar as the model of administration that EU agencies characterise remains hidden beyond the black letter provisions of the Treaties, these checks-and-balances will frame EU agencies' action and ensure that administrative discretion is not used for purposes other than the effective attainment of the goals prescribed by law.

The organisation of EU agencies and their political accountability, the proceedings they follow in the exercise of administrative powers and the substantive review of such powers ensure that administrative action is compatible with individual rights as protected in a democratic legal order. The chapter aims to identify the key legal guarantees under EU administrative law that entrench administrative powers, both in the making of administrative action and in the judicial review. When analysing the administrative level, on the one hand, the chapter discusses the autonomy of EU agencies (section II) with the aim of understanding how this organisational principle concretely affects EU agencies' composition, action and accountability. On the other hand, the chapter considers the legal guarantees that shape the exercise of administrative powers in the decision-making process, with particular reference to the enforcement of the right to good administration (section III) and the articulation of impartial and fair administrative proceedings (section IV). The emerging bundle of principles guiding the exercise of administrative discretion is thus analysed in the specific context of composite administration where EU agencies generally operate and the procedural issues of this complex method of administration are highlighted (section V).

Moving to the side of remedies, the chapter considers the internal administrative review by EU agencies' Boards of Appeals as a relevant but still underdeveloped instrument of administrative protection. The scope of these remedies and the reach of their scrutiny on administrative discretion (section VI) are

[6] Article 298 TFEU and Charter of Fundamental Rights, Art 41; but see also Art 15 TFEU.

[7] Article 263 TFEU and Charter of Fundamental Rights, Art 47.

analysed as key issues that contribute to identifying their still limited impact. When analysing the judicial level, the effectiveness of the existing legal remedies is addressed (section VII) and the emerging standard of judicial review is discussed (section VIII). Because EU agencies' acts may be both hard law and soft law, these key legal guarantees are adequately considered for all the EU agencies' activities with the aim of leaving no room for areas of administrative irresponsibility. Section IX emphasises that a more coherent entrenchment of EU agencies' action would protect against the concerns of the *Meroni* doctrine and make decentralised administration more sustainable within the (weak) framework of the Treaties.

II. PRINCIPLE OF AUTONOMY

To ensure the accomplishment of their tasks, the principles of impartiality and fairness in the pursuit of the legal goals have significant implications on the organisation of administration. The functional aspect of these principles related to the objective and reasonable pursuit of the public interest must be supported by organisational arrangements. Organisation affects the EU agencies' own possibilities to accomplish the tasks that EU law confers on them. Independence is the claimed legal requirement that ensures the capability of the organisation to accomplish its mission and tasks with impartiality and fairness. The concept of independence, however, has blurred boundaries and substantially covers institutional and functional autonomy.

Although the structure of EU agencies is not the same in every sector and reflects sectorial specificities and the political momentum of their establishment, clearly, all decentralised agencies are autonomous legal entities. Their legal personality structures the capability of their organisation to take autonomous decisions with effects regarding third parties. Autonomy does not involve the insulation of EU agencies from the relevant EU institutions and the national competent authorities, nor from the market.

In the generality of cases, however, this does not mean that they are independent from the central executive of the Commission. They mostly work for or under the supervision of the Commission, as their powers are instrumental to the decision-making of the Commission or provide technical assistance to national authorities. The Commission's policy and practice is to strengthen the relationships with EU agencies through formal and informal connections with its departments (Directorates General).[8] Expertise justifies their autonomous organisation and structures the scientific independence of their evaluations, but not their separation from the EU executive.

[8] M Egeberg, J Trondal and NM Vestlund, 'The Quest for Order: Unravelling the Relationship Between the European Commission and European Union Agencies' (2015) 22 *Journal of European Public Policy* 609, 616–24.

Technically, they are not legally independent from the influence of the Commission.[9] This emerges organisationally, from the participation of the Commission's representatives in agencies' management boards, and functionally, from the supervision of the Commission of agencies' work programmes and performance. Nonetheless, EU legislation and the narrative of the Commission have promoted the idea of independence to explain their decentralised position and their non-hierarchical relationship with the Commission.[10] EU legal scholarship has, however, emphasised the independent character of EU agencies' autonomous action, making interchangeable use of these terms. For instance, Vos has considered EU agencies to be functionally independent because of their autonomy to implement policies with no undue interference from EU institutions, Member States and market actors.[11] Scholten evaluated this aspect of independence as the core of EU agencies' competence and it is connected to their capability to exercise discretionary powers.[12] Lavrijssen and Ottow have suggested that institutional independence supports functional independence by providing EU agencies with an autonomous organisation, separated from the Commission and the Council.[13] This prevents other institutions from disposing of EU agencies and, crucially, preserves them from abolition.[14]

The principle of independence dismissing the EU executive's influence becomes more relevant where EU agencies exercise stronger autonomous powers. The European Aviation Safety Agency (EASA)'s quasi-regulatory powers rely on some independence in the design of the relationship between the Agency and the Commission. European Supervisory Authorities (ESAs)' powers point in this direction and they may also lead to the exercise of the Commission's powers. In these cases, EU agencies are not influenced by the Commission in the adoption of their administrative acts. However, they still cooperate closely as peers with other EU institutions, especially with the Commission. This qualified-autonomy or semi-independence, however, is not well-defined and its reach is not crystal-clear. Its legal articulation and limits contribute to designing the exercise of

[9] E Chiti, 'An Important Part of the EU's Institutional Machinery: Features, Problems and Perspectives of European Agencies' (2009) 46 *Common Market Law Review* 1395, 1399–1400.

[10] See COM(2008)135, which refers to EU regulatory agencies as 'independent bodies', but endowed with 'autonomous power'. See also M Shapiro, 'The Problems of Independent Agencies in the United States and the European Union' (1997) 4 *Journal of European Public Policy* 276, who emphasises that in the United States independence has meant the disconnection of administrative authorities from the political circuit, whereas in the EU it has been 'a matter of separation of powers', so that 'agencies are "independent" because they are (partially) independent from the Commission' (281).

[11] See E Vos, 'Independence, Accountability and Transparency of European Regulatory Agencies' in D Geradin, R Muñoz and N Petit (eds), *Regulation Through Agencies in the EU: A New Paradigm of European Governance* (Elgar Publishing, 2005) 120, 123.

[12] M Scholten, *"Independence vs. Accountability": Dilemma or Misconception*, (2010) 22, available at https://ssrn.com/abstract=1718584. See also M Scholten, '"Independent, Hence Unaccountable"?' (2011) 4 *Review of European Administrative Law* 5.

[13] S Lavrijssen and A Ottow, 'Independent Supervisory Authorities: A Fragile Concept' (2012) 39 *Legal Issues of Economic Integration* 419, 428.

[14] Scholten '"Independence vs. Accountability": Dilemma or Misconception' (n 12) 12.

EU agencies' powers in a new accountability framework, but do not dare to disconnect these agencies from the EU central executive and create independent authorities.

The structure of their Boards, the integration of interest representation in the decision-making process and the instruments ensuring political accountability are key elements that contribute to understanding to what extent EU agencies are architecturally prepared to set up sector-specific regulation.

A. Design of EU Agencies' Boards

As seen in Chapter 3, the composition of the Boards may influence the identification of the relevant public interest and the means to pursue it. As Chiti observed, the core participation of the heads of national competent authorities in these Boards and the presence of a representative of the Commission makes EU agencies the clear expression of an institutionalised cooperation between Member States and the Commission.[15] This model admits some variances. For instance, the national members of the Agency for the Cooperation of Energy Regulators (ACER) administrative board are appointed by the Council and it also includes representatives not only from the Commission, but also from the European Parliament.[16] However, the leading role of the Administrative Board is balanced by the establishment of the Board of Regulators,[17] with key responsibilities in the Agency's decision-making process.[18] Comprising senior representatives of the national competent authorities and one representative from the Commission with no voting rights, the Board of Regulators reaffirms the key relevance of national interests but in a different organisational setting.

The comparison between the EASA's Management Board and the ESAs' Boards of Supervisors show different modules of cooperation: in the EASA, the representative of the Commission is a full member of the Management Board with voting rights,[19] whereas in the ESAs, the member of the Board of Supervisors

[15] Chiti, 'An Important Part of the EU's Institutional Machinery' (n 9) 1398.

[16] Regulation 713/2009/EC of the European Parliament and of the Council of 13 July 2009 establishing an Agency for the Cooperation of Energy Regulators, art 12 [2009] OJ L 211/1. The Administrative Board of ACER is composed of nine members, five of which are appointed by the Council and the remaining four are equally divided between the Commission and the European Parliament.

[17] The Board of Supervisors is 'formally' appointed by the Administrative Board, which means that the latter has no substantive power to choose the members of the former; Regulation 713/2009/EC, art 13(2).

[18] Regulation 713/2009/EC, art 15. The Board of Supervisors particularly approves the appointment of the Director of the Agency and the work programme, and assists the Director by issuing binding opinions and providing binding guidance in the execution of his tasks.

[19] Regulation 216/2008/EC, arts 34 and 37. Article 90 of the 2015 legislative proposal for a new EASA Regulation, COM(2015)613, has established an Executive Board composed of the Chairperson of the Management Board, two representatives of the Commission and six other members appointed by the Management Board from among its members with the right to vote with the mission of assisting the Management Board in the preparation and the implementation of its decisions.

from the Commission has no voting rights.[20] In addition, representatives from the European Systemic Risk Board and the other ESAs participate in the ESAs' Boards with no voting rights.[21] These variances in the composition and voting rights highlight the different sets of interests that cooperation aims to compromise and identify different organisational models: autonomy, in the case of the EASA, and the embryonic model of independence structuring their capability to act 'in the sole interest of the Union as a whole'[22] in the case of the ESAs. Busuioc investigated the influence that individual Member States and the Commission may exercise on the quality of the debate in such Boards.[23] If some national representatives have no specific interest in the issues at stake, they do not commit to the analysis of the case and other (more interested) states or the Commission may milk the situation. Insofar as the composition of their Boards excludes the neutrality of EU agencies to national interests, they institutionally become centres of mediation of interests in light of internal market integration. Busuioc featured this as a definite problem for the functioning of the Boards, because the large national membership of the Boards shifts the focus from strategic discussion on the Agency's performance to micro-management and issues affecting national interests.[24] As Lavrijseen and Ottow have emphasised, the principle of independence yet also autonomy is the legal safeguard preventing the unjustified transferral of national problems at the EU level and vice versa.[25] However, the justiciability of this principle is not straightforward, as national interests seem to affect the quality of the discussion within the Boards, rather than the activities of the Boards in themselves.

B. Institutionalisation of Stakeholders' Participation

Besides national interests, market interests are also relevant for EU agencies and may affect their independence. Although capture of EU agencies by private interests is to be avoided, consultation and participation of private parties is key in the functioning of EU agencies. They are able to consider all the relevant public and private interests at stake, with a view to achieving sound evaluations. The representation of the regulated interests has assumed different forms at the level of EU agencies. For instance, in the case of the European Railway Agency (ERA), the rail-sector categories participate as non-voting members in the

[20] ESAs Founding Regulations, art 40(1)(c).
[21] Ibid art 40(1)(d) and (e).
[22] Ibid art 42.
[23] Busuioc, *European Agencies: Law and Practices of Accountability* (n 2) 99–103.
[24] M Busuioc, 'European Agencies and their Boards: Promises and Pitfalls of Accountability Beyond Design' (2012) 19 *Journal of European Policy* 719, 728–29.
[25] Lavrijssen and Ottow, 'Independent Supervisory Authorities: A Fragile Concept' (n 13) 440.

Administrative Board.[26] In the case of the EASA and the ESAs, such representation has been institutionalised. The EASA's Management Board establishes an Advisory Body of Interested Parties to be consulted on specific issues of its activity,[27] whereas the Founding Regulations of the ESAs directly establish sector-specific Stakeholder Groups operating within the ESAs.[28]

The institutionalisation of the relations between EU agencies and private interests is accompanied by different levels of flexibility according to the reach and the relevance of consultation. In the case of the EASA, consultation is mandatory, but not binding on a series of activities that may directly concern private parties, such as the Agency's work programme, the procedures for the Executive Director's decisions, the Agency's budget and the fees and charges applicable to the services provided by the Agencies. In the case of ESAs, instead, Stakeholder Groups representing the prominent interests of intermediate bodies and categories are to be consulted on the administrative action with a regulatory impact that only generally affects private parties, such as the draft of regulatory and implementing technical standards as well as the adoption of guidelines and recommendations. Participation therefore has a more strategic value: it is able to influence the content of general acts and it also contributes to justifying and making more acceptable the relevant categories of EU hard and soft standards. Busuioc particularly emphasised that the institutionalisation of 'participatory regulatory networks' can decisively contribute to 'serving as a potential legitimizing source, even more so given agencies' low democratic credentials' and to enhancing efficiency by 'secur[ing] input legitimacy and generat[ing] trust among major stakeholders'.[29]

However, as Chiti has pointed out, the 'stable and institutionalized representation of private subjects within European agencies presents a number of shadows' that point to the risks of neo-corporative models of governance, such as the creation of pressures that hinder the independent decision-making of the Agency, or the risks of unequal access to representation.[30] The composition and functioning of the Stakeholder Group therefore assumes strategic relevance. For this reason, this has not been left to the discretion of the Agency, but has been directly regulated by EU legislation.

The ESAs' Founding Regulations provide that every Stakeholder Group shall represent 'in balanced proportions' the relevant industry and its employees, consumers and users of the relevant services and representatives of the SMEs and 'shall, to the extent possible, ensure an appropriate geographical and gender

[26] Regulation 881/2004/EC of the European Parliament and of the Council of 29 April 2004 establishing a European railway agency, art 26 [2004] OJ L 220/3.

[27] Regulation 216/2008/EC, art 33(4).

[28] ESAs Founding Regulations, recital 48 and art 37.

[29] Busuioc, *European Agencies: Law and Practices of Accountability* (n 2) 34.

[30] Chiti, 'An Important Part of the EU's Institutional Machinery' (n 9) 1402.

balance and representation of stakeholders across the Union'.[31] The difficulties of such a balanced appointment emerged in the evidence in the cases submitted to the European Ombudsman on the composition of the Banking Stakeholder Group at the EBA.[32] When declaring the EBA's maladministration in the process of selection of the members of the Banking Stakeholder Group, the Ombudsman emphasised the need to ensure the geographical and gender balance within each category of membership.[33] The Ombudsman also clarified the reach of some categories, emphasising that consumers may also include experts not belonging to consumer associations, and that the users of banking services are retail users of services provided by the financial/banking sector, and not accounting and audit firms and credit rating agencies that provide services to the financial/banking sector.[34] On the grounds of these remarks, the Ombudsman suggested that the EBA should strengthen the selection process by enhancing the transparency of the process and indicating how it has complied with the legal requirements, by requiring applicants to indicate only one of the six categories represented in the Stakeholder Group, by giving the most possible diffusion of its calls for expression of interest so as to increase gender balance.[35]

C. Instruments of Political Accountability

The last critical element that shapes the reach of EU agencies' autonomy is their accountability to the EU institutional framework. As supranational bodies, EU agencies must be kept accountable to the audience of EU institutions for the exercise of their powers, but they cannot be fully controlled if the specificity of this administrative model is to be preserved. As anticipated, the principle of autonomy is articulated in differentiated accountability regimes. As Chiti observed in a broader analysis of EU administrative networks, these accountability regimes vary according to the organisation and the powers exercised by such networks.[36] When analysing the institutional controls of EU institutions on such networks, Chiti noted their use either as a means to ensure the reliability of the instrumental activities aimed to serve institutional action of EU institutions or

[31] ESAs Founding Regulations, art 37(2), (3).

[32] Decision of the European Ombudsman of 7 November 2013 closing her inquiry into complaint 1966/2011/(EIS)LP against the European Banking Authority ('UNI Europa Decision'); Decision of the European Ombudsman of 19 December 2013 closing her inquiry into complaint 1321/2011/(PMC)(EIS)LP against the European Banking Authority ('Consumatori Associati Decision').

[33] UNI Europa Decision (n 32) paras 24–34; Consumatori Associati Decision (n 32) paras 28–29.

[34] UNI Europa Decision (n 32) paras 51–54; Consumatori Associati Decision (n 32) para 23.

[35] UNI Europa Decision (n 32) Further remarks 1–2; Consumatori Associati Decision (n 32) Further remarks 1–3.

[36] E Chiti, 'L'accountability delle reti di autorità amministrative dell'Unione Europea' (2012) *Rivista Italiana di Diritto Pubblico Comunitario* 29.

national authorities,[37] or as instruments assessing the 'political acceptability' of network activities.[38] He also pointed out the substantive inability of the established institutional controls to effectively entrench administrative action.[39]

The system of institutional controls fails to counter-balance the growing autonomy of EU agencies, and it does not seem to give autonomy to the wider framework of EU institutions' powers. The control exercised by EU institutions rather reflects the still uncertain place of EU agencies in the framework of the Treaties and the tensions in the checks-and-balances on their discretion. The instruments of political accountability do not ensure a strong oversight of EU agencies' powers by the EU legislature conferring such powers, nor by the Commission as a key actor of the EU executive. Nonetheless, they still aim to anchor EU agencies to the EU institutional circuit. For instance, the Commission plays a substantive role in the control of EU agencies' performance. EU agencies' Founding Regulations ensure the technical control on their operation through the instrument of periodic evaluations. The ESAs' Founding Regulations and the 2012 Common Approach have passed this task to the Commission, which must forward the report and any accompanying proposals, as appropriate, to the European Parliament and to the Council.[40] In contrast, the EASA's Founding Regulation took a more prudent approach aimed at preserving the autonomy of the Agency against the Commission.[41] The EASA's Management Board commissions an independent external evaluation on the implementation of its regulation and then it evaluates the reported findings and issues recommendations regarding changes to the regulation, the Agency and its working practices to the Commission. However, the Commission keeps some discretionary powers in the evaluation process, as it decides whether to forward the EASA's proposal to the European Parliament and to the Council and to add its own opinion as well as appropriate proposals.

Chamon has not disregarded the opportunity for the Commission as 'the primary core executive' to take on the responsibility to control EU agencies.[42] He particularly claimed 'a general prerogative for the Commission to annul or suspend agency decisions' and its 'greater involvement in the agency's decision-making'.[43] Considering EU agencies as a political compromise for the Member States to transfer powers at the EU level but not to the Commission, Scholten

[37] Ibid 63–65.

[38] Ibid 66.

[39] Ibid 76–77.

[40] ESAs Founding Regulations, art 81. See also Common Approach, Annex to the Joint Statement of the European Parliament, the Council and the European Commission of 19 July 2012 on Decentralised Agencies, para 60.

[41] Regulation 216/2008/EC, art 62.

[42] M Chamon, *EU Agencies: Legal and Political Limits to the Transformation of the EU Administration* (Oxford University Press, 2016) 320–21.

[43] Ibid 321.

has criticised this approach as affecting their independence.[44] These opposing conceptions aim to address different risks; respectively, the absence of a legal justification of EU agencies' powers in the framework of the institutional balance designed in the Treaties, and the political obstacles to keep EU agencies within the domain of the Commission. These risks highlight the blurred boundaries of EU agencies' organisational model and the reach of their autonomy. Chamon constructed autonomy as a weak condition, which does not preclude the exercise of hierarchical powers from the Commission, whereas Scholten had a stronger conception, which does not admit interference with powers.

The current political accountability regime may legitimately cover both interpretations. In my view, where agencies have stronger powers and enjoy reinforced autonomy touching upon independence, the Commission cannot exercise general hierarchical powers over EU agencies for legal and practical reasons. Although the Commission may legitimately be involved in some controls over EU agencies and may practically influence their work programmes, the hierarchical substitution would in fact imply the capability of the Commission to exercise the powers of EU agencies and, in particular, produce on its own comparable technical evaluations. This clearly clashes with the functional reasons for the establishment of EU agencies with stronger, quasi-regulatory powers. Under the same logic, the Commission can depart from EU agencies' evaluations only by providing reasons that justify the necessity of a different approach. Their relationship, therefore, requires more sophisticated means of control which must have regard to the epistemic and legal autonomy of EU agencies. As Lavrijssen and Ottow pointed out, accountability mechanisms ensure that when pursuing their delegated tasks independently, EU agencies satisfy 'the delegator's original intention' and this may result in the enhancement of their independence in practice.[45] It is not by chance that EU institutions exercise most of their control through the supervision of EU agencies' activities. The European Parliament and the Commission are particularly informed of the activities of EU agencies through the powers to summon their key officials, such as the Chairperson of the Board of Supervisors or the Executive Directors. Scholten noted the enhanced role of the European Parliament in making EU agencies' top officials personally accountable, as an effect of its growing role as part of the EU legislative power.[46] For instance, in the case of the ESAs, the European Parliament and the Council may invite the Chairperson to make statements, answer questions and report in writing on the main activities carried out.[47] In addition, the European Parliament must confirm the

[44] M Scholten, 'Publication Review: "M Chamon, *EU Agencies. Legal and Political Limits to the Transformation of the EU Administration* (Oxford University Press 2016)"' (2017) 42 *European Law Review* 139, 140; Scholten, *The Political Accountability of EU and US Independent Regulatory Agencies* (n 2) 170–71.

[45] Lavrijssen and Ottow, 'Independent Supervisory Authorities: A Fragile Concept' (n 13) 421.

[46] Scholten, *The Political Accountability of EU and US Independent Regulatory Agencies* (n 2) 105–6.

[47] ESAs Founding Regulations, art 50.

appointment of the ESAs' Executive Directors appointed by the Board of Supervisors[48] and in charge, among others, of drafting the work programmes, the budget and the annual report.[49] Similarly, the European Parliament and the Council may invite the EASA's Executive Director to report on his/her tasks,[50] but the Commission is to propose the candidates for this role to be appointed or dismissed by the Management Board.[51]

In addition, after the legislative definition of the mandate of EU agencies, the EU legislature and the Commission may supervise the activities of EU agencies through their work programmes as a means to enhance the coherence of EU agencies' activities with regard to EU policies. In the case of the EASA, the annual work programme will be adopted by the Management Board after receiving the opinion of the Commission and it is then submitted to the European Parliament, the Council, the Commission itself and the Member States.[52] The same applies to the ESAs, which, however, do not need the opinion of the Commission for the adoption of their work programme.[53]

Despite the different organisational arrangements, the ESAs show a lower degree of accountability to the Commission, but this does not involve the existence of stronger relations with the European Parliament and the Council. In practice, insofar as the accountability instruments at their disposal are the same, they acquire more independence from the EU executive as a whole. However, as seen in Chapter 2, the 2012 Joint Statement of the European Parliament, the Council and the Commission on a common approach to EU decentralised agencies placed on the Commission the power to intervene in the Management Board and raise the question of compatibility of EU agencies' acts with EU law and policies.[54] In practice, therefore, the Commission may retain a key role in the control of the legality of EU agencies' action. The compatibility of the Commission's powers under the 2012 Common Approach with the ESAs' Founding Regulation, however, is not easy to demonstrate. In fact, the ESAs may claim their independence on the grounds that their regulations do not envisage such a supervisory role for the Commission, and may contest the validity of the Common Approach as a non-binding source of law.

The most visible political accountability instrument tempering control and autonomy are the annual reports that EU agencies submit to the relevant institutions; ie the European Parliament, the Council, the Commission and the Court of Auditors. In addition, the EASA also submits its annual general report to the Member States,[55] whereas the ESAs also give their account of the activities

[48] Ibid art 51(2).
[49] Ibid art 53(4), (5), (6) and (7).
[50] Regulation 216/2008/EC, art 38.
[51] Ibid art 39(1).
[52] Ibid art 33(2)(c).
[53] Ibid art 43(4) and (6).
[54] Common Approach (n 40) para 59.
[55] Regulation 216/2008/EC, arts 33(2)(b) and 57.

carried out to the European Economic and Social Committee.[56] Annual reports allow EU institutions to 'pass judgement on the conduct' of EU agencies.[57] By applying Bovens' reconstruction of the concept of accountability as a social relation between an actor and a forum, through annual reports EU agencies explain and justify their activities and the forum of EU institutions can question such reports and approve or publicly contest them.[58]

If annual reports are the traditional instruments ensuring the accountability of independent agencies in the Member States, they show the disconnection between control and transparency that affects the capability of reconnecting EU agencies to the democratic principle. According to Bovens, accountability incorporates the specific method of control operating through the procedures of explanation and justification of an actor's conduct.[59] Being not necessarily aimed at this procedure of scrutiny, 'transparency as such does not qualify as a genuine form of accountability'.[60] Nonetheless, transparency is relevant as it can be conceived as 'a prerequisite for accountability or sometimes even as part of accountability',[61] a means facilitating the accountability control by giving administrative action 'constant visibility'.[62]

The problem is that this accountability mechanism does not bring about a substantive judgement of the political acceptability of EU agencies' activities. It rather brings back the idea of separation between political responsibilities and technical tasks on which the allocation of powers to EU agencies has been construed. In fact, annual reports do not secure the substantive control of the EU legislature and the executive on the performance of EU agencies. Reports are mainly descriptive of the activities carried out and do not focus on the (issues in the) achievement of scheduled objectives.[63] Scholten pointed out that, generally,

[56] ESAs Founding Regulations, arts 43(5), 16(4) and 17(8), respectively, which also require ESAs to clarify future plans and include any information requested by the European Parliament on an ad hoc basis.

[57] M Bovens, 'Analysing and Assessing Accountability: A Conceptual Framework' (2007) 13 *European Law Journal* 447, 451.

[58] As Bovens observed, the judgment of the forum may have some consequences for the actor held accountable, but sanctions are only one of the possible consequences. Being a social relation, accountability may involve implicit or informal consequences, and may not necessarily be brought upon the actor by the forum itself. See ibid 451–52.

[59] Ibid 453–54.

[60] Ibid 453.

[61] Vos, 'Independence, Accountability and Transparency of European Regulatory Agencies' (n 11) 129; see also C Scott, 'Accountability in the Regulatory State' (2000) 27 *Journal of Law and Society* 38, 58; HCH Hofmann, 'Agency Design in the European Union' (2010) 28 *Windsor Yearbook of Access to Justice* 309, 321.

[62] D Curtin, 'Holding (Quasi-)Autonomous EU Administrative Actors to Public Account' (2007) 13 *European Law Journal* 523, 533.

[63] See European Court of Auditors, *The European Union's Agencies: Getting Results*, Special Report no 5 (2008), 24–25 and 31; see also Rambøll, Euréval and Matrix Insight, *Evaluation of the EU Decentralised Agencies in 2009, Final Report* (2009) vol I, 23 and *Final Report* (2009) vol IV, 6, which point out the difficulty to assess and compare EU agencies' performances.

Founding Regulations do not select the kind of information that such reports shall provide and make reporting merely a procedural burden.[64] It is not by chance that, as in the cases of the EASA and the ESAs, where stronger powers are allocated, Founding Regulations require disclosure of information about performance, ensuring more significant control. Wider autonomy and, *a fortiori*, embryonic independence are to some extent compensated by enhanced supervision. The technical nature of reports may nonetheless affect the understanding of politicians and officers with different expertise.[65] Control therefore is more likely to focus on the legitimacy of EU agencies' actions, rather than on the merits of their choices. From this standpoint, the reconnection to the democratic principle rests on the recognition that EU agencies have discretion on the merit based on their administrative expertise, but their actions need to be legally framed and controlled. The principle of legality therefore becomes the key instrument reconnecting the administration of EU agencies to the democratic principle.

This legal approach to democracy relies on transparency as a means to make administrative action acknowledgeable to the forum that has to scrutinise it. In the absence of a substantive control, however, accountability can only formally contribute to enhancing the transparency of administrative action, but it is not able to strengthen its public awareness. If transparency aims to lessen the divide between technocracy and democracy, a concise version of the report in layman's terms could usefully be submitted, so as to enhance the understanding of administrative activities and practices, as well as their results in terms of implementation of the policy goals. Where transparency can operate as a means of public awareness, it can contribute to strengthening the democratic grip on administrative action.

As Bovens has pointed out, accountability instruments need to be directed to overcome the typical agency problems that disconnect administration from the democratic circuit.[66] Bovens particularly emphasised the need to assess whether accountability arrangements provide the political principal with sufficient information and offer enough incentives to the agent to commit to the political agenda.[67] In my view, the quality of the information is also relevant and structures the capability of the political principal to control the conduct of the agent. In addition, the commitment of EU agencies to EU policy goals (and not to national interests) can be ensured only by the combination of the clear formulation of policy goals and the wise use of the accountability instruments at the disposal of EU institutions. However, the current accountability regime does not design a clear-cut relationship between accountability and autonomy and offers indecisive evidence of the entrenchment of EU agencies' powers in the EU institutional framework.

[64] Scholten, *The Political Accountability of EU and US Independent Regulatory Agencies* (n 2) 109–10.
[65] See Busuioc, *European Agencies: Law and Practices of Accountability* (n 2) 125–26.
[66] Bovens, 'Analysing and Assessing Accountability' (n 57) 465.
[67] Ibid.

III. PROCEDURAL PROTECTION AND THE RIGHT TO GOOD ADMINISTRATION

The principles of impartiality and fairness are to guide EU agencies in the adoption of administrative acts. As part of the EU administration, EU agencies will comply with those primary rules that shape administrative action and design a specific legal relationship between administration and individual rights. The principles of impartiality and fairness ensure that administration pursues the public interest in an objective and reasonable way. Procedural requirements will in particular ensure the fairness and impartiality of the decision-making so as to keep under control the exercise of administrative discretion.

The Treaties provide key legal guarantees setting administrative checks-and-balances on the exercise of discretionary powers, but no general EU administrative procedural law consistently implements the Treaties' principles. Procedural rights and duties emerged in the case law of the Court of Justice of the European Union (CJEU) and framed EU administrative action. On the one hand, the rights to defence of the parties affected by administrative action, the reasonable duration of the proceedings and the duty of the administrative body to give reasons for its own decisions particularly serve as key procedural requirements ensuring the fairness of administrative action.[68] The Treaties strongly emphasise the need for public participation and transparency as means to ensure such fairness.[69] On the other hand, the principles of impartiality and due care in the pursuit of the public interest ensure the consideration in the proceedings and the protection of interested third parties who do not enjoy the same rights as the directly affected parties.[70] The diligent and impartial examination of the case emerged, therefore, as a key condition for a fair decision.

The EU case law associated all these rights and duties with the principle of sound or good administration. Nehl emphasised that procedural rights ensure the protective function of the principle, whereas the principles of impartiality and due care and duty to give reasons are process standards that ensure the reasonableness of the decision.[71] Although the principle struggled to be recognised as an enforceable legal principle beyond the recognition of procedural failures in administrative

[68] See J Schwarze, 'Judicial Review of European Administrative Procedure' (2004) 68 *Law and Contemporary Problems* 85, 91–93. Alongside these requirements, Schwarze rightly considers also the confidentiality of the attorney-client correspondence.

[69] Article 11 TEU and Art 15 TFEU.

[70] See L Azoulai, 'Le principe de bonne administration' in J-B Auby and J Dutheil de la Rochère (eds), *Droit administratif européen* (Bruylant, 2007) 493, 499; E Barbier de La Serre, 'Procedural Justice in the European Community Case-law concerning the Rights of the Defence: Essentialist and Instrumental Trends' (2006) *European Public Law* 225, 239.

[71] HP Nehl, 'Good Administration as Procedural Right and/or General Principle?' in HCH Hofmann and AH Türk (eds), *Legal Challenges in EU Administrative Law: Towards an Integrated Administration* (Elgar Publishing, 2009) 322, 349.

practice,[72] it clearly portrays the key need to control the exercise of administrative discretion, so that the power to make value judgements and technical assessments in the implementation of EU (secondary) law is not arbitrary but well-founded in the context of the different public and private interests at stake. Advocate General van Gerven recognised in *Nolle* that the wide discretion of the Commission in the establishment of anti-dumping duties had to be reviewed in light of 'essential formalities and the principles of good administration, which include the duty of care'.[73] The CJEU endorsed this approach[74] and further specified its application in technical matters in *Technische Universität München*, which strongly connected the administrative duty to careful and impartial examination of the case to the rights of the defence.[75]

The reach of the principle has been questioned in courts. In the *Syntraval* case, the CJEU recognised against the General Court's appraisal that the principle of impartial and careful examination of a state aid case cannot be interpreted as requiring the Commission to engage on its own motion in the potential objections of the complainant.[76] The extensive approach of the General Court appeared also in *Tideland Signal v Commission*, where the principle of good administration transformed the power of the Commission to seek clarification on a tender offer into an obligation 'in circumstances where clarification of a tender is clearly both practically possible and necessary'.[77] In *max.mobil v Commission*, the General Court associated to the principles of impartiality and care the right of bringing judicial action for the enforcement of the administrative duty to impartial and diligent treatment of the case.[78] The CJEU restricted this approach by restating the prevalence of the standing rules as stated in the Treaties on the extension of rights through the principle of sound administration.[79] However, in *Area Cova SA v Council and Commission*, the General Court limited the reach of the principle and recognised that the infringement of the principle of sound administration cannot in itself amount to the infringement of a rule of law intended to confer

[72] 96–102/82, 104/82, 105/82, 108/82 and 110/82 *IAZ v Commission* [1983] ECR 3369, para 15, where the CJEU blamed the Commission for failing to respond to the interested parties in a competition case, but did not infer the illegality of its decision because it was not vitiated by the procedural defect; 64/82 *Tradax Graanhandel BV v Commission* [1984] ECR 1359, Opinion of AG Slynn, 1385–86, who considered that in the absence of an enforceable right to information, the CJEU should have recognised a non-binding rule of good administration requiring the disclosure of information as a matter of administrative practice. The CJEU, however, did not address the argument and rejected the plea.

[73] C-16/90 *Detlef Nölle, trading as "Eugen Nölle" v Hauptzollamt Bremen-Freihafen* [1991] ECR I-5163, Opinion of AG van Gerven, para 28.

[74] Ibid para 13.

[75] C-269/90 *Technische Universität München* [1991] ECR 1-5469, para 14.

[76] C-367/95P *Commission v Chambre Syndicale Nationale des Entreprises de Transport de Fonds et Valeurs (Sytraval) and Brink's France SARL* [1998] ECR I-1719, paras 60–62; T-95/94 *Sytraval and Brink's France SARL v Commission* [1995] ECR II-2651, para 78.

[77] T-211/02 *Tideland Signal Ltd v Commission* [2002] ECR II-3781, para 37.

[78] T-54/99 *max.mobil v Commission* [2002] ECR II-313, para 56.

[79] C-141/02P *Commission v max.mobil* [2005] ECR I-1283, paras 70–73.

rights upon individuals, which is a necessary condition for the recognition of the non-contractual liability of EU institutions.[80]

Despite the attempt of the General Court to extend the reach of the principle of good administration, judicial interpretation demonstrates its limited reach. As Azoulai emphasised, EU case law considered the principle of good administration as a 'regle d'intérêt public spéciale' covering the general need under EU law to protect private rights and interests against the abuse of administrative powers, but unable to create further individual rights.[81] Kańska observed that the notion of good administration emerged as an 'umbrella principle, comprising an open-ended source of rights and obligations', that has not remarkably changed with the acquisition of binding force under Article 41 of the Charter of Fundamental Rights affirming the right to good administration.[82] Kańska particularly pointed out that the Charter of Fundamental Rights transformed the principle of good administration into an enforceable right.[83] However, Nehl correctly noted that this fundamental right must be interpreted as a pool of procedural rights serving the fundamental values of modern legal systems adhering to the rule of law.[84] Wakefield also recognised the right under the Charter as 'the first enunciation of a right to good administration in the western legal tradition', but its innovation 'imposed no new obligations'.[85] In *Tillack v Commission*, the General Court referred to this right (before its acquisition of binding force) as:

> the expression of specific rights such as the right to have affairs handled impartially, fairly and within a reasonable time, the right to be heard, the right to have access to files, or the obligation to give reasons for decisions.[86]

Article 41 of the Charter generalised the protection of procedural rights 'providing an umbrella for a non-exhaustive list of procedural guarantees',[87] but it did not outline an original concept of good administration. Its open character allows the judicial expansion of the substantive standard of good administration,[88] so as to potentially include further rights and principles that implement the rule of law at the potential expense of legal certainty.[89] In light of the *max.mobil* judgment, the

[80] T-196/99 *Area Cova SA and others v Council and Commission* [2001] ECR II-3597, paras 42–44.

[81] Azoulai, 'Le principe de bonne administration' (n 70) 506–7, 509.

[82] K Kańska, 'Towards Administrative Human Rights in the EU: Impact of the Charter of Fundamental Rights' (2004) 10 *European Law Journal* 296, 305.

[83] Ibid 300 and 303–4.

[84] Nehl, 'Good Administration as Procedural Right and/or General Principle?' (n 71) 342.

[85] J Wakefield, *The Right to Good Administration* (Kluwer, 2007) 63.

[86] T-193/04 *Tillack v Commission* [2006] ECR II-3995, para 127.

[87] Lord PJ Millett, 'The Right to Good Administration in European Law' (2002) *Public Law* 309, 318. See also Wakefield, *The Right to Good Administration* (n 85) 69–70.

[88] Kańska, 'Towards Administrative Human Rights in the EU' (n 82) 325.

[89] Identified in the judicial interpretation of the notion of good administration as a source of legal uncertainty, see MP Chiti, 'The Role of the European Court of Justice in the Development of General Principles and their Possible Codification' (1995) *Rivista Italiana di Diritto Pubblico Comunitario* 661, 664.

fragmentation of the right to good administration into a series of procedural rights may reduce the chances to invoke this right. Insofar as the Charter of Fundamental Rights applies within the limits of the Treaties,[90] the right to good administration seems to be unable to expand the standing rights of third parties. It does apply to adjudicatory proceedings as well as to executive rule-making, but it may struggle to be enforced in the latter. For instance, the right to good administration omits reference to participation of third parties in the administrative proceedings.

The development of a fair and impartial administration requires both adjudication and executive rule-making to fulfil the core requirements that shape the right to good administration,[91] but with the necessary procedural adjustments due to the different settings.[92] In practice, the implementation of this principle serves the fragmented structure that participation assumes in the different sector-specific regimes and their effective capacity to fulfil the objectives pursued by the administrative proceedings.[93]

In the absence of a general EU administrative procedural law implementing the general principle and the resulting rights, the substantive standard of good administration remains ambiguous and susceptible to different interpretations according to the adjudicative or regulatory nature of the proceedings. Mendes emphasised that 'the meaning of good administration as a right remained obscure', whereas the concept of good administration has been construed on three different levels: the procedural rights, the legal rules structuring the exercise of administrative powers, and the non-legal rules defining the standards of conduct.[94] The European Ombudsman particularly implemented the substantive standard of good administration with a view to assessing maladministration. On the one hand, it works cooperatively with EU institutions and agencies to remove unlawful situations. For instance, it successfully advised the EASA to repeal a decision on the recognition of type-certifications[95] and to revise airworthiness Directives on safety belts and torso restraint systems.[96] As Busuioc emphasised, the cooperative working method of the Ombudsman reduces the information asymmetries in the understanding of technical matters[97] and together with the reputation of the Ombudsman makes its legal action effective. On the other hand, the Ombudsman's

[90] Charter of Fundamental Rights Art 52.

[91] See Kańska, 'Towards Administrative Human Rights in the EU' (n 82) 310.

[92] J Mendes, *Participation in EU Rule-Making: A Right-Based Approach* (Oxford University Press, 2011); but see also E Chiti, 'La disciplina procedurale della regolazione' (2004) 54 *Rivista Trimestrale di Diritto Pubblico* 679.

[93] See ibid.

[94] J Mendes, *Good Administration in EU Law and the Code of Good Administrative Behaviour*, EUI Working Papers Law 2009/09 (2009), 3–5.

[95] Decision of the European Ombudsman of 1 August 2007 on complaint 1103/2006/BU against the European Aviation Safety Agency, which also considered the absence of an appropriate legal basis for the adoption of the decision.

[96] Decision of the European Ombudsman of 23 November 2010 on complaint 407/2010/(FS)BEH against the European Aviation Safety Agency.

[97] Busuioc, *European Agencies: Law and Practices of Accountability* (n 2) 233.

Code of Good Administrative Behaviour contributes to enhancing the standard of good administration by advising on the good rules of conduct.[98] Mendes pointed out that this has critically shaped the concept of good administration beyond the legal enforcement of the right to good administration.[99] For instance, it extended the grounds of participation beyond the judicial interpretation of the right to be heard as a right reserved to adversely affected parties.[100] Although this Code is not legally binding on EU institutions and bodies, it pragmatically shaped the administrative behaviour of EU institutions and worked as a basis for EU agencies' proceedings.

IV. PROCEDURAL REQUIREMENTS AND ADMINISTRATIVE DISCRETION

Against this general backdrop, sector-specific administrative procedures enforce the procedural guarantees that meet the requirements of good administration. EU legislation sets the key legal guarantees that must be ensured in the performance of administrative action, but leaves EU agencies able to further develop their own administrative procedure and specify how such procedural requirements shall apply. In the case of the ESAs, the Founding Regulations set out only the principles of the ESAs' decision-making[101] and, on these general grounds, each ESA adopts its own procedural rules to govern the exercise of its powers.[102] Similarly, the EASA has established its own administrative procedure in compliance with the principles set out in its Basic Regulation that shapes the 'working methods'.[103]

The identification of core general principles on procedure in the Regulations is a necessary condition to ensure the effectiveness of procedural requirements, but it may not be sufficient. EU agencies' decisions setting sector-specific administrative procedures do not have the same legal value as EU legislation as sources of law and this affects the effectiveness of protection. The substantive issue in the legislative definition of administrative procedures is that the choice of procedural requirements is not neutral to the final decision. The way the procedure is articulated allows some interests rather than others to be taken into account.

[98] Resolution of the European Parliament of 6 September 2001, C50438/20002000/2212 (COS), approving the European Ombudsman's 'European Code of Good Administrative Behaviour'.

[99] Mendes, *Good Administration in EU Law and the Code of Good Administrative Behaviour* (n 94).

[100] European Code of Good Administrative Behaviour, art 16.

[101] ESAs Founding Regulations, art 39.

[102] See ESMA, Decision of the Management Board, Code of Good Administrative Behaviour, ESMA/2011/MB/6 (11 January 2011); EBA, Decision of the Management Board, EBA Code of Good Administrative Behaviour, EBA DC 006 (12 January 2011); EIOPA, Decision of the Management Board, EIOPA Code of Good Administrative Behaviour, EIOPA-MB-11/043 (10 February 2011).

[103] See Regulation 216/2008/EC, art 52. The current rule-making procedure is disciplined by EASA Management Board Decision 01-2012, amending and replacing Decision 08-2007 concerning the procedure to be applied by the Agency for the issuing of opinions, certification specifications and guidance materials ('rule-making procedure').

This affects both fact-finding and decision-making.[104] Giving EU agencies the chance to decide how to reach their decisions means conferring on them the prioritisation of interests. This autonomy may represent a potential threat to the impartiality of the decision-making process, because EU agencies are empowered to decide, on their own, if and how to accept the competing rights and interests in the decision-making process. On the contrary, the legislative definition of administrative procedures reconnects administrative action to the democratic principle, as the EU legislature can decide what interests require protection and how the administration shall take them into consideration. This would respond from a procedural standpoint to the concerns of the *Meroni* doctrine and would help both the parties who may want to be involved in the procedures, and the judges who are called to review EU agencies' action.

Consider, for instance, that the ESAs' Founding Regulations set a time limit within which the addressee may exercise his rights to the defence to be dependent on 'the urgency, complexity and potential consequences of the matter',[105] with no general criteria about the concrete application of these concepts. Moreover, the publication of the ESAs' decisions are to be made public:

> unless such publication is in conflict with the legitimate interests of financial market participants in the protection of their business secrets or could seriously jeopardise the orderly functioning and integrity of financial markets or the stability of the whole or part of the financial system of the Union.[106]

Even if transparency is a key principle of administrative action and the protection of operators' rights and the security of financial markets is a priority, the letter of this provision, in practice, is able to frustrate the general principle of publicity by conferring on the ESAs discretionary powers as to its concrete application. In the Founding Regulations, there are no criteria which effectively limit the procedure while ensuring its flexibility.

Likewise, the ESAs' consultation process is undeveloped: details about the parties who are to be consulted, the structure and the timeframe of the consultation, and the application of the proportionality principle to the procedure, are all missing.[107] From this standpoint, the EASA has elaborated more structured participation arrangements that apply not only to the adjudication, but also to the rule-making and standardisation based on the mechanism of notice and comment. The EASA issues a Notice of Proposed Amendment (NPA), containing an explanatory memorandum and a regulatory proposal, for public consultation. Subsequently,

[104] See G della Cananea, 'The European Union's Mixed Administrative Proceedings' (2004) 68 *Law and Contemporary Problems* 197, 207, who emphasised that the interests at stake shape administrative proceedings.

[105] ESAs Founding Regulations, art 39(1).

[106] Ibid art 39(5).

[107] See E Chiti, 'European Agencies' Rulemaking: Powers, Procedures and Assessment' (2013) 19 *European Law Journal* 93, 107–8.

the comments to the NPA are reviewed by experts not directly involved in the drafting of the proposed rule, together with Agency staff or a drafting group.[108] The responses to the comments are exposed in a Comment Response Document (CRD) and an explanatory memorandum should accompany the proposal if the final text significantly differs from the first draft published in the NPA.[109]

The relevant differences between EU agencies show that the introduction of a general EU administrative procedural law implementing the key procedural rights and duties covered by the Treaties, the Charter of Fundamental Rights and the principles of EU law would certainly constrain the exercise of their administrative powers and further ensure the legality of administrative action. The current procedural autonomy might also limit the transparency of administrative action and favour the pitfalls of regulatory complexity. As legal scholarship pointed out, the codification of administrative procedure at the EU level would enhance the coherence of principles and procedures and strengthen the consistency of administrative action.[110] The legal basis for codification has been consensually identified in Article 298(2) of the Treaty on the Functioning of the European Union (TFEU),[111] which allows the European Parliament and the Council, acting by means of regulations in accordance with the ordinary legislative procedure, to adopt provisions fostering an open, efficient and independent European administration.

The European Parliament adopted two Resolutions under Article 225 TFEU inviting the Commission to adopt a general EU administrative procedure: in 2013, it laid down a series of recommendations concerning the key principles ensuring the right to good administration by means of an open, efficient and independent administration;[112] in 2016, after the commissioned ReNEUAL project concerning the development of model rules on EU administrative procedure

[108] EASA Management Board Decision 01-2012, art 7.

[109] Ibid art 8.

[110] See DU Galetta, HCH Hofmann, O Mir Puigpelat and J Ziller, 'Context and Legal Elements of a Proposal for a Regulation on the Administrative Procedure of the European Union's Institutions, Bodies, Offices and Agencies' (2016) 26 *Rivista Italiana di Diritto Pubblico Comunitario* 313, 315–20; R Meads and L Allio, 'A "Win-Win-Win" Scenario: Reaping the Benefits of an EU Law on Administrative Procedure' (2014) 5 *European Journal of Risk Regulation* 87, 89–90; P Craig, 'A General Law on Administrative Procedure, Legislative Competence and Judicial Competence' (2013) 19 *European Public Law* 503; BG Mattarella, 'The Concrete Options for a Law on Administrative Procedure Bearing on EU Direct Administration?' (2012) 22 *Rivista Italiana di Diritto Pubblico Comunitario* 537; J Ziller, 'Is a Law of Administrative Procedure for the Union Institutions Necessary?' (2011) *Rivista Italiana di Diritto Pubblico Comunitario* 699, 710–15; J Ziller, *Alternatives in Drafting EU Administrative Procedure Law* (Policy Department C: Citizens' Rights and Constitutional Affairs, 2011); MP Chiti, 'Towards a New EU Regulation on Administrative Procedure?' (2011) 21 *Rivista Italiana di Diritto Pubblico Comunitario* 1, 10; but see also C Harlow, 'Codification of EC Administrative Procedures? Fitting the Foot to the Shoe or the Shoe to the Foot' (1996) 2 *European Law Journal* 3.

[111] Craig 'A General Law on Administrative Procedure, Legislative Competence and Judicial Competence' (n 110) 511–12; Ziller, 'Is a Law of Administrative Procedure for the Union Institutions Necessary?' (n 110) 722, who also recognised Charter of Fundamental Rights, art 52(1) as an additional legal basis.

[112] European Parliament Resolution of 15 January 2013 with recommendations to the Commission on a Law of Administrative Procedure of the European Union, 2012/2024(INL).

delivered its findings,[113] the European Parliament built upon the previous Resolution unheeded by the Commission and offered a more structured proposal for an EU administrative procedural law.[114] The latter Resolution refined the scope of the proposed regulation by expressly excluding alongside legislative and judicial proceedings and national administrative proceedings, those 'procedures leading to the adoption of non-legislative acts directly based on Treaties, delegated acts or implementing acts'.[115] As one of the reasons for the failure to adopt a general administrative procedure was the reluctance of the Commission to constrain its own discretionary powers, the exclusion of the Commission's proceedings may become key to ensuring the political success of the European Parliament's legislative initiative. At the same time, such an exclusion makes EU agencies the most prominent actors to which the general administrative procedure would be addressed.

This proposal for a general EU administrative procedure is even more relevant as it applies as the bottom-line protection for administrative activities, but covers all the administrative implementation with no distinction between adjudication and rule-making. Although the proposal would apply 'without prejudice to other legal acts of the Union providing for specific administrative procedural rules',[116] nonetheless it would be able to substitute the conflicting specific procedures autonomously adopted by the individual EU agencies and effectively limit their administrative discretion. In addition, the proposal ensures the implementation of the key procedural rights also in the context of administrative acts of general scope.[117] Interpretation suggests that soft law acts may also be subject to the legal guarantees of the proposed administrative procedure. In fact, administrative activities are broadly defined as all those implementing activities not expressly excluded from the scope of application of the proposed regulation,[118] and a specific definition of administrative acts is missing. In addition, the proposed regulation requires the form of administrative acts to be in writing and signed by

[113] The ReNEUAL research network's project was developed between 2009 and 2014 and drafted a structured and detailed proposal for binding legislation implementing the general principles of EU law and identifying best practices. The findings of the project are available at reneual.eu/index.php/projects-and-publications/reneual-1-0 and have been published in P Craig, H Hofmann, J-P Schneider and J Ziller (eds), *ReNEUAL Model Rules on EU Administrative Procedure* (Oxford University Press, 2017).

[114] European Parliament Resolution of 9 June 2016 for an open, efficient and independent European Union administration, 2016/2610(RSP).

[115] Ibid art 2(2). Considering the 2016 Resolution an expression of the willingness of the European Parliament to claim and exercise its legislative initiative, see DU Galetta, 'Attività e procedimento nel diritto amministrativo europeo, anche alla luce della risoluzione del Parlamento europeo sulla disciplina del procedimento per istituzioni, organi ed organismi dell'Unione europea' (2017) *Rivista Italiana di Diritto Pubblico Comunitario* 391, 408–12.

[116] European Parliament Resolution 2016/2610(RSP), art 3.

[117] Ibid art 26.

[118] Ibid art 4(b).

competent authority,[119] but it does not dictate the specific legal effects of the acts. As Chiti has observed, the existence of a single decision-making process with no distinction between formal and informal activities would enhance the coherence of administrative action.[120]

In the case of administrative acts of general scope, the proposed regulation subordinates the entry into force to publication 'by means directly accessible to those concerned'.[121] This provision seems to presuppose the binding character of these acts, confirming the applicability of the provisions under Article 277 TFEU to EU agencies' acts and burying the non-delegation doctrine as stated in *Romano*. However, this does not rule out that non-binding recommendations and guidelines may ensure the same procedural rights. The choice between formal and informal instruments would then depend on opportunity reasons rather than on legal requirements.

V. PROCEDURAL ISSUES OF COMPOSITE ADMINISTRATION

The tasks and responsibilities conferred on EU agencies highlight their fundamental role of coordination and harmonisation in the EU multilevel governance. Where both supranational and national administrations participate in composite or mixed administrative proceedings, the development of a fair and impartial administration must deal with the existence of multiple administrative proceedings that take place at different administrative levels and ensure different procedural requirements.[122] EU agencies' commitment to a fair and impartial administration has therefore to cope with the uncertainties, gaps and duplications that the search for administrative integration between the EU and its Member States present. In fact, EU agencies participate in these composite proceedings with 'parallel, non-exclusive legal powers'[123] entirely regulated by EU law.[124] Administrative functions distributed among a plurality of national and supranational administrations generate interdependences that EU agencies coordinate. However, the increasing powers allocated to EU agencies complicate the application of this scheme and challenge the procedural fairness of the composite administrative proceedings. As seen in Chapter 2, the quasi-regulatory powers of EU agencies operating in a

[119] Ibid art 18.

[120] Chiti, 'European Agencies' Rulemaking' (n 107) 106.

[121] European Parliament Resolution 2016/2610(RSP), art 27(2).

[122] On the notion of composite administration see C Franchini, *Amministrazione italiana e amministrazione comunitaria. La coamministrazione nei settori di interesse comunitario*, 2nd edn (Cedam, 1993) 174; S Cassese, 'European Administrative Proceedings' (2004) 68 *Law and Contemporary Problems* 21; della Cananea, 'The European Union's Mixed Administrative Proceedings' (n 104).

[123] Cassese, 'European Administrative Proceedings' (n 122) 22.

[124] See E Chiti, 'Administrative Proceedings Involving European Agencies' (2004) 68 *Law and Contemporary Problems* 219, 222–23; HCH Hoffman and AH Türk, *Legal Challenges in EU Administrative Law: Towards an Integrated Administration* (Elgar Publishing, 2009) 28–29.

multilevel administrative framework, as well as in relation to private business, can produce autonomous legal effects.

When the increasing role of EU agencies in composite administrative proceedings is not taken into account, the juxtaposition of supranational and national administrative proceedings may create an incoherent framework of protection, where the informal character of some EU agencies' activities is not adequately controlled. National competent authorities are particularly subject to the procedural tensions that originate in the multilevel system of administration as they are the nerve centre in the relations between supranational decentralised agencies and the regulated parties. In fact, several EU agencies' acts are enforced by national administrations accepting EU agencies' recommendations and guidelines, whereas adjudication procedures do not rule out the participation of national authorities. The functioning of the multilevel system clearly presupposes cooperation and networking between the EU agencies and national competent authorities. However, formally, their proceedings remain distinct and the organisational model of reference remains the traditional one; that is, implementation by the Member States.

This is particularly evident in the 'comply or explain' mechanism in the implementation of ESAs' guidelines and recommendations. National authorities are first called to cooperate with the ESAs' Boards of Supervisors in the adoption of the relevant soft law acts. Following the ESAs' administrative procedures, public and private interests are addressed and evaluated in light of the relevant EU legislation. However, national authorities are then required to implement such guidelines and recommendations in their own jurisdictions and to give reasons for their non-compliance. At the domestic level, a new administrative procedure therefore takes place, and its conclusion will be the acceptance or the motivated rejection of the ESAs' guidelines. The national decision-making may have to follow an administrative procedure that considers the position of the national industry. Procedural requirements and procedural rights provided under national law are key to the industry having a say in the decision-making process and for challenging and/or supporting the national enforcement of EU soft law. In the economy of the procedure, this enhances the chances of protection of those interests that are distinctive of individual Member States. National authorities must therefore evaluate the guidelines and recommendations in light of the national stakeholders' competing interests, and justify why these private interests cannot be protected or are to prevail over EU soft law. Conversely, if the participation of the relevant industry is excluded from the adoption of acts of general application, the private interests can be effectively protected only at the supranational level in the ESAs' Stakeholder Groups, which, however, represent cross-country interests. The burden on national authorities would be reduced, but the chances of protection for local stakeholders are considerably reduced.

This two-level model of administration based on the formal separation between the EU procedure and the national ones presents some challenges when the effective achievement of the EU objectives relies on a substantially composite administration. When EU agencies' soft law has quasi-regulatory content, the juxtaposition of national and supranational administrative procedures does not ensure the effective protection of individual rights and interests at stake and affects cooperation. The flexibility of the informal 'comply or explain' mechanism does not rule out the procedural issues hidden behind the duty to give reasons. These proceedings add a new category to the phenomenology of mixed administrative proceedings as proposed by della Cananea in 2004.[125] Alongside the 'top-down' proceedings initiated by a decision of European authorities, the 'bottom-up' proceedings that terminate with a decision of the European administration, and the 'hybrid' proceedings which contemplate mechanisms for moving the executive functions between the different levels of government, the 'comply or explain' mechanism creates circular soft law proceedings that include hard law national proceedings. The integration purpose of EU administrative law generates procedural issues that derive from the interconnection of different levels of government with different legitimation and legal sources to achieve the common administrative goals.[126]

When the EU level adopts hard law decisions, the legal issues embedded in this circularity become even more apparent. The European Banking Union (EBU) offers a clear-cut example, as national competent authorities closely assist the European Central Bank (ECB) in the role of day-to-day supervisor. To avoid procedural gaps and strengthen cooperation, the ECB—in consultation with national competent authorities—has set in motion a special administrative procedure which applies to both the single supervisor and national competent authorities when dealing with such significant banks.[127] When national authorities have a fact-finding role or an executive function within the ECB's decision-making, the Single Supervisory Mechanism (SSM) Framework Regulation applies as the unified procedure of administration. National administrative procedures are relevant only in the (possible) preliminary phase of fact-finding, before the initiation of the ECB procedure.[128] The unified procedure, however, does not necessarily enhance

[125] della Cananea, 'The European Union's Mixed Administrative Proceedings' (n 104) 199–205.

[126] MP Chiti, 'Lo Spazio amministrativo europeo' in MP Chiti and A Natalini (eds), *Lo spazio amministrativo europeo. Le pubbliche amministrazioni dopo il Trattato di Lisbona* (Il Mulino, 2012) 1, 10; MP Chiti, *Diritto Amministrativo Europeo*, 3rd edn (Giuffrè, 2008) 179–82; MP Chiti, 'Lo spazio giuridico europeo' (2001) *Rivista Italiana di Diritto Pubblico Comunitario* 979.

[127] Regulation 1024/2013/EU, arts 6(3) and (7). These provisions have been implemented by Regulation 468/2014/EU of the ECB of 16 April 2014 establishing the framework for cooperation within the Single Supervisory Mechanism between the ECB and national competent authorities and with national designated authorities ('SSM Framework Regulation').

[128] This is for instance the case of the authorisation for the access to the activity of credit institutions and of the acquisition of qualifying holding in credit institutions, where national competent authorities are required to start the proceedings by submitting their draft decision to the ECB according to the requirements set out in their national law, including the relevant EU law. See Regulation 1024/2013/EU, arts 14 and 15, and Regulation 468/2014/EU ECB/2014/17, art 73. See A Magliari, 'I procedimenti amministrativi di vigilanza bancaria nel quadro del Single Supervisory Mechanism. Il caso dell'applicazione dei diritti nazionali da parte della BCE' (2015) *Rivista di Diritto Bancario* 1, 13 and 18.

the level of protection. It has been observed that the exclusion of the exercise of the ECB's investigative powers from the scope of the SSM Framework Regulation opens a potential gap in the protection of the right to good administration.[129] In addition, legally speaking, since in many Member States the administrative procedure applied by national competent authorities is state law, the SSM Framework Regulation might also involve a reduction of protection in terms of legitimacy and hierarchy of legal sources. As it was not adopted by ordinary legislative procedure under Article 289 TFEU, the SSM Framework Regulation is an atypical regulation. This may create some inconsistencies in the composition of conflicts between legal sources, as supranational procedural law does not have the consolidated characteristics to automatically prevail over national procedural law on the grounds of the principle of supremacy of EU law.

Where administrative integration sees the allocation of relevant powers between the national and the EU level, procedural requirements must ensure procedural consistency between the different levels of government. The search for coherence inspires the SSM Framework Regulation. The advisory role traditionally reserved for EU agencies has so far avoided the establishment of more comprehensive proceedings for their activities. The steady development of EU agencies' powers suggests that stronger procedural requirements ensuring the consistency between national and supranational proceedings will be adopted. The conferral of quasi-regulatory powers on EU agencies requires the introduction of legal guarantees that foster cooperation, regardless of the formal or informal character of agencies' action. This does not mean the ossification of informal proceedings, but the coordination of the relevant procedural requirements.

VI. INTERNAL ADMINISTRATIVE REVIEW OF EU AGENCIES' ACTS

The Treaties ensure the opportunity to submit EU agencies' acts not only to judicial review, but also to review by the administration itself. The Treaties design the reach and the extent of the administrative review of EU agencies' acts. On the one hand, the organisation and the function of the judiciary are clearly outlined. Article 256 TFEU defines the two-tier system of judicial review composed of the General Court and the Court of Justice, and Article 257 TFEU confers on EU legislation the power to establish 'specialised courts attached to the General Court to hear and determine at first instance certain classes of action or proceeding brought in specific areas', which can be appealed before the General Court only on a point of law. On the other hand, Article 263(5) TFEU confers on EU legislation the capability to lay down 'specific conditions and arrangements concerning actions brought by natural or legal persons against the acts of these bodies, offices

[129] See B Wolfers and T Voland, 'Level the Playing Field: The New Supervision of Credit Institutions by the European Central Bank' (2014) *Common Market Law Review* 1463, 1494.

and agencies intended to produce legal effects in relation to them'. This provision has legitimised the existing legal practice of securing the internal review of EU agencies' acts under secondary law in the absence of any Treaties' provision ensuring the justiciability of EU agencies' acts.[130] In doing so, Article 263(5) TFEU has ensured that a further level of administrative protection precedes judicial review of EU agencies' acts.

Nevertheless, this Treaty provision leaves wide discretion to the EU legislature to design the bodies and the proceedings of the administrative review. The system of administrative remedies therefore is not structured as a coherent level of protection preceding judicial review, but as a sector-specific device ensuring a further level of control in specific areas of the exercise of the technical expertise of EU agencies.[131] The specificity of these internal remedies significantly emerges from the differentiation of requirements that govern the procedure, such as the standard of evidence, burden of proof and investigative powers.[132] Yet some common features can be distinguished.

EU agencies' Boards of Appeal (BoAs) are generally appointed by the Management Boards, but they perform the adjudicating function independently. In fact, the decision-making function of EU agencies and the internal administrative review of their decisions pursue different objectives: active administration aims to realise the goals set out in the EU legislation, whereas the administrative review ensures both the compatibility of the decision-making with the rights of

[130] As regards the CPVO, see Council Regulation 2100/94/EC of 27 July 1994 on Community plant variety rights, arts 45–48 [1994] OJ L 227 and Commission Regulation 874/2009/EU of 17 September 2009 establishing implementing rules for the application of Council Regulation (EC) 2100/94 as regards proceedings before the Community Plant Variety Office, arts 11, 12 and 45–52 [2009] OJ L 251/3; as regards OHIM, see Council Regulation 6/2002/EC of 12 December 2001 on Community designs, arts 55–61 [2002] OJ L 3/1, and Council Regulation 207/2009/EU of 26 February 2009 on the Community trade mark, arts 58–65 [2009] OJ L 78/1; as regards the ECHA, see Regulation 1907/2006/EC of the European Parliament and of the Council of 18 December 2006 concerning the registration, evaluation, authorisation and restriction of chemicals (REACH), establishing a European Chemicals Agency, amending Directive 1999/45/EC and repealing Council Regulation (EEC) 793/93 and Commission Regulation (EC) 1488/94 as well as Council Directive 76/769/EEC and Commission Directives 91/155/EEC, 93/67/EEC, 93/105/EC and 2000/21/EC, arts 89–93 [2006] OJ L 396 and Regulation 528/2012/EU of the European Parliament and of the Council of 22 May 2012 concerning the making available on the market and use of biocidal products, art 77 [2012] OJ L 167; as regards the EASA see Regulation 216/2008/EC, arts 40–49; as regards the ACER, see Regulation 713/2009/EC of the European Parliament and of the Council of 13 July 2009 establishing an Agency for the Cooperation of Energy Regulators, arts 18–20 [2009] OJ L 211/1. In the literature see Chamon, *EU Agencies* (n 42) 334 and 338.

[131] This model of BoAs has been effectively compared with the original model of UK administrative tribunals, before their juridification in the Tribunals, Courts and Enforcement Act 2007. Like administrative tribunals, in fact, BoAs are very differentiated, composed of legal and sector experts, and have general procedural rules. See B Marchetti, 'La tutela non giurisdizionale' (2017) *Rivista Italiana di Diritto Pubblico Comunitario* 423,434.

[132] See Marchetti, 'La tutela non giurisdizionale' (n 131) 429–30; B Marchetti, 'Administrative Justice Beyond the Courts: Internal Reviews in EU Administration' in B Marchetti (ed), *Administrative Remedies in the European Union: The Emergence of a Quasi-Judicial Administration* (Giappichelli, 2017) 1, 8–9.

the claimants and the correct implementation of the EU policy-goals.[133] Yet, there is administrative continuity between active administration and internal administrative review, which means that the BoA's decisions express the conclusive position of the Agency.[134] The General Court has thus recognised such 'continuity in terms of their functions',[135] as they both contribute from different angles to the implementation of the relevant EU legislation. The Court of Justice confirmed this approach, showing that the independence of the administrative review is still an internal administrative procedure whose findings can be usefully submitted to the two-tier level of judicial review.[136]

This is a significant difference to the ECB Administrative Board of Review, which is empowered in the administrative review of the SSM decisions taken by the ECB Supervisory Board only through non-binding opinions.[137] Nonetheless, the Supervisory Board must take into account the opinion of the Administrative Board of Review and must in any case promptly submit a new draft decision to the Governing Council. As scholarship has pointed out, this choice aims to preserve the independent status of the ECB as an EU institution, which cannot be bound by the decisions of a technical body composed of external experts.[138]

[133] See P Chirulli and L De Lucia, 'Specialised Adjudication in the EU Administrative Law: The Boards of Appeal of EU Agencies' (2015) 40 *European Law Review* 832, 838; A Cassatella, 'Appeals Before the European Aviation Safety Agency' in B Marchetti (ed), *Administrative Remedies in the European Union: The Emergence of a Quasi-Judicial Administration* (Giappichelli, 2017) 21, 37; Marchetti, 'La tutela non giurisdizionale' (n 131) 430.

[134] Chirulli and De Lucia 'Specialised Adjudication in the EU Administrative Law' (n 133) 837; Cassatella 'Appeals Before the European Aviation Safety Agency' (n 133) 38. See also A Magliari, 'Administrative Remedies in European Financial Governance' in B Marchetti (ed), *Administrative Remedies in the European Union: The Emergence of a Quasi-Judicial Administration* (Giappichelli, 2017) 99, 108–9, who sees reduced continuity of function between the ESAs and their Joint Board of Appeal, on the grounds that the organisation of the BoA is external (although still connected) to each individual Authority and its review does not extend to the merit.

[135] See T-163/98 *Procter & Gamble v OHIM (Baby Dry)* [1999] ECR II-2383, paras 36–39; T-63/01 *Procter & Gamble v OHIM (Soap Bar Shape)* [2002] ECR II-5255, paras 21–23; T-308/01 *Henkel KGaA v OHIM* [2003] ECR II-3253, para 25; T-252/04 *Caviar Anzali v OHIM* [2006] ECR II-2115, paras 30–31; T-609/13 *Blackrock v OHIM* ECLI:EU:T:2015:54, para 35.

[136] C-29/05P *OHIM v Kaul GmbH* [2007] ECR I-2213, para 51. See also T-273/02 *Krüger GmbH & Co KG v OHIM* [2005] ECR II-1271, para 62, which emphasised that the 'proceedings before the Boards of Appeal are administrative and not judicial in nature'.

[137] Council Regulation 1024/2013/EU, art 24(7). Magliari pointed out that when reviewing the ECB's decisions, the ECB Administrative Board of Review might also happen to indirectly evaluate the effects of the national administrative procedure on which the ECB's decision was based, as well as to assess the correctness of the ECB's interpretation and application of national law for those decisions taken under art 4(3) of the SSM Regulation 1024/2013/EU. See Magliari, 'Administrative Remedies in European Financial Governance' (n 134) 115. See also C Brescia Morra, R Smits and A Magliari, 'The Administrative Board of Review of the European Central Bank: Experience After 2 Years' (2017) 18 *European Business Organisation Law Review* 567, 582.

[138] C Harlow and R Rawlings, *Process and Procedure in EU Administration* (Hart Publishing, 2014) 292–94. As the Governing Council has veto powers on the decisions of the Supervisory Board, the binding nature of the internal administrative review would indirectly affect the independence of the Governing Council itself. However, Harlow and Rawlings suggested that the Administrative Board of Review might have been binding only on the Supervisory Board and not on the Governing Council. *Contra*, Brescia Mora who considers that this substantive approach would have nonetheless affected

The advantage of EU agencies is that their unentrenched constitutional status allows the flexible application of administrative remedies with the extension of their binding force. Whereas judicial review is crucial for the ECB's decisions under the SSM, EU agencies' acts can benefit from a further level of administrative protection.[139]

The object of internal administrative review is generally limited to the decisions of EU agencies; that is, to those acts adopted in the exercise of adjudication powers. For instance, in the case of the EASA, administrative review covers all the certification activities, the investigation of undertakings and the levy of fees and charges.[140] In the case of the ESAs, the twin Founding Regulations submit to the scrutiny of the Joint BoA the decisions on the breach of EU law, the action in emergency situations and the settlement of disagreements, as well as any other decision addressed or of direct and individual concern to someone.[141]

This approach significantly affects both the nature of the acts that can be submitted to the internal administrative review and the standing before the BoAs. On the one hand, the focus on decisions clearly excludes all the prominent standardisation activities of EU agencies and their participation in rule-making procedures. This has a significant effect on individual protection, which is deferred either to the national law implementing the soft law acts of EU agencies or to the capability to challenge EU legislation.[142] In addition, acts 'merely confirmatory of the earlier decision' are excluded from the appeal.[143]

On the other hand, appeal is reserved to those parties who can demonstrate that the decision in question affected their rights. First, parties must have an interest

the 'formal competence of the Governing Council to take decisions, by means of the non-objection procedure': see C Brescia Morra, 'The Administrative and Judicial Review of Decisions of the ECB in the Supervisory Field' in R D'Ambrosio (ed), *Scritti sull'Unione Bancaria* (Banca d'Italia, Quaderni di Ricerca Giuridica della Consulenza Legale, 2016) 120. See also Brescia Morra, Smits and Magliari, 'The Administrative Board of Review of the European Central Bank' (n 137) 573.

[139] See M Clarich, 'Il riesame amministrativo delle decisioni della Banca Centrale Europea' (2015) *Rivista Italiana di Diritto Pubblico Comunitario* 1513, 1518–19 and 1521–22, who pointed out that this difference shows that ECB internal review is not conceived as a filter in the access to justice, but is both a swift instrument of administrative protection and a further chance for the Supervisory Board to assess SSM decisions, because in the preparation of the new draft decision, it 'shall not be limited to examination of the grounds relied upon by the applicant as set forth in the notice of review, but may also take other elements into account in its proposal for a new draft decision'; see Decision ECB/2014/16 of the ECB of 14 April 2014 concerning the establishment of an Administrative Board of Review and its Operating Rules, art 17(1) [2014] OJ L 175/47.

[140] Regulation 216/2008/EC, art 44(1).

[141] ESAs Founding Regulations, art 60.

[142] Here the limitation of Art 263(4) TFEU applies, as individuals can challenge regulatory acts in courts if they are of direct concern to them and do not entail implementing measures. See *Stephen Luck v EASA*, Decision of the EASA BoA of 30 April 2013, AP/03/2012/LUCK, paras 43–46 (which require the challengeable act to be legally binding by producing legal effects) and para 48 (which states that national courts must ensure protection against decisions of national authorities, even by preliminary reference to the CJEU).

[143] *Onix Asigurari SA and Simone Lentini v EIOPA*, Decision of the Joint ESAs BoA of 24 November 2014, EIOPA, BOA 2015 001, para 54; *Stephen Luck v EASA* (n 142) paras 50–51.

in the appeal. They must benefit from the annulment of the contested decision. As the Joint BoA has clarified in *Investor Protection Europe Sprl v ESMA*, an association may have a right of appeal where it 'represents the interests of natural or legal persons who would be entitled to bring proceedings in their own right', or it 'is sufficiently individually concerned in its own interests as an association being affected by the contested measure'.[144]

Secondly, parties will have a right to appeal. The *SV Capital OÜ v EBA* case clarified the limited standing in appeals to the ESAs' Joint BoA for breach of EU law under article 17 of the EBA Founding Regulation. According to the General Court's ruling, as confirmed by the Court of Justice,[145] a complaint to the EBA to initiate an investigation into an alleged breach or failure to apply EU law cannot give rise to a right of standing before the ESAs' BoA if it is not raised by one of the privileged actors expressly referred to in article 17(2) of the EBA Founding Regulation; that is, the European Parliament, the Council, the Commission or the Banking Stakeholder Group.[146]

Private parties may legitimately request the EBA to start an investigation, but the EBA has discretion in commencing it, as its action would legally be on its own initiative. The result is that such parties cannot be considered the addressees of the decision not to initiate an investigation and therefore they have no right of appeal.[147] In light of this case law, the Joint BoA has substantially reversed its decision in *Investor Protection Europe Sprl v ESMA*, which recognised standing rights against the decisions on opening investigations under article 60 of the ESMA Founding Regulation.[148] Dismissing the idea that such decisions were 'purely preparatory' to the issue of a recommendation to the competent authority concerned according to article 17(3) of the ESMA Founding Regulation, the Joint BoA considered this a decision addressed to the applicant as 'the final conclusion' of the procedure under article 17.[149] In *Kluge and others v EBA*, the Joint BoA restricted its approach to standing rights in light of the General Court's findings in *SV Capital OÜ v EBA*. The BoA particularly clarified that its internal proceeding rules have only set out good practices in dealing with complaints, but they cannot confer appeal rights not included in the EBA Founding Regulation.[150] Only where

[144] *Investor Protection Europe Sprl v ESMA*, Decision of the Joint BoA of 10 November 2014, BoA 2014 05, BOA 2012 002, para 59.

[145] T-660/14 *SV Capital OÜ v EBA* ECLI:EU:T:2015:608; C-557/15P *SV Capital OÜ v EBA* ECLI:EU:C:2016:947.

[146] T-660/14 *SV Capital OÜ v EBA* (n 145) paras 69–71; C-557/15P *SV Capital OÜ v EBA* (n 145) para 40.

[147] T-660/14 *SV Capital OÜ v EBA* (n 145) paras 45–49; C-557/15P *SV Capital OÜ v EBA* (n 145) para 41. See also *Andrus Kluge, Boris Belyaev, Radio Elektroniks OÜ and Timur Dyakov v EBA*, Decision of the Joint ESAs BoA of 19 August 2016, EBA/2015/D/2015, BOA 2016 001, paras 23–24, 31–32.

[148] *Investor Protection Europe Sprl v ESMA* (n 144) paras 42–49.

[149] Ibid paras 48–49.

[150] *Andrus Kluge, Boris Belyaev, Radio Elektroniks OÜ and Timur Dyakov v EBA* (n 147) paras 33–35.

the EBA takes a decision identifying a breach of EU law, private parties may have a right of appeal with regard to the protection of their own interests with regard to the identified breach.[151]

The judicially induced restrictions on the standing rights affect the ESAs Joint BoA's capability to review ESAs' decisions in favour of the recognition of the ESAs' administrative discretion to decide whether to open an investigation. If the letter of the Founding Regulations justifies this legal conclusion, the emerging gap in the standing rights shows the still limited role of the Joint BoA in the enforcement of the ESAs' mandate. In addition, this gap makes it difficult to characterise a coherent relationship between the internal administrative review and judicial review. As the Joint BoA has emphasised in *Kluge and others v EBA*, the General Court in *SV Capital OÜ v EBA* (and also the CJEU in the appeal case) did not discuss this issue.[152] Legal scholarship has highlighted that, so far, internal administrative review works as a 'de facto filter' of judicial review.[153] If their exhaustion aims to be a necessary condition for action in courts, the clear identification of BoAs' jurisdiction is a preliminary issue which may affect the compliance with time-limits required for the action in courts. Likewise, the limited acts covered by appeal proceedings show that the BoA is not designed as a general instrument to ensure the justiciability of EU agencies' acts, but rather as a specific remedy aimed to protect specific interests.

A. Nature of Internal Administrative Review and Administrative Discretion

The reach and the limits of internal administrative review depend on the relevant EU legislation, so that BoAs' powers cover different aspects of review. Generally, the appeal has a devolutive effect, so that the full reappraisal of the contested decision is required. This means that BoAs assess not only the lawfulness of the contested decision, but also the facts of the dispute and consider the new facts and evidence that the parties may introduce on appeal.[154] Only the request filed in the application limits the powers of the BoAs, whereas the time limit for the submission of evidence makes the acquisition of later evidence a discretionary choice of the BoAs.[155] As noted by Chirulli and De Lucia, these limits express the principle

[151] T-660/14 *SV Capital OÜ v EBA* (n 145) para 67; C-557/15P *SV Capital OÜ v EBA* (n 145) para 37.

[152] *Andrus Kluge, Boris Belyaev, Radio Elektroniks OÜ and Timur Dyakov v EBA* (n 147) para 38.

[153] See M Lamandini, 'The ESAs' Board of Appeal as a Blueprint for the Quasi-Judicial Review of European Financial Supervision' (2014) 11 *European Company Law* 290, 293; A Witte, 'Standing and Judicial Review in the New EU Financial Markets Architecture' (2015) 1 *Journal of Financial Regulation* 1, 21–22.

[154] See T-252/04 *Caviar Anzali v OHIM* (n 135) paras 31–32.

[155] T-415/09 *New Yorker SHK Jeans GmbH & Co KG v OHIM* [2011] ECR II-336, para 31; C-621/11P *New Yorker SHK Jeans GmbH & Co KG v OHIM* ECLI:EU:C:2013:484, paras 21–24.

of procedural good faith.[156] BoAs retain all powers in the competence of the relevant EU agencies, and amend or substitute their decisions, or also remit the case to the decision of the Agency.[157]

The two most prominent exceptions to the full review in law and in fact are the Joint BoA of the ESAs[158] and the Single Resolution Board (SRB) Appeal Panel, whose expert legal advices are limited to the legality of the SRB's exercise of its powers.[159] However, the review is still technical in nature, as these bodies are mainly composed of members with sector-specific expertise. The presence of members with technical and legal backgrounds is key to ensuring that the review covers both legal and technical criteria.

As Brescia Morra pointed out with regard to the ECB Administrative Board of Review, the presence of experts has added value to 'the "well qualified" assessment of the prudential aspect of the case underlying the supervisory decision'.[160] *Mutatis mutandis*, this also applies to EU agencies' Boards of Appeal. Nonetheless, the internal review of the administrative discretion exercised by EU agencies shows a legal approach. Despite the range of their powers, BoAs have borrowed the principles of administrative review from the EU case law (see below). They particularly elaborated on the CJEU's case law on the recognition of the broad discretion of the Commission on complex assessments.[161] On the one hand, BoAs ensure an intense control on the facts structuring EU agencies' decisions. They evaluate that evidence is factually accurate, reliable and consistent, but recognise that the finding of the basic facts may involve some discretion. On the other hand, they ensure that the decision under review has taken into consideration all the relevant factors and circumstances of the situation the act was intended to regulate,

[156] Chirulli and De Lucia, 'Specialised Adjudication in the EU Administrative Law' (n 133) 849. However, in some cases such as the EASA, the BoA's inspection powers are so wide that they are not necessarily limited to the legal question raised in the application for review. See Marchetti, 'La tutela non giurisdizionale' (n 131) 430.

[157] As regards the EASA, see Regulation 216/2008/EC, art 49.

[158] ESAs Founding Regulations, art 58(2). See also *Global Private Rating Co 'Standing Rating' Ltd v ESMA*, Decision of the Joint BoA of 10 January 2014, BoA 2013-4, paras 180–83, which clarify that the BoA can alternatively confirm the decision of the ESMA or remit the case to the Agency, and has no power to order payment of monetary compensation to an appellant.

[159] Regulation 806/2014/EU of the European Parliament and of the Council of 15 July 2014 establishing uniform rules and a uniform procedure for the resolution of credit institutions and certain investment firms in the framework of a Single Resolution Mechanism and a Single Resolution Fund and amending Regulation (EU) 1093/2010, art 85(2) [2014] OJ L 225/1.

[160] Brescia Morra, 'The Administrative and Judicial Review of Decisions of the ECB in the Supervisory Field' (n 138) 121.

[161] See *Dow Benelux BV Netherlands v ECHA*, Decision of the ECHA BoA of 19 June 2013, A-001-2012, para 110, referring to C-15/10 *Etimine SA* [2011] ECR I-6681, para 125; *Heli-Flight GmbH & Co KG v EASA*, Decision of the EASA BoA of 17 December 2012, AP/01/2012, para 63, referring to C-326/05P *Industrias Químicas del Vallés SA v Commission* [2007] ECR I-6557, para 75; *Honeywell Belgium NV Belgium v ECHA*, Decision of the ECHA BoA of 29 April 2013, A-005-2011, para 76 referring to C-386/10P *Chalkor v Commission* [2011] ECR I-13085, para 54.

so as to ascertain its impartiality and fairness.[162] As a result, BoAs do not substitute the Agency's assessment of the case, but assess its compatibility with the goals of the relevant legislation.

VII. EFFECTIVE JUDICIAL PROTECTION AGAINST EU AGENCIES' ACTS

Judicial protection is a key condition to ensure the compatibility of the allocation of powers to administrative bodies with the democratic principle and the rule of law. Article 47 of the Charter of Fundamental Rights ensures the right to an effective remedy and to a fair trial as a fundamental right to justice. By protecting individuals against the abuse and misuse of administrative powers, the justiciability of administrative acts ensures the legal accountability of administrative action. Only recently, however, has this right become binding on EU institutions and bodies and, in particular, before the TFEU no legal provision ensured the judicial review of EU agencies' acts.

Before the Lisbon Treaty, distinguished scholarship[163] advocated the extension of judicial protection to EU agencies' acts on the grounds of the recognition in the *Les Verts* case law of the inescapable principle of judicial review in a Community based on the rule of law.[164] The Court of Justice embraced this approach in *Commission v European Investment Bank*[165] and extended to this 'Community body established and endowed with legal personality by the EC Treaty' the system of judicial remedies envisaged in *Les Verts*. Only later did the General Court uphold this approach in *Solgema*.[166] Only recently, therefore, has judicial review been secured as a means of protection against EU agencies' acts, with the adoption of the Lisbon Treaty, which filled this gap in the protection. To ensure the effective application of EU law and protection against abuses of power, the General Court proclaimed the coherent application of judicial remedies to administrative bodies of the EU producing acts with legal effects on third parties and extended to EU agencies the *Les Verts* doctrine.

Chamon observed that such judicial interpretation is not undisputed, as EU agencies were not included amongst the institutions under the EC Treaty and, particularly, the acts of the European Agency for Reconstruction (EAR) in *Solgema*

[162] On the principles of impartiality and due care and on the recognition of limits in the scrutiny of facts, see *Honeywell Belgium NV Belgium v ECHA* (n 161) paras 76–77, which particularly refer to C-269/90 *Technische Universität München* (n 75) para 14 and T-96/10 *Rütgers Germany GmbH and others v ECHA* ECLI:EU:T:2013:109, para 100; *Dow Benelux BV Netherlands v ECHA* (n 161) para 114, which particularly refers to C-343/09 *Afton Chemical Ltd* [2010] ECR I-07027, paras 33–34.

[163] See K Lenaerts, 'Regulating the Regulatory Process: "Delegation of Powers" in the European Community' (1993) 18 *European Law Review* 23, 45–46.

[164] 94/83 *Parti écologiste 'Les Verts' v European Parliament* [1986] ECR 1339, para 23.

[165] C-15/00 *Commission v EIB* [2003] ECR I-7281, para 75.

[166] T-411/06 *Solgema* [2008] ECR II-2771, paras 36–37.

could have been referred to the Commission.[167] In addition, the General Court itself refused to extend judicial protection against the Ombudsman, as his/her acts did not produce legal effects on third parties and it was not an EC Treaty institution.[168] In my view, the reasons for the ruling in *Solgema* will not be found in the subjective nature of the body whose acts were challenged. The General Court rather focused on the nature of the acts in question; that is, their capability to produce binding legal effects.[169] The cancellation of a tender procedure in *Solgema* was an act:

> which adversely affects the applicant and brings about a distinct change in his legal position, since the result is that the applicant can no longer expect to be awarded the contract for which he has submitted a tender.[170]

Conversely, by definition a decision of the Ombudsman concerning the substantive examination of a complaint:

> does not constitute a measure capable of being challenged by an action for annulment, since such a decision does not produce legal effects on third parties, within the meaning of Article 230 EC.[171]

Understanding what acts may produce legal effects is therefore key to grasping the boundaries of judicial review.

As seen, today Article 263(1) TFEU explicitly extends the guarantee of judicial review of the acts of bodies, offices or agencies of the Union intended to produce legal effects vis-à-vis third parties. As Advocate General Jääskinen pointed out in the *ESMA Short Selling* case, the only remedy which is not explicitly referred to agencies by the Treaty is non-contractual liability; however, the *Solgema* case law covers compensation for the damage produced by measures taken by agencies.[172] The legal existence of the remedies, however, does not ensure the full justiciability of all EU agencies' action.

[167] M Chamon, 'EU Risk Regulators and EU Procedural Law' (2014) 5 *European Journal of Risk Regulation* 324, 325; Chamon, *EU Agencies* (n 42) 329–30.

[168] T-196/08 *Srinivasan v European Ombudsman* ECLI:EU:T:2008:470, paras 10–13.

[169] This interpretation finds confirmation in T-70/05 *Evropaïki Dynamiki—Proigmena Systimata Tilepikoinonion Pliroforikis kai Tilematikis AE v EMSA* [2010] ECR II-313, paras 64–66.

[170] T-411/06 *Solgema* (n 166) para 38. In addition, the General Court relied on the relation of delegation that connects the EAR and the Commission, so that the acts of the tender procedure and the awarding of contracts could not be referred to the Commission as they had been lawfully delegated to the Agency (para 39).

[171] T-196/08 *Srinivasan v European Ombudsman* (n 168) para 12. See also T-193/04 *Tillack v Commission* (n 86) para 128, where the maladministration sanctioned by the Ombudsman was found not to constitute, 'in itself … a sufficiently serious breach of a rule of law within the meaning of the case-law'. See Wakefield, *The Right to Good Administration* (n 85) 117–19, who expresses the dichotomy between illegality and maladministration on the Ombudsman's accountability model, subject to parliamentary control and assisting the European Parliament, with no own enforcement power.

[172] C-270/12 *United Kingdom v Council and Parliament*, Opinion of the AG Jääskinen (n 5) para 73. Note that the 2015 legislative proposal for a new EASA Regulation introduces a provision on non-contractual liability which replicates Art 340 TFEU and confers on the CJEU the relevant jurisdiction; see COM(2015)613, art 84(3) and (4).

When ensuring judicial protection against EU agencies' acts, their capability to produce legal effects filters the distinction between hard law and soft law. As seen in Chapter 2, although not-binding, soft law may produce indirect or incidental legal effects that can be justiciable. As the Court of Justice held in *Grimaldi*, when any concerned person is affected by any national measure which is taken on the grounds of soft law, such recommendations should be taken into account by the courts. Recommendations 'cannot therefore be regarded as having no legal effect', 'in particular where they are capable of casting light on the interpretation of other provisions of national or Community law'.[173] In *Dansk Rørindustri*, the CJEU considered the Commission's guidelines on the calculation of fines under competition law as 'rules of conduct, which are of general application' and are 'designed to produce external effects'.[174] In addition, the CJEU recognised the availability of the action for annulment for 'all measures adopted by the institutions, whatever their nature or form, which are intended to have legal effects'.[175] Case law on the protection of fundamental rights has particularly demonstrated the pursuit of substantive interpretation of the Treaties to ensure the full application of EU law and to give protection to procedural rights regardless of the formal status of the challenged acts.[176] The CJEU has also held that the soft nature of the law cannot affect the substantive classification of the rules contained therein as essential elements of a policy.[177] This means that formally non-binding acts may be subject to judicial review. If producing legal effects, soft law will be subject to judicial review.[178]

[173] C-322/88 *Grimaldi v Fonds des maladies professionnelles* [1989] ECR 4407, paras 18–19.

[174] C-189/02P, C-202/02P, C-205-208/02P and C-213/02P *Dansk Rørindustri and others v Commission* [2005] ECR I-5425, paras 209–11.

[175] 22/70 *Commission v Council* [1971] ECR 263, para 42.

[176] C-354/04P *Gestoras Pro Amnistia v Council* [2007] ECR I-1579, paras 52–54; C-355/04P *Segi Araitz Zubimendi Izaga and Aritza Galarraga v Council* [2007] ECR I-1657, paras 53–54.

[177] C-355/10 *European Parliament v Council* ECLI:EU:C:2012:516, para 80.

[178] An opposite approach to the justiciability of soft law acts is present in the Italian legislation on public procurement. Under Law 28 January 2016, no 11, art 1(1)(t), as implemented by Legislative Decree 18 April 2016, no 50, art 213(2) (Codice dei contratti), all the directives adopted by the Autorità nazionale anticorruzione (ANAC), whether binding or not, are amenable to judicial review. Under Italian law, therefore, the problem is not the possibility to challenge these acts in courts, but the regime of judicial protection. In its Opinion on the legislative draft, the Consiglio di Stato considered non-binding acts as better specified as 'ordinary administrative acts' (*ordinari atti amministrativi*), and binding acts as 'administrative acts of general application' (*atti amministrativi generali*); see Consiglio di Stato, Special Commission, 1 April 2016, no 855, 39–41. Legal scholarship, however, contested the sector-specific regulatory nature of binding acts, and recognised their general and innovative force of law (*regolamenti*): see MP Chiti, 'Il sistema delle fonti nella nuova disciplina dei contratti pubblici' (2016) *Giornale di diritto amministrativo* 436, 441–43; G Morbidelli, 'Linee guida dell'ANAC: comandi o consigli?' (2016) *Diritto amministrativo* 273, 287–91; L Torchia, 'La regolazione del mercato dei contratti pubblici' (2016) *Rivista della Regolazione dei Mercati* 72; F Cintioli, 'Il sindacato del giudice amministrativo sulle linee guida, sui pareri c.d. precontenzioso e sulle raccomandazioni di ANAC' (2017) *Diritto processuale amministrativo* 381; C Deodato, 'Nuove riflessioni sull'intensità del sindacato del giudice amministrativo. *Il caso delle linee guida dell'ANAC*' (2017) *Federalismi.it*, 18–25, available at www.federalismi.it/nv14/articolo-documento.cfm?Artid=33244&content=Nuove+riflessioni+sull%27intensit%C3%A0+del+sindacato+del+giudice+amministrativo&content_author=%3Cb%3ECarlo+Deodato%3C/b%3E; F Marone, 'Le linee guida dell'autorità nazionale

If binding measures are clearly challengeable as definitive acts, the capability of non-binding soft law to produce legal effects must be contextualised case-by-case. The quasi-regulatory nature of most EU agencies' action makes judicial review particularly problematic, because the attribution of legal force does not causally follow the adoption of the act. Preparatory acts are a specific category of administrative measures that creates such a problem.[179] Where EU agencies' acts are preparatory acts of a broader decision-making procedure, the possibility of bringing an action against these acts is limited by the role of the act in the procedure. In some cases, the General Court refused to review those scientific opinions adopted by EU agencies that did not produce legally binding effects[180] or it considered such acts within the responsibility of the Commission. With regard to the European Medicines Agency (EMA)'s decisions on refusals of applications for variation of the terms of marketing authorisations, in *Dr Karl Thomae GmbH v Commission*[181] the General Court upheld the action for annulment against the Commission which was entrusted with the adoption of the final decision, whereas the EMA was formally entrusted only with the scientific opinion on the case. Likewise, it rejected the action against the EMA in *Schering Plough Ltd v Commission.*[182] In other cases, the Court of Justice has, however, recognised the justiciability of EU agencies' opinions, where they structured the decision of the Commission or their content constituted an integral part of the motivation of the decision in question, such as the EMA's opinions on the withdrawal or the suspension of the marketing authorisations of medicinal products.[183] In these cases, EU agencies' acts could be reviewed together with the relevant binding decision of the Commission.

The justiciability of standardisation acts is also particularly problematic. Insofar as soft law is not intended to directly produce binding legal effects, the action for annulment becomes difficult under the CJEU's case law.[184] Article 263(4) TFEU,

anticorruzione nel sistema delle fonti' (2017) *Rivista Trimestrale di Diritto Pubblico* 743. The different taxonomy changes the legal regime for the acts in question and affects judicial powers. For instance, only administrative acts with the force of law (*regolamenti*) can be disapplied by administrative judges and challenged for infringement of law before the Supreme Court of Cassation (Corte di Cassazione); in addition, individuals are expected to comply with them (*ignorantia legis non excusat*) and judges to know and apply them (*iura novit curia*). In a more recent Opinion on ANAC's negotiated procedure, the same administrative court admitted the possibility that some guidelines may also have the force of law, showing that the legal qualification of ANAC's binding acts is still not settled: see Consiglio di Stato, Special Commission, 3 November 2016, no 2284, para 5.1.

[179] On the general issues of reviewability of preparatory acts under EU law see HCH Hofmann, GC Rowe and AH Türk, *Administrative Law and Policy of the European Union* (Oxford University Press, 2011) 803–5.

[180] T-311/06 *FMC Chemical and Arysta Lifesciences v EFSA* [2008] ECR II-88; T-312/06 *FMC Chemical v EFSA* [2008] ECR II-89; T-397/06 *Dow AgroSciences v EFSA* [2008] ECR II-90.

[181] T-123/00 *Dr Karl Thomae GmbH v Commission* [2002] ECR II-5193.

[182] T-133/03 *Schering Plough Ltd v Commission and European Agency for the Evaluation of Medicinal Products (EMEA)* ECLI:EU:T:2007:365, paras 22–23.

[183] T-74/00 *Artegodan v European Commission* [2000] ECR II-2583, paras 197–99; T-326/99 *Olivieri v European Commission and EMA* [2003] ECR II-6053, para 55.

[184] C-521/04P (R) *Tillack v Commission* [2005] ECR II-3995, para 31. See Hofmann, Rowe and Türk, *Administrative Law and Policy of the European Union* (n 179) 806–7 and 865.

in fact, requires the act in question to be either addressed or of direct and individual concern to any natural or legal persons, or to be a regulatory act of direct concern to them and not entailing implementing measures. As Hofmann, Rowe and Türk noted, although 'any act of general application irrespective of its form' can be conceived as a regulatory act, only where no 'indirect means of review' is available, private parties are ensured direct judicial protection.[185] EU agencies' soft law acts, however, generally require implementation from national competent authorities. Different means of judicial protection should therefore apply.

The recognition of the legal effects of soft law has induced the Court to admit other actions, such as the incidental review of illegality as in the *Dansk Rørindustri* case,[186] and the preliminary reference as in *Grimaldi*.[187] The coordination role of EU agencies makes these actions particularly relevant. Where EU agencies adopt standardisation acts, their soft powers may produce some legal effects on national authorities and, where applicable, on private parties. In the case of the EASA, for instance, national authorities have an obligation to ensure a consistent interpretation of national law with the recommendations and technical specifications provided by the Agency, unless they demonstrate that they can ensure the expected level of safety with another equivalent means. In the case of the ESAs, the 'comply or explain' mechanism introduces an obligation either to enforce such recommendations and guidelines or to state the reasons for non-compliance. Insofar as national law implementing EU law must also enforce soft law provisions, the action against national measures and its compatibility with EU law may also bring into question the legitimacy of soft law. National courts must take into account EU agencies' recommendations when assessing the legality of national law in light of EU law, so their legal interpretation matters in the application of EU law. Likewise, EU agencies' soft law acts may also matter in preliminary reference proceedings, as their validity may be questioned by the CJEU when examining the validity of the (secondary) legislation on which the soft law is based.

The legal effects produced by soft law make soft law able to be challenged in courts together with the relevant EU law which the contested decision implements.[188] However, if soft law anticipates the relevant EU legislation, as happened in the case of the EIOPA's preparatory guidelines discussed in Chapter 2, the risk is that the non-binding character of soft law makes direct legal action more difficult. In addition, incompetence and trespass on the delegated powers of the Commission may not be legally detected because of the non-binding nature of guidelines and recommendations. The soft character of the measures may protect

[185] Ibid 814.

[186] C-189/02P, C-202/02P, C-205-208/02P and C-213/02P *Dansk Rørindustri and others v Commission* (n 174) paras 212–14.

[187] C-322/88 *Grimaldi* (n 173) para 8.

[188] T-123/00 *Dr Karl Thomae GmbH v Commission* (n 181) para 97; 32/58 and 33/58 *Snupat v High Authority* [1959] ECR 127, para 141.

them from justiciability. Nonetheless, the non-implementation of soft law may lead to EU agencies' decisions, which then could be challenged as binding acts producing clear legal effects and therefore subject to judicial review.

The identification of legal effects is therefore key to ensuring judicial protection against EU agencies' acts regardless of their nature. However the legal effects of EU agencies' acts are recognised, the issue then becomes the nature of the judicial scrutiny, so that effective legal protection can be ensured against EU agencies' acts.

VIII. STANDARD OF JUDICIAL REVIEW

The judicial control over the exercise of administrative powers is key to ensuring the compatibility of EU agencies' action with the democratic principle and the rule of law. As seen in Chapter 3, without the recognition of the existence of administrative discretion, the judicial acknowledgement of wide discretion in EU agencies' complex decisions would have paradoxical effects on the coherence of the *Meroni* doctrine.[189] Administrative discretion will be legally constrained within a normative framework setting the hierarchy of the interests and the priorities of administrative action. Only in this framework is administrative action legitimate. The Court of Justice has employed both substantive criteria and procedural guarantees to review the exercise of EU administrative action. Substantive criteria concern the control over the legitimacy of the exercise of powers, whereas procedural guarantees ensure the accuracy of the decision-making process.

As Türk emphasised, the control over the exercise of EU agencies' discretion is articulated in three different stages: the interpretation of the statutory provisions framing the administrative competence; the scrutiny of the facts founding the administrative decisions; and the conclusions reached by the administration connecting the facts and the law.[190] On the first stage of judicial review concerning the questions of law, Craig has pointed out that the CJEU has the monopoly on the interpretation and may accordingly substitute the legal interpretation of the proceeding authority.[191] In the case of EU agencies, the review on the point of law strongly depends on the constitutional limits to delegation. The *Meroni* doctrine plays a key role in setting the boundaries of administrative action and in the control over the legitimacy of EU agencies' powers. The validity of the delegation and the compliance of the administrative action with the delegation criteria are crucial grounds of review.

[189] See T-102/13 *Heli-Flight GmbH & Co KG v EASA* ECLI:EU:T:2014:1064; C-61/15P *Heli-Flight GmbH & Co KG v EASA* ECLI:EU:2016:296.

[190] AH Türk, 'Oversight of Administrative Rulemaking: Judicial Review' (2013) 19 *European Law Journal* 126, 136.

[191] P Craig, *EU Administrative Law*, 2nd edn (Oxford University Press, 2012) 405.

Conversely, EU courts tend not to substitute their judgments for that of the initial decision-maker on issues of fact and discretion.[192] The scrutiny of facts is generally limited to the examination of their procedural accuracy, so that evidence is correctly acquired and used. Especially where complex technical assessments are at stake, courts do not substitute their particular appraisal of the case with the one of the competent institution.[193] Nonetheless, the intensity of the review of facts varies according to the complexity of the measure in question and the discretion conferred on the decision-making authority. When EU administrative acts require complex evaluations, judicial review is limited to the control of the manifest error of appraisal, misuse of powers or excess of the discretion limits.[194] This standard of review has, however, been articulated differently according to the willingness of the courts to review the accuracy of the facts founding the administrative actions.

The manifest error test for the revision of complex factual assessments has probably reached its highest intensity in the *Tetra Laval* case, introducing an enhanced scrutiny on evidence.[195] In a merger procedure, the General Court required the Commission to provide 'sufficiently convincing evidence' for its factual assessments in support of the manifest error review[196] and the Court of Justice confirmed that the judicial standard of review includes the examination that evidence is 'factually accurate, reliable and consistent' and 'contains all the information which must be taken into account in order to assess a complex situation', so as to check that 'it is capable of substantiating the conclusions drawn from it'.[197] According to Mendes, the *Tetra Laval* test emerged as 'a quite hands-on judicial approach' but still moving within the realm of the manifest error review.[198] Craig claimed that the *Tetra Laval* test 'conceals more than it reveals', as the standard of proof required for decision-makers could become apparent only after the judicial enquiry.[199]

[192] T-123/00 *Dr Karl Thomae GmbH v Commission* (n 181) paras 82 and 105; T-74/00, 76/00, 83/00, 85/00, 132/00, 137/00 and 141/00 *Artegodan GmbH v Commission* [2002] ECR II-4945, para 200; T-13/99 *Pfizer Animal Health SA v Council* [2002] ECR II-3305, para 139. In the literature, see Craig, *EU Administrative Law* (n 191) 408; J Scott and S Sturm, 'Courts as Catalysts: Rethinking the Judicial Role in New Governance' (2007) 13 *Columbia Journal of European Law* 565, 583.

[193] See C-425/08 *Enviro Tech (Europe)* [2009] ECR I-10035, para 47; C-343/09 *Afton Chemical Ltd* (n 162) para 28.

[194] C-55/75 *Balkan-Import Export GmbH v Hauptzollamt Berlin-Packhof* [1976] ECR 19, para 8.

[195] T-5/02 *Tetra Laval v Commission* [2002] ECR II-4389.

[196] Ibid paras 162 and 223.

[197] C-12/03P *Commission v Tetra Laval* [2005] ECR I-987, para 39.

[198] J Mendes, 'Discretion, Care and Public Interests in the EU Administration: Probing the Limits of Law' (2016) 53 *Common Market Law Review* 419, 430.

[199] Craig, *EU Administrative Law* (n 191) 436. Although the subsequent case law confirmed the validity of the *Tetra Laval* test in different areas of competition law and state aid, the difficulty of its application emerged in the case law of the Court of Justice recognising the errors in law committed by the General Court. See C-413/06P *Bertelsmann AG and Sony Corporation of America v Independent Music Publishers and Labels Association (IMPALA)* [2008] ECR I-4951, para 95; C-382/12P *MasterCard Inc and others v Commission* ECLI:EU:C:2014:2201, para 169.

Conversely, courts need to make clear the standard of proof in order to ensure the legal certainty of administrative action.[200]

A comparable intense approach to the scrutiny of facts has been applied in risk regulation. As far as EU agencies' acts are concerned, their competence suggests that the judicial review of facts is likely to rely on the principles that emerge in risk regulation. In the seminal *Pfizer* case, the General Court focused on the need for experts to provide an accurate risk assessment which should be based on the principles of excellence, independence and transparency,[201] and should be updated to the best scientific information available and the most recent results of international research.[202] Only insofar as the scientific risk assessment is grounded on these key principles can it provide 'sufficiently reliable and cogent information' to the competent public authorities 'to understand the ramifications of the scientific question raised and decide upon a policy in full knowledge of the facts'.[203] EU institutions must show that regulation has been adopted on the grounds of a scientific risk assessment 'as thorough as possible' and that on the basis of that assessment, they disposed of 'sufficient scientific indication to conclude, on an objective scientific basis, that there was a risk to human health'.[204] In the subsequent case law, the General Court focused this approach particularly on the compliance of risk assessment with procedural guarantees and the control of the (ir-)regularities in the processing of scientific information.[205] By arguing that there should be coherence between the scientific evidence that constitutes the basis of the decision and the content of the decision itself, the General Court indirectly confirmed that even if scientific risk assessment was not binding for EU institutions, any departure from scientific evidence should be justified. The Court of Justice upheld the substance of this scrutiny, but it treated scientific uncertainty more flexibly, both relaxing the intensity of the review and reducing the procedural review of facts.[206]

[200] Craig, *EU Administrative Law* (n 191) 432–33.

[201] T-13/99 *Pfizer Animal Health SA v Council* (n 192) para 159.

[202] Ibid para 158.

[203] Ibid para 162.

[204] Ibid para 165. The burden of proof that is imposed on EU institutions is grounded on what the General Court considers to be a key issue in the assessment of the risk at stake, the criterion of the tenability of the risk. EU institutions are entitled to determine 'what level of risk is deemed unacceptable' for society (paras 149 and 155) and accordingly set the threshold of protection. To set this threshold, EU institutions 'may take into account, inter alia, the severity of the impact on human health were the risk to occur, including the extent of possible adverse effects, the persistency or reversibility of those effects and the possibility of delayed effects as well as the more or less concrete perception of the risk based on available scientific knowledge' (para 153).

[205] T-229/04 *Kingdom of Sweden v Commission* [2007] ECR II-02437, paras 108–10, 119–21. In this case the General Court accepted that the Commission's evaluation report, stating no indication of the neurotoxicity of the herbicide paraquat to be authorised as a plant protection product, should be considered inaccurate, because its conclusions were not founded on the necessary procedural requirements (eg inaccurate analysis of the relevant scientific literature, procedural errors in the evaluation of the information).

[206] C-343/09 *Afton Chemical Ltd* (n 162) paras 30 and 33 (where the CJEU excluded 'to some extent, … the finding of the basic facts'); C-77/09 *Gowan Comércio International* [2010] ECR I-13533, para 60. See Craig, *EU Administrative Law* (n 191) 438–39.

Even though EU agencies are not institutions, one can legitimately expect that the CJEU will adopt the same scrutiny of their acts, as the technical complexity of facts affects the capability of courts to review the evidence of their complex technical assessments.

When revising how discretionary powers have been concretely applied, the criteria of judicial review have been consolidated in the case law on the revision of technical decisions, particularly in the leading case *Technische Universität München*. In this case, EU courts reviewed administrative action on the grounds of 'the duty of the competent institution to examine carefully and impartially all the relevant aspects of the individual case'.[207] As Türk pointed out, this duty has both a procedural aspect and a substantive dimension: procedurally, it ensures the appropriateness of the evidence acquired, whereas substantively it ensures that all the relevant issues are considered in the evaluation of the case.[208] This duty therefore directs the administrative balance of competing public interests and the fair pursuit of public interest. As Mendes emphasised, this duty should be interpreted as a 'legal duty that derives from the attribution of administrative discretion to act in a certain way'.[209]

The principles of impartiality and due care are key to controlling the correct exercise of administrative discretion under the notion of good administration, but the deeper scrutiny of administrative choices requires their application with the general principle of proportionality. Schwarze noted the complementarity of these principles in the government of administrative action, as they assist judicial review from different angles: proportionality 'sets material limits to the interference of public authorities into the private sphere of citizens', whereas impartiality focuses on 'objective standards of executive procedures'.[210] When ensuring the reasonable adjustment of public measures to the pursued public goals set by the law, the proportionality test is a means to check that individual rights are not over-restricted by administrative action, but in doing so it also assesses whether that administrative power is correctly implemented.[211] In fact, the choice of the instrument which is least intrusive for private parties relies on complete and accurate fact-finding. This commits public administration to the correct understanding of the different

[207] C-269/90 *Technische Universität München* [1991] ECR 1-5469, para 14.

[208] Türk, 'Oversight of Administrative Rulemaking' (n 190) 141.

[209] Mendes, 'Discretion, Care and Public Interests in the EU Administration' (n 198) 440.

[210] J Schwarze, 'The Principle of Proportionality and the Principle of Impartiality in European Administrative Law' (2003) *Rivista Trimestrale di Diritto Pubblico* 53.

[211] Seminal studies on the proportionality principle in EU law remain, see G de Búrca, 'The Principle of Proportionality and its Application in EC Law' (1993) 13 *Yearbook of European Law* 105; T Tridimas, *The General Principles of EU Law*, 2nd edn (Oxford University Press, 2006) chs 3–5; Craig, *EU Administrative Law* (n 191) ch 19; in a comparative perspective see M Cohen-Eliya and I Porat, 'Proportionality and the Culture of Justification' (2011) 59 *American Journal of Comparative Law* 463; DU Galetta, *Principio di proporzionalità e sindacato giurisdizionale nel diritto amministrativo* (Giuffrè, 1998); A Sandulli, *La proporzionalità dell'azione amministrativa* (Cedam, 1998).

public and private interests at stake and structures the public decision-making in light of individual rights' protection.[212]

The implementation of the proportionality test has, however, been critically limited by the recognition of the EU institutions' discretion. Although EU agencies have a different status, it cannot be ignored that the three-tier test affirmed in *Fedesa*[213] would assume different intensity according to the degree of administrative discretion allocated to the proceeding authority. Controls over the suitability and the necessity of the measure are the most relevant grounds for review, whereas the control over the tolerability of the burden imposed on individual competing rights (that is, proportionality in the strictest sense) is less significant. The proportionality test therefore falls within the realm of the manifest error standard of review. It creates a burden of proof on the applicant that EU institutions' action is vitiated by manifest error and reduces the burden on the EU institutions to demonstrate the individual fairness of the measure.[214]

Procedural guarantees therefore supplement the substantive review of administrative discretion with further grounds of judicial review. In *Technische Universität München*, the CJEU held that the enforcement of procedural rights and the duty to give reasons were complementary guarantees ensuring the fairness of administrative action. The control over the concrete implementation of all these guarantees crucially guides the judicial scrutiny of the factual and legal elements upon which the exercise of the administrative power of appraisal is based. Clearly, the intensity of the scrutiny varies according to the nature of administrative proceedings. As seen, procedural rights and the specificity of the motivation in fact are more stringent with individual proceedings leading to the adoption of administrative decisions, rather than with rule-making activities. Nonetheless, the control over these guarantees ensures the procedural fairness of administrative action.

IX. *MERONI* DOCTRINE GOING FORWARD

The analysis of the principles and the rights limiting administrative action and the remedies to the wrongful exercise of administrative discretion show a patchy

[212] See J Jowell QC, 'The Two Faces of Proportionality', paper delivered at the Institute of Advanced Legal Studies, London, 23 November 2007.

[213] C-331/88 *Fedesa and others* [1988] ECR I-040023, para 13. In this leading case, the proportionality review was based on the control over the suitability of the measure for the purpose of facilitating or achieving the pursued goal; the necessity of the measure in the sense that the authority concerned had no other mechanism (with the same effectiveness) at its disposal which was less restrictive of freedom; and proportionality in the strict sense, so that the measure should not impose an intolerable burden on the affected individuals. This also involved the assessment of adequacy on the basis of a costs-benefits analysis. See also C-11/70 *Internationale Handelsgesellschaft mbH v Einfuhr- und Vorratsstelle für Getreide und Futtermittel* [1970] ECR 1125, paras 12 and 16.

[214] T-13/99 *Pfizer Animal Health SA* (n 192) paras 419 and 450; C-77/09 *Gowan Comércio International* (n 206) para 83.

implementation of the legal guarantees that apply to EU agencies' action. On the one hand, the rules applying to EU institutions validly apply to EU agencies and cover their action in conformity with the framework of the Treaties; on the other hand, the legal status of EU agencies makes these guarantees still unable to justify the confident allocation of strong administrative powers in the absence of a clear recognition of their competence in the Treaties. Even though EU agencies' administrative powers comply with the principle of institutional balance as their powers can be legally distinguished in nature from those belonging to EU institutions under the Treaties, the absence of a coherent system of procedural guarantees regulating their action makes the allocation of such powers a legal risk.

The analysis of the organisation, the administrative procedures and the remedies show that EU administrative law aims to entrench administration through EU agencies to the key legal guarantees that a modern system of administration requires. This legal effort, however, has not yet succeeded in the attempt to create a mature structure of decentralised administration. The organisation and the responsibilities of EU agencies still present grey areas that may create concrete problems where further enhanced administrative powers are conferred on them. The conferral of regulatory powers on EU agencies would therefore require the reconsideration of those elements that fuel the unchecked and unbalanced allocation of power.

As seen, the organisation of EU agencies and the enforcement of procedural rights are core elements in the recognition of the impartiality and accountability of administration. In the current regime, however, their implementation presents some gaps. The principle of autonomy is not structured so as to enhance coherence in administrative decision-making and the pursuit of the identified European public interest. Conversely, it tempers the divergent interests gravitating to EU agencies. Insofar as autonomy is required as a condition for the operation of EU administration, the political accountability framework should be strengthened accordingly. Conversely, the current regime demonstrates little awareness of the political relevance of the technical tasks exercised by EU agencies. Nonetheless, several accountability mechanisms apply. As Scholten correctly observed, the diversification of EU agencies' political accountability regimes creates 'no genuine consensus as to what minimum set of accountability mechanisms EU agencies should be subject to and what (minimum) involvement the Council and the European Parliament should have in relation to EU agencies'.[215] The result is that it is difficult to measure the actual value of single accountability instruments and to assess their effective contribution to the control over EU agencies' functions. Hence, the legal risk is that although formally accountable, EU agencies are uncontrolled because no comprehensive understanding of the substance of their account is in place.

215 Scholten, *The Political Accountability of EU and US Independent Regulatory Agencies* (n 2) 173. See also Busuioc, *European Agencies: Law and Practices of Accountability* (n 2) 152–53, 250–52.

Administrative proceedings are also key to ensuring that discretion is fairly exercised. If the bundle of the rights and principles under EU law is already able to ensure fair adjudication proceedings, the case would be more complicated where EU agencies may adopt acts of general application. Participation in executive rule-making is still in search of a model and it is divided between the corporative representation of interests and broader modules of notice-and-comment.

In addition, several EU agencies' acts are soft law. The fact that these recommendations and guidelines need formal endorsement from other institutions relieves EU agencies from the full application of procedural rights and procedural transparency. Pragmatically, if soft law acts aim to be effective, they require EU agencies to comply with the principles covered by good administration, especially, impartiality and due care. Legally speaking, however, compliance with these principles in the exercise of (soft) administrative powers cannot be left to the institutional capacity of individual EU agencies to implement essential rules of administrative law. The principle of legality requires law to set out clearly defined conditions that ensure the compatibility of the exercise of administrative powers with the democratic principle. When exercising hard law powers, EU agencies enforce procedural rights more carefully, as they follow an administrative procedure that must comply with the guarantees of good administration. However, an EU agency itself and not the EU legislature defines the articulation of the administrative procedure. This affects the justification of administrative powers in itself, which is based on the legislative establishment of their conditions and limits.

As long as the model of administration which characterises EU agencies remains hidden beyond the black letter provisions of the Treaties, the implementation of a general procedural law regulating their action would ensure both administrative and judicial occasions of legal protection that would be sufficient to procedurally defeat the objections to the exercise of administrative powers by EU agencies. An EU administrative procedural law would in fact enhance the visibility of EU agencies' action by making it more transparent and verifiable. The European Parliament's call for a European administrative procedure should be welcomed as a precious instrument to strengthen the legitimacy of EU administrative powers and a legal support to enhance EU agencies' role in internal market integration.

The introduction of clear-cut guarantees would assure that EU agencies work according to the rule of law within the framework of competences stated in the Treaties. The enforcement of legal guarantees clearly entails the hardening of administrative action and the connected problems related to the growth of bureaucracy and bureaucratic powers. However, this operation of legal certainty could be carried out so as to include some flexibility in the decision-making process. For instance, a general administrative procedural law based on principles, rather than on detailed rules and bureaucratic requirements, would ensure the flexible implementation of the guarantees of protection. The American problem of the 'ossification' of administrative procedures through the enhancement of legal requirements and their judicial review[216] is still far from being a European problem. Yet, it can be taken into account when designing appropriate rules. Nonetheless, weak legal guarantees do not make *agencification* compatible with the Treaties and do not serve the development of legitimate administration by EU agencies.

If EU legislation may intend to increase EU agencies' powers as internal market regulators, coherent legal guarantees about their role and functioning would contribute to legitimising their action, making it more justiciable. The long-lasting relaxation of the *Meroni* doctrine should therefore pass through the consistent enhancement of the guarantees of EU agencies' action. From this perspective, the implementation of the principles of autonomy, accountability, participation and transparency become the fundamental benchmarks for a modern interpretation of the *Meroni* doctrine, as their combination would bundle the concrete standard of legality.[217] On the one hand, the coherent implementation of the principles that could strengthen the democratic compatibility of administrative action contributes to enhancing confidence in decentralised administrative action. As Lenaerts pointed out, the general principles concerning the relationship between citizens and government may consolidate the individual trust in Union governance as these 'trust-enhancing principles constitute primarily different expressions of the meta-fundamental right of due process'.[218] On the other hand, the rule of law and the accountability mechanisms make EU agencies responsible for their acts as autonomous bodies within a plural EU executive in a system of multilevel governance. The concerns about the unity of the regulatory function could be addressed procedurally. Although the development of administrative responsibilities requires the differentiation and pluralisation of administrative tasks, legal guarantees as to their exercise could maintain the coherence of the executive function.

[216] In the vast American debate on the ossification of administrative law see particularly PL Strauss, 'The Rulemaking Continuum' (1992) 41 *Duke Law Journal* 1463; PR Verkuil, 'Comment: Rulemaking Ossification: A Modest Proposal' (1995) 47 *Administrative Law Review* 453; S Mee, 'Negotiated Rulemaking and Combined Sewer Overflows (CSOs): Consensus Saves Ossification' (1997) 25 *Boston College Environmental Affairs Law Review* 213; SM Johnson, 'Ossification's Demise: An Empirical Analysis of EPA Rulemaking from 2001–2005' (2008) 38 *Environmental Law* 767; M Seidenfeld, 'Why Agencies Act: A Reassessment of the Ossification Critique of Judicial Review' in (2009) 70 *Ohio State Law Journal* 251; J Webb Yackee and S Webb Yackee, 'Testing the Ossification Thesis: An Empirical Examination of Federal Regulatory Volume and Speed, 1950–1990' (2012) 80 *George Washington Law Review* 1414; RJ Pierce, Jr, 'Rulemaking Ossification is Real: A Response to Testing the Ossification Thesis' (2012) 80 *George Washington Law Review* 1493; SA Shapiro, 'Rulemaking Ossification and the Debate over Reforming Hard Look Review' (2015) 41 *Administrative and Regulatory Law News* 13.

[217] See M Simoncini, 'Legal Boundaries of European Supervisory Authorities (ESAs) in the Financial Markets: Tensions in the Development of True Regulatory Agencies' (2015) 34 *Yearbook of European Law* 319, 348–51.

[218] K Lenaerts, '"In the Union We Trust": Trust-enhancing Principles of Community Law' (2004) 41 *Common Market Law Review* 317, 343. The same link between the guarantees of administrative procedure and the growth of confidence is also considered in the 2013 European Parliament Resolution 2012/2024(INL) (n 112), letters L and R and recommendation 3 in the paragraph codifying the principle of fairness.

Conclusions: The 'Long and Winding Road' to EU Administrative Regulation

ADMINISTRATIVE GOVERNANCE through EU decentralised agencies is the product of several compromises. On an organisational level, it compromises the EU executive's interest in the supranational sector-specific regulation aimed at internal market integration with the national interests in the control over the services to be 'communitarised'. Autonomy is the legal figure of such organisational compromise. On a functional level, the reach of EU agencies' powers is the result of a compromise between the political and functional needs for decentralised governance and the non-delegation doctrine setting precise limits to the delegation of the competences allocated to EU institutions under the Treaties. In the absence of an explicit legal basis in the Treaties for the establishment of EU agencies, judge-made law has governed the competence of EU agencies under the so-called *Meroni* doctrine. Even though the *Meroni* case referred to the delegation of powers from the High Authority to private law agencies under the European Coal and Steel Community (ECSC) Treaty, it has lasted as the principle preserving the democratic legitimacy of administration under the Community Treaties and in the general consensus it has continued to rule the legislative conferral of powers upon the agencies established under EU law. However, the *Meroni* doctrine as the law governing the evolving phenomenon of *agencification* has in practice failed to predict and explain the growth of EU agencies' powers. Compromises have steadily eroded the substance of this legal barrier.

The coordination and the management of the interdependences in a complex system of multilevel administrative governance made EU agencies the centres of mediation between supranational and intergovernmental interests. They emerged as non-hierarchical yet apical hubs for internal market governance and operate in what Sabel and Zeitlin called a 'directly deliberative polyarchy', a network of actors whose constant exchange of expertise and interests' negotiation led to new (harmonised) rules and practices.[1] The fact that they have been developing beyond any express provision in the Treaties hints at both the political and technical reasons that justify their existence beyond the black letter provisions of the Treaties.

[1] CF Sabel and J Zeitlin, 'Learning from Difference: The New Architecture of Experimentalist Governance in the EU' in CF Sabel and J Zeitlin (eds), *Experimentalist Governance in the European Union* (Oxford University Press, 2010) 1, 5–6.

Their growth through different 'waves' of agencification shows that they have become key assets in the development of internal market integration, especially for services. Their role in the polyarchy has slightly changed with the legally unexpected growth of their apical competence. The latest generations of EU agencies have acquired significantly enhanced powers in the direction of the polyarchy, and hybrid administrations with increased autonomy have been established. Chapter 2 particularly focused on the European Aviation Safety Agency (EASA) and the European Supervisory Authorities (ESAs) as case studies unequivocally demonstrating that key quasi-regulatory powers have been allocated to EU agencies, which only with (political and technical) difficulties could be allocated to other institutional actors. Adjudication activities structuring the access to the internal market, independent standardisation practices and reinforced participation in the formal rule-making of the EU institutions emerged as key instruments shaping individual prospects and opportunities in internal market regulation.

These emerging methods of administrative quasi-regulation by EU agencies question the constitutional foundations of EU agencies' competence. In the leading *Meroni* and *Romano* cases, the Court of Justice of the European Union (CJEU) strictly limited agencies' contribution to internal market regulation, but this could not prevent the practical expansion of their tasks. Although the validity of the *Meroni* doctrine survived 60 years of European integration, its capability to effectively govern EU agencies' action in the internal market has been debated. In practice, the *Meroni* doctrine has become the formal requirement for the legitimacy of EU agencies' powers in hidden conflict with the substance of the allocated powers. The laconic *adagio* of the *Meroni* case concerning 'clearly defined executive powers' not 'implying a wide margin of discretion which may, according to the use which is made of it, make possible the execution of actual economic policy', has been recited as a mantra in legal practice. Yet it has not prevented the innovative expansion of EU agencies' competence, but it has nonetheless trapped agencification in an unfortunate compromise between legality and reality.

The emerging situation is the typical relationship between a dominant paradigm and anomalies that Kuhn effectively illustrated in his study on the structure of scientific revolutions.[2] Kuhn considered scientific knowledge as governed by the embracing of paradigms intended as 'universally recognized scientific achievements that for a time provide model problems and solutions to a community of practitioners'.[3] The interpretation of scientific phenomena produces dominant paradigms that explain the succeeding reality. Following this approach, the *Meroni* doctrine can be considered as the emerged dominant paradigm for the compatibility of EU agencies' powers with EU law, as it has provided the rule to explain and guide the delegation of power to EU agencies.

[2] TS Kuhn, *The Structure of Scientific Revolutions*, 2nd edn (International Encyclopedia of Unified Science, University of Chicago Press, 1962).

[3] Ibid vii.

At a certain point, however, this dominant paradigm may become unable to explain new phenomena and 'anomalies, or violations of expectations' may start to emerge.[4] Whereas persistent anomalies cannot be aligned to the dominant paradigm, they generate a crisis in the epistemic community and new scientific theories emerge. The crisis questions the dominant paradigm and may alternatively be resolved in the context of normal science or lead to a scientific revolution intended as a paradigm shift. Where a new theory succeeds to be established as a new paradigm, the crisis is over, a new stage of 'normal science' is achieved and phenomena are explained in light of the new paradigm. The Copernican, Newtonian, chemical, electromagnetic and Einsteinian revolutions are all interpreted as paradigm shifts.[5] The reality of EU integration has somehow outreached the legal prediction of the *Meroni* doctrine, questioning the capability of this paradigm to entrench the exercise of EU agencies' powers. This opens a crisis in the application of the *Meroni* doctrine that 'loosens the rules of normal puzzle-solving in ways that ultimately permit a new paradigm to emerge'.[6]

Kuhn significantly pointed out the resistance of the epistemic community to a paradigm change based on both factual and theoretical reasons. On a factual level, the decision to abandon a dominant paradigm is based on the emergence of a new paradigm and 'the comparison of both paradigms with nature *and* with each other'.[7] On a theoretical level, the crisis of a dominant paradigm triggers 'epistemological counterinstances' introducing 'numerous articulations and *ad hoc* modifications of their theory in order to eliminate any apparent conflict'.[8] In the factual absence of a new paradigm replacing the *Meroni* doctrine, the non-binding nature of EU agencies' powers and the avoidance of direct conflict of competence with the Commission have so far worked as theoretical justifications for the compatibility of such powers with the EU legal order. Nonetheless, such compromises fail to structure a credible response to the legitimacy and the reach of EU agencies' powers in the face of their most recent developments. Uncertainty has therefore been the distinctive mark of governance. In Kuhn's words, 'insecurity is generated by the persistent failure of the puzzles of normal science to come out as they should. Failure of existing rules is the prelude to a search for new ones'.[9]

The weakness of the 'top-down transmission of power and democratic legitimacy' justification brought about competing readings, partly replacing the *Meroni* doctrine's approach with 'bottom-up alternatives to traditional political representation, which rely more heavily on participation of stakeholders in the regulatory

[4] Ibid ix.
[5] Ibid 66–71.
[6] Ibid 80.
[7] Ibid 77.
[8] Ibid 78.
[9] Ibid 68.

process, accountability and transparency … completed by the possibility of judicial review'.[10] Although the bottom-up approach significantly identifies the constitutional issues in the functioning of the polyarchic governance, it cannot justify the legislative allocation of powers to EU agencies and does not erase the limits set by the *Meroni* doctrine. A structured reflection on the place of EU agencies in the EU constitutional framework is therefore the inescapable issue hidden behind the search for justification of any single EU agencies' power.

This study took the challenge to appraise the dominant paradigm explaining EU agencies' democratic legitimacy and investigate the tenability of the *Meroni* doctrine under the current system of EU agencies' governance. The study recognised the centrality of the *Meroni* doctrine as the dominant paradigm embedding the key legal principles still governing the development of administrative governance through EU agencies, but proposed an innovative reading that might contribute to shifting the paradigm for their administrative powers.

The critique to the dominant paradigm of the *Meroni* doctrine moves from the reflection that its application has not secured the growth of EU agencies' tasks and responsibilities to their legal recognition as centres of administrative powers. Reasons lie in the pragmatic approach that dominant EU administrative law has used to understand the reality of EU agencies. On the one hand, the non-binding nature and the advisory function of most of their powers, as well as the limited reach of their decision-making in highly technical matters, contributed to their tolerance as a 'light' form of administration in the silence of the Treaties. On the other hand, the *Meroni* doctrine filtered any chance to enhance their regulatory functions beyond the cooperation and the commitment to implementation of the relevant EU regulation. Going beyond this consolidated approach of EU administrative law, this study aimed to discuss the competence and the organisation of EU agencies as centres of administrative powers.

The *Meroni* doctrine aimed to respond to the key questions of the delegation of powers to EU agencies: the nature of the delegated power and its amenability to judicial review. Codifying lawful delegation on the *adagio* of the 'clearly defined executive powers', in EU administrative law the *Meroni* case has been interpreted as restricting EU agencies' powers to technical powers not involving discretionary evaluations of a political nature. In addition, the *Romano* case has ensured that EU agencies do not adopt 'acts having the force of law'. In the recent *ESMA Short Selling* case, the CJEU has revisited this consolidated interpretation of the *Meroni* doctrine in light of the new space acquired by EU agencies in the Lisbon Treaty, but it has not taken the opportunity to wipe out the ambiguities of the case law regarding the nature of EU agencies' powers and their entrenchment in the rule of law. The CJEU rather built upon the ambiguity of *Meroni*

[10] R van Gestel and T van Golen, 'Enforcement by the New European Supervisory Agencies: Quis Custodiet Ipsos Custodes?' in K Purnhagen and P Rott (eds), *Varieties of European Economic Law and Regulation, Liber Amicorum for Hans Micklitz* (Springer, 2014) 757, 760.

and *Romano* to find justification for EU agencies' powers under the current framework of the Treaties.

Chapter 1 of this study innovatively demonstrated that some continuity between the *ESMA Short Selling* case and the *Meroni* ruling exists, because the ambiguity of *Meroni* allows different interpretations of the nature of powers that can be delegated that may accommodate administrative powers. This study proposed that the dichotomy between political powers discretionary in nature, and technical powers neutral to the balance of interests, which emerged under the dominant *Meroni* paradigm, is a false myth derived from a specific narrative of EU administrative law at the beginning of the EU integration process. Conversely, the vague language of *Meroni* can effectively ground the legitimacy of delegation on the administrative nature of the powers that can be delegated and the existence of effective systems of political and legal accountability that ensure their entrenchment in the democratic principle and the rule of law. In addition, the *Romano* test concerning the nature of the powers has not proved to be sufficiently grounded in the CJEU's interpretation to preclude the ESMA from the adoption of acts with some normative content. This approach to the *Meroni* doctrine revitalises the key legal principles that govern the allocation of administrative powers, but dismisses its stalling interpretation. In doing this, my study is theoretically linked to those studies that 'question the functional determinist narratives of EU law' in the development of EU constitutional practices.[11] Rasmussen has particularly emphasised how European public law is the historical product of political actors and societal forces operating in the cause of integration and reinterpreted key cases of EU law in light of their historical momentum.[12] When discussing such cases, Rasmussen identified the leading role of the Legal Service of the High Authority and then the Commission since 1954 in the 'construction of a European legal order solid enough to constitute the foundation for European co-operation and policy-making'.[13] The centrality of the powers of the Commission in the development of the integration project also played a key role in the support of the strict interpretation of the *Meroni* doctrine.[14] Yataganas has strongly criticised the Commission's ambition to safeguard its own executive powers in the integration process as the political reason behind its opposition to the development of EU agencies.[15] There is some empirical evidence that the Legal Service has long

[11] See FG Nicola, 'Critical Legal Histories in EU Law' (2013) 28 *American University International Law Review* 1173, 1178.

[12] M Rasmussen, 'Rewriting the History of European Public Law: The New Contribution of Historians' (2013) 28 *American University International Law Review* 1187, 1202–11.

[13] M Rasmussen, 'Establishing a Constitutional Practice of European Law: The History of the Legal Service of the European Executive, 1952–65' (2012) 21 *Contemporary European History* 375, 378.

[14] See G Majone, 'The Credibility Crisis of Community Regulation' (2000) 38 *Journal of Common Market Studies* 273, 286; D Geradin and N Petit, 'The Development of Agencies at EU and National Levels: Conceptual Analysis and Proposal of Reform' (2004) 23 *Yearbook of European Law* 137, 148.

[15] XA Yantaganas, *Delegation of Regulatory Authority in the European Union: The Relevance of the American Model of Independent Agencies*, Jean Monnet Working Paper 3/2001 (2001), 20 and 26.

maintained an 'orthodox' approach to the *Meroni* doctrine, and only in the 2000s did it start to support the allocation of limited tasks to EU agencies, which then paved the way for the following agencification waves.[16]

My take is that at a different stage of European integration, the *Meroni* doctrine may accommodate a different legal interpretation based on the changed historical and legal reality of EU law. My critical approach to the consolidated interpretation of the *Meroni* doctrine also challenged the established categories of EU administrative law, which so far failed to characterise the core of administrative power and to shed light on the ambiguity of the EU case law. I have proposed a new taxonomy of administrative powers at the EU level, which makes it possible to investigate whether the allocation of substantive powers with regulatory impact on EU agencies is compatible with EU law and its constitutional principles without forcing EU agencies' powers into unrealistic dichotomy between political and technical powers.

My study moved from the recognition of the quasi-regulatory powers that some more recently-established EU agencies retain, and reconstructed the specific model of administrative governance that they represent. These agencies have been found to exercise some administrative discretion in the pursuit of their mission. By focusing on the nature of the powers that EU agencies exercise, Chapter 3 reversed the dominant idea that these are only technical in nature, as opposed to the political powers exercised by EU institutions, and detected their administrative nature. The analysis pointed out that as the centre of mediation of different interests, EU agencies make some choices regarding how to exercise the competence that EU legislation conferred upon them for the pursuit of a specific EU public interest. Their enforcement powers therefore express some marginal choices within the legal framework of priorities and hierarchy of rights and interests defined in the EU legislation, which qualify as administrative discretion. EU agencies contribute to implementing policies by taking some decisions on the best way to accomplish their goals concretely.

The model of governance emerging from EU agencies' administration revolves around the recognition of their specific competence as autonomous entities under EU law that complement direct administration by the Commission and support national competent authorities in the achievement of EU policy goals. In the words of Advocate General Jääskinen, they represent 'a midway solution between vesting implementing authority in either the Commission or the Council, on the one hand, or leaving it to the Member States, on the other'.[17] Their sector-specific

[16] Legal Service, *The Community Agencies*, Note of 20 February, 2001 SEC(2001)340. According to Yantaganas, this Note represents a welcomed evolution in the Commission's approach to EU agencies' competence; see Yantaganas, *Delegation of Regulatory Authority in the European Union* (n 15) 56. See also European Commission, *White Paper on Governance, Establishing a Framework for Decision-making Regulatory Agencies*, Report by Working Group 3a, SG-8597/01-EN (June 2001); Communication from the Commission, *European Governance: Better Lawmaking*, COM(2002)275 (5 June 2002) 5.

[17] C-270/12 *United Kingdom v Council and European Parliament* ECLI:EU:C:2014:18, Opinion of AG Jääskinen, para 86.

expertise is embedded in an administrative organisation which gives their powers the force to impose autonomously in the context of EU administrative regulation. Unlike European standardisation bodies, EU agencies are public entities that definitely operate in a system of public governance. Their standardisation practices do not need to be commissioned by the Commission in order to produce legal effects on the sector-specific administrations and operators, because other non-binding mechanisms in the realm of public enforcement apply. At the same time, the administrative nature of their organisation represents the structural limit to the reach of the powers they can be allocated. No chance, then, that EU agencies can set the priorities and the criteria for the exercise of their powers, as happens in other systems of administrative governance led by EU institutions, such as the Single Supervisory Mechanism (SSM) under the European Central Bank (ECB). As demonstrated in Chapter 3, the specific administrative character of their organisation and functions makes EU agencies an autonomous model of administration within the EU governance of the internal market.

A consequence of this approach is a change in the interpretation of the general principle of institutional balance between the EU public powers. Unlike under the dominant paradigm, institutional balance can be effectively construed on the recognition of the hierarchy in EU legal sources, rather than on the enumeration of institutional competences. In the absence of Treaties' provisions spelling out the powers of EU agencies, the operation of legal criteria in the distinction between the sources of law may make their activities compatible with the EU legal order. On the one hand, the EU legislature confers upon EU agencies powers that are administrative in nature and cannot innovate EU legislation. The establishment of priorities and criteria for the exercise of EU agencies' powers is the *condition sine qua non* for the lawful conferral of administrative powers. The principle of hierarchy in the legal sources therefore defines the limits of competence. On the other hand, the allocation of administrative tasks to EU agencies cannot intrude on the non-legislative and implementing powers assigned by the Treaties to the Commission under Articles 290 and 291 of the Treaty on the Functioning of the European Union (TFEU). The principle of competence hence distinguishes the reach of powers. This principle makes the differentiation of the EU executive legally possible, insofar as it does not involve the fragmentation of the Commission's powers, but allows the EU legislature to confer further administrative responsibilities on other administrative actors. Indirect confirmation of this possibility can be envisaged in the reference in the Treaties to the judicial review of acts of general application adopted, among others, by EU agencies. The application of this principle is, however, legally problematic. How the EU legislature decides which procedures shall be chosen to carry out a specific task remains legally unclear.

The underdevelopment of executive rule-making in the Treaties makes the distinction of administrative competences a thorny issue for EU administrative law. First, the legal criteria defining the allocation of delegated and implementing powers to the Commission are not crystal-clear in the black letter provisions of the

Treaties and legal scholarship has speculated about their interpretation.[18] Secondly, EU agencies may participate in the Commission's executive rule-making changing the balance of powers as designed in the Treaties. As seen, the ESAs' strong input in both regulatory and implementing technical standards adopted by the Commission makes them the factual owners of the regulatory process and pragmatically erodes the monopoly of the Commission on executive rule-making. Thirdly, the absence in the Treaties of a secure legal basis for EU agencies' competence makes the search for a general distinction prone to failure. Conversely, the absence of well-defined legal rules on competence makes it easy for inter-institutional conflicts to arise. Treaty amendments would certainly be key to solving the legal gap, but to be effective it should provide meaningful criteria to distinguish the respective competence of EU agencies and the Commission. Practice may suggest that expertise should play a key role in the allocation of responsibility to EU agencies and the pluralisation of the EU executive should be the functional result of organisational arrangements aimed at satisfying the growing complexity of the European Union. The choice between centralised implementation by the Commission and decentralised governance by EU agencies should therefore be regarded as matters of political convenience and functional opportunity based on the proportionality principle. The necessity of delegation, which emerged as a key requirement in the *Meroni* case, therefore encompasses the decision to entrust decisions to an EU agency, rather than the Commission, on the grounds of the evaluation of the substance of the subject matter, its level of technicality and its political impact.

Pragmatically speaking, EU agencies already participate in formulating internal market regulation along with the Commission's rule-making powers. However, this happens through legal stratagems of informal instruments that accommodate Kuhnian anomalies under the dominant paradigm of the *Meroni* doctrine. The enforcement of EU law therefore occurs through 'naming and shaming' mechanisms, and not through the traditional mechanisms of public enforcement. Scott particularly emphasised that these informal powers challenge EU administrative law, as they combine hard and soft measures blurring the allocation of legal responsibilities.[19] For instance, soft law harmonisation creates informal settings

[18] See P Craig, 'Delegated Acts, Implementing Acts and the New Comitology Regulation' (2011) 36 *European Law Review* 671; S Peers and M Costa, 'Accountability for Delegated and Implementing Acts' after the Treaty of Lisbon' (2012) 18 *European Law Journal* 427; P Craig, *The Lisbon Treaty: Law, Politics, and Treaty Reform*, 2nd edn (Oxford University Press, 2013) 260 ff; T Christiansen and M Dobbels, 'Non Legislative Rule Making after the Lisbon Treaty: Implementing the New System of Comitology and Delegated Acts' (2013) 19 *European Law Journal* 42; J Mendes, 'Delegated and Implementing Rule Making: Proceduralisation and Constitutional Design' (2013) 19 *European Law Journal* 22, 31–35.

[19] J Scott, 'In Legal Limbo: Post-Legislative Guidance as Challenge for European Administrative Law' (2011) 48 *Common Market Law Review* 329, 354; D Curtin and T Manucharyan, 'Legal Acts and Hierarchy of Norms in EU Law' in A Arnull and D Chalmers (eds), *The Oxford Handbook of European Union Law* (Oxford University Press, 2015) 103.

for compliance and commits national administrations and operators through incentives and reputational mechanisms. The analysed 'comply or explain' mechanism of the ESAs is particularly emblematic of the capability of legally non-binding instruments to generate a framework for compliance.

The proposed taxonomy of EU agencies' powers does not ignore this qualitative difference of EU agencies' enforcement powers, but it does not see it as a substantive obstacle to the characterisation of their administrative nature. Where informal instruments produce legal effects, effective accountability principles will operate and make administrative action controlled and justiciable. Informal powers may have been used to avoid direct encroachment on the Commission's powers and the preservation of the institutional balance, but the nature of the power should not be misunderstood because of the form in which powers are exercised. Disregarding the administrative nature of these instruments because of their formally non-binding character would mean ignoring the distinctiveness of EU agencies' administrative governance, constrained as it is by the *Meroni* doctrine and the internal market integration goals. Conversely, it is key to understanding the very substance of the power despite its informal character. Circumscribing administrative powers to the unilateral exercise of authoritative power, as happens in the national administrative laws, would severely affect the comprehension of the substance of EU agencies' action. The study thus identified an exercise of administrative powers in those implementing activities of EU agencies that are the result of complex evaluations and produce legal effects on third parties through formal or informal frameworks.

Accountability must therefore catch both formal and informal instruments of enforcement, so as to ensure that no abuse in the exercise of administrative powers occurs. Chapter 4 focused on the checks-and-balances that entrench EU agencies' governance. My argument is that a composite accountability regime, comprising organisational, procedural and judicial controls, must govern their action. So long as the variety of administrative proceedings may favour areas of administrative irresponsibility, sector-specific guarantees and procedures need to reflect a general approach aimed at securing the legality of administrative action.[20] As accountability instruments operate in a polyarchic governance, they also contribute to strengthening the bottom-up legitimacy of EU agencies, providing fora for participation and multiple control and offering justification to the exercise of enforcement powers under the governance approach.

The analysis of the current accountability regime revealed a fragile elaboration of the relationships between EU agencies and the actors of the governance; namely, EU institutions, Member States, the relevant sector-operating stakeholders. Notwithstanding the several accountability mechanisms in place, inconsistencies

[20] See also J Mendes, 'Executive Rule-making: Procedures in Between Constitutional Principles and Institutional Entrenchment' in C Harlow, P Leino and G della Cananea (eds), *Research Handbook on EU Administrative Law* (Elgar Publishing, 2017) 371, 372.

and margins of legal uncertainty emerge in the control over the complex system of administrative governance. This study aimed to point out the key legal principles that apply to EU agencies' governance and showed how their current application does not entrench EU agencies' administrative powers in a crystal-clear accountability framework. The reach of the autonomy structuring the organisation, the general principles of administrative proceedings and the justiciability of acts are issues that will disentangle the coherence of the accountability framework.

The more structured adherence of EU agencies' functioning to the general principles of impartiality and fairness is a necessary condition for the allocation of administrative powers. The proposal of an EU administrative procedural law is particularly welcomed as it would remove from the EU agencies' appraisal the selection of the interests that are to be protected in the administrative proceedings and set the minimum legal guarantees that will necessarily govern EU agencies' action. Insofar as the principles of impartiality and fairness in the organisation and functioning are not made completely clear, EU agencies' powers may come into conflict with the rule of law and endanger their compatibility with the democratic principle. This also affects the compliance of EU agencies' action with the second limb on which the *Meroni* doctrine relies; that is, the existence of an accountability framework that ensures the institutional and procedural compatibility of delegation with the rule of law and the democratic principle.

From this standpoint, my approach to the constitutional principles of the *Meroni* doctrine values not only the existence of judicial review as a guarantee against the arbitrary exercise of power, but also the existence of a wider accountability system that justifies and constrains the administrative power. This reading emphasises aspects that are not considered in the *Meroni* case law and that are only implicitly advanced in the more recent *ESMA Short Selling* case. In the latter, the CJEU expressly reiterated the statements in the *Meroni* case on the need to subject EU agencies' powers to judicial review in light of objective criteria, but it also mentioned other relevant circumstances that indirectly substantiate the importance of the accountability framework. The CJEU distinguished the significance of EU agencies' organisation as being a 'European Union entity, created by the EU legislature', but it did not expressly attach legal effects to this status.[21] In addition, the reconstruction of the boundaries and conditions for the exercise of the power explicitly pointed towards qualifying its nature, but only indirectly pinpointed the relevant accountability framework. The aspects that are implicit in the case law need to emerge distinctly in the law to ensure that EU agencies' powers are tenable under the current EU legal order.

My reassessment of the compatibility of EU agencies' powers with the *Meroni* doctrine can therefore only reach provisional conclusions. Even though EU agencies' discretionary powers may be compatible with the limits to delegation set out in *Meroni*, the general accountability regime that currently surrounds

[21] C-270/12 *United Kingdom v Council and European Parliament* (n 17) para 43.

the operation of EU agencies does not seem to be able to consistently sustain the allocation of significant regulatory powers. Even the most powerful agencies are not structured as independent regulators. The illustrated cases of the EASA and the ESAs show that these agencies combine the functioning and accountability mechanisms of bodies that informally coordinate the implementation of sector-specific internal market policies with the autonomous exercise of quasi-regulatory powers that have some potential to create more powerful regulators. They are the evidence of the compromises that characterise their institution.

This may suggest a reasoned approach to EU agencies' governance. Any further allocation of administrative powers should require partial organisational reform and the introduction of ad hoc guarantees that hold and entrench their (regulatory) powers. Whereas the model of EU agencies happens to move towards the model of independent authorities, a stronger accountability framework will support such an institutional and functional change. Clearly the amendment of the Treaties with specific provisions clarifying the boundaries of EU agencies' administrative action would be the perfect scenario able to produce the Kuhnian paradigm shift. It would dissolve the issue of their legitimacy as administrative organisations, and could design the institutional balance of EU administrative tasks, as well as provide some key aspects of EU agencies' accountability framework. However, this legal revolution might not be feasible in the short term and it might not be sufficient to circumscribe the reach and the limits of EU agencies' action.[22]

A coherent system of procedural rights and remedies would structure the exercise of such power, and EU legislation would be the most attractive source of law. The disentanglement of the legal issues would have strong effects on the polyarchic governance through EU agencies. It would definitely put the dominant interpretation of the *Meroni* doctrine to rest, and it would make room for the development of administrative regulation in conformity with the rule of law and the democratic principle. The new legal framework would revolutionise the application of the dominant paradigm and may also bring about a shift of paradigm. Where administrative discretion is kept within the boundaries of legality through a solid accountability framework, the fear of EU agencies' powers may not be legally justified.

Such a legal change might structurally affect the function of EU agencies in the internal market and the model of governance. From a cooperation role, they would be able to acquire stronger regulatory tasks and may ultimately approximate to the status of independent regulators in the internal market. As soon as they are conferred powers to adopt sector-specific acts of general application, they would

[22] See also D Geradin, 'The Development of European Regulatory Agencies: Lessons from the American Experience' in D Geradin, R Muñoz and N Petit (eds), *Regulation Through Agencies in the EU: A New Paradigm of European Governance* (Elgar Publishing, 2005) 215, 221, who considered that a Treaty amendment may not be sufficient to recognise the discretionary powers of EU agencies.

be legally able to govern internal market integration from a hierarchical position. The system of administrative governance would therefore include stronger hierarchical elements in the relationships between EU agencies, on the one hand, and national competent authorities and market operators, on the other hand. Their enhanced powers would also reduce the role of the Commission and they might acquire a higher degree of autonomy, if not an independent status.

This institutional innovation is not remote. Legal scholarship has recognised that the *ESMA Short Selling* case has opened a new era in EU agencification. The epistemic community is therefore prepared to accept changes in the governance through EU agencies. Institutional innovation, however, carries a deeper constitutional change in the conception of EU agencies' tasks and responsibilities, which more broadly concerns the EU administrative identity. Constitutional change requires a more general understanding of the role of EU agencies in the wider context of the EU legal order. The increasing complexity of the reality substantiates the sophistication of administrative powers, but requires adequate models of legality that justify and control administrative phenomena. The search for a new paradigm must therefore confront the conception of law and democracy that the EU legal order aims to embrace.

The search for a democratic justification of administrative powers questions the foundations of the relationship between EU law and society. The non-majoritarian character of the administration makes its democratic legitimacy necessarily weak, but the challenge is how to make the discontinuity acceptable for democratic systems. Clearly, this is not a problem peculiar to the EU legal order, but it also applies to states and their conception of public administration. However, in the case of the EU it resounds with the 'original sin' of the democratic deficit of the EU[23] and its more recent disconnection from the popular sentiments on the wave of multiple crises.[24] The underlying risk in advancing administrative competence is that in a context where output legitimacy is recessive, the conferral of stronger administrative powers upon EU agencies may further undermine the state of EU input legitimacy. This theoretical approach, however, under-estimates the functional benefits that increased administrative integration may generate in

[23] See JHH Weiler, 'The Community System: The Dual Character of Supranationalism' (1982) 1 *Yearbook of European Law* 267; JHH Weiler, 'The Transformation of Europe' (1991) 100 *Yale Law Journal* 2403; D Grimm, 'Does Europe Need a Constitution?' (1995) 1 *European Law Journal* 282; J Habermas, 'Remarks on Dieter Grimm's "Does Europe Need a Constitution?"' (1995) 1 *European Law Journal* 303; G Majone, *The European Community as a Regulatory State* (Nijhoff, 1995); G Majone, *Regulating Europe* (Routledge, 1996); G Majone, 'Europe's 'Democratic Deficit': The Question of Standards' (1998) 4 *European Law Journal* 5; A Moravcsik, *The Choice for Europe: Social Purpose and State Power from Messina to Maastricht* (Cornell University Press, 1998).

[24] See L Papadopoulou, I Pernice and JHH Weiler (eds), *Legitimacy Issues of the European Union in the Face of Crisis* (Hart Publishing, 2017); M Simoncini and G Straetmans (eds), 'Sixty Years Later. Rethinking Competing Paradigms for EU Law in Times of Crisis' (2017) 9 *Perspectives on Federalism*, Special Issue no 2.

the internal market regulation, especially of network services,[25] as well as in the management of network crises.[26]

The search for a suitable model of legality that accommodates democratic concerns can therefore be conveniently narrowed down to the issue of how administrative power can be defined and limited in a democratic legal order. This means discussing EU 'administrative constitutionalism'; that is, the legal culture and the constitutional structure that govern administrative action.[27] Fisher proposed two different paradigms that may illustrate to what extent EU agencies can express value judgements in the process of interpreting statutes. The 'rational-instrumental' approach is based on the idea of 'transmission-belt' administration entrusted with a series of tasks that are regulated by the legislative scheme as much as possible and keep discretion to a minimum; whereas the 'deliberative-constitutive' model confers on the administration substantive discretion to tailor the implementation of the legislation.[28] The first paradigm embraces a model of legality seriously concerned about the democratic legitimacy of administrative action, whereas the second is more pragmatically concerned with effective problem-solving.

The question is, what model of administrative constitutionalism is the EU legal order prepared to accept? So far, EU administrative law under the specific narrative of the *Meroni* doctrine has functionally (and passively) embraced the 'rational-instrumental' approach to identify EU agencies' tasks. The growth of EU agencies' powers, however, may suggest that it is time to engage in a wider reflection on the sustainability of such a model. The identification of the discretionary content of EU agencies' powers does not affect by itself the dominance of that model, as the quantity of administrative discretion conferred on EU agencies is still limited. However, the qualitative recognition of such discretion beyond the dichotomy between political and technical powers opens the discussion on the deliberation process for (hard or soft) administrative decisions. This offers a significant chance to elaborate on the 'deliberative-constitutive' paradigm and its limits.

The findings of this study suggest that the current reality of EU administrative constitutionalism is an unfortunate compromise between the two models

[25] Geradin and Petit, 'The Development of Agencies at EU and National Levels' (n 14) 145–47; J Pelkmans and A Renda, 'Single eComms Market? No Such Thing …' (2011) 2 *Communications and Strategies* 21; J Pelkmans, *The Case for 'More Single Market'*, CEPS Policy Brief no 234 (2011), available at http://aei.pitt.edu/29749/1/No%20234%20JP%20on%20EU%20Single%20Market.pdf; J Pelkmans and G Luchetta, *Enjoying a Single Market for Network Industries?*, Notre Europe Studies and Report no 9 (2013), available at www.notre-europe.eu/media/singlemarketnetworkindustries-pelkmansluchetta-ne-jdi-feb13.pdf?pdf=ok.

[26] On the case of European aviation and the volcanic ash crisis see M Simoncini, 'Governing Air Traffic Management in the Single European Sky: The Search for Possible Solutions to Safety Issues' (2013) 38 *European Law Review* 209, 215–16; on the case of the financial crisis and the financial markets institutional reforms, see N Moloney, *EU Securities and Financial Markets Regulation*, 3rd edn (Oxford University Press, 2014) 30–36.

[27] See E Fisher, *Risk Regulation and Administrative Constitutionalism* (Hart Publishing, 2007) 35.

[28] Ibid 28–32.

of administration that Fisher has identified, as it aims to reduce the necessary administrative balance of interests in light of the legislative goals in the absence of a legal culture that stands for the manifest acknowledgement of the democratic compatibility of EU agencies' powers. Freezing the development of EU agencies' regulatory powers, the dominant paradigm of the *Meroni* doctrine, has blocked the elaboration of the EU administrative discourse. The pragmatic result is a system of governance by uncertainty, where the EU agencies have been vested with limited powers with no clear foundation in EU constitutionalism. By elaborating on the nature of such powers and the accountability framework for their lawful exercise, this study aimed to contribute to the development of a legal culture that does not fear the theoretical discussion of the factual growth of EU agencies' responsibilities and tasks beyond their original model. I have asserted that it is time to abandon the anachronistic pattern set by the consolidated reading of the *Meroni* doctrine and engage in the discussion of administrative regulation by EU agencies even in the weak framework of the Treaties. There will probably be a 'long and winding road' to follow before arriving at a paradigm shift that accepts the regulatory powers of EU agencies, but it is worth doing to give a more structured answer to the growth of EU agencies and, more generally, to understand the potential and the limits to EU administrative integration.

Bibliography

Albanese, A, 'Il ruolo del principio di proporzionalità nel rapporto fra amministrazione e amministrati' (2016) 37 *Istituzioni del Federalismo* 697.

Alcubilla, RG and Del Pozo, JR, *Credit Rating Agencies on the Watch List* (Oxford University Press, 2012).

Amiel, H, 'L'examen particulier des circonstances: contribution à l'étude du contrôle du pouvoir discrétionnaire par le juge administratif français dans la jurisprudence récente' (1979) *Revue de droit prospectif* 25.

Azoulai, L, 'Le principe de bonne administration' in J-B Auby and J Dutheil de la Rochère (eds), *Droit administratif européen* (Bruylant, 2007) 493.

Bachelet, V, *L'attività tecnica della pubblica amministrazione* (Giuffrè, 1967).

Bachof, O, 'Beurteilungsspielraum, Ermessen und unbestimmter Rechtsbegriff im Verwaltungsrecht' (1955) *Juristenzeitung* 97.

—— *Verfassungsrecht, Verwaltungsrecht, Verfahrensrecht in der Rechtsprechung des Bundesverwaltungsgerichts* (Mohr Siebeck 1964) vol I.

Baldwin, R, Cave, M and Lodge, M, *Understanding Regulation*, 2nd edn (Oxford University Press, 2011).

Barbier de La Serre, E, 'Procedural Justice in the European Community Case-law Concerning the Rights of the Defence: Essentialist and Instrumental Trends' (2006) *European Public Law* 225.

Benedetti, A, *Certezza pubblica e "certezze private". Poteri pubblici e certificazioni di mercato* (Giuffrè, 2010).

Bergström, CF, 'Introduction' in CF Bergström and D Ritleng (eds), *Rulemaking by the European Commission* (Oxford University Press, 2016) 1.

Black, J, 'Paradoxes and Failures: "New Governance" Techniques and the Financial Crisis' (2012) 75 *Modern Law Review* 1037.

Bourgois, JP, *L'erreur manifeste d'appréciation: la décision administrative, le juge et la force de l'évidence* (L'Espace juridique, 1988).

Bovens, M, 'Analysing and Assessing Accountability: A Conceptual Framework' (2007) 13 *European Law Journal* 447.

Brescia Morra, C, 'The Evolution of the Banking Supervision Architecture in Europe' in R Virzo and I Ingrallo (eds), *Evolutions in the Law of International Organizations* (Brill Nijhoff, 2015) 224.

—— 'The Administrative and Judicial Review of Decisions of the ECB in the Supervisory Field' in R D'Ambrosio (ed), *Scritti sull'Unione Bancaria* (Banca d'Italia, Quaderni di Ricerca Giuridica della Consulenza Legale, 2016) 120.

Brescia Morra, C, Smits, R and Magliari, A, 'The Administrative Board of Review of the European Central Bank: Experience After 2 Years' (2017) 18 *European Business Organisation Law Review* 567.

Brüggemeier, G, *Common Principles of Tort Law: A Pre-Statement of Law* (BIICL, 2004).

Buess, M, 'European Union Agencies and their Management Boards: An Assessment of Accountability and Demoi-cratic Legitimacy' (2015) 22 *Journal of European Public Policy* 94.

Bullinger, M, 'Le pouvoir discrétionnaire de l'administration publique fédérale d'Allemagne' (1988) 4 *Revue Francaise de Droit Administratif* 684.
Burrow, N and Hiram, H, 'Legal Articulation of Policy in the EC' in T Daintith (ed), *Implementing EC Law in the UK: Structures for Indirect Rule* (Wiley, 1995) 29.
Busuioc, M, 'European Agencies and their Boards: Promises and Pitfalls of Accountability Beyond Design' (2012) 19 *Journal of European Policy* 719.
—— 'Rule-making by the European Financial Supervisory Authorities: Walking a Tight Rope' (2013) 19 *European Law Journal* 111.
—— *European Agencies: Law and Practices of Accountability* (Oxford University Press, 2013).
Byrne, D, 'The Genesis of EFSA and the First 10 Years of EU Food Law' in A Alemanno and S Gabbi (eds), *Foundations of EU Law and Policy: Ten Years of the European Food Safety Authority* (Routledge, 2014) 17.
Camus, G, 'Réflexions sur le détournement de procédure' (1966) *Revue du Droit Public* 65.
Caranta, R, 'On Discretion' in S Prechal and B van Roermund (eds), *The Coherence of EU Law: The Search for Unity in Divergent Concepts* (Oxford University Press, 2008) 185.
Carmassi, J, Luchetti, E and Micossi, S, *Overcoming Too-Big-to-Fail: A Regulatory Framework to Limit Moral Hazard and Free Riding in the Financial Sector, Report of the CEPS-ASSONIME Task Force on Bank Crisis Resolution* (CEPS, 2010).
Cassatella, A, 'Appeals Before the European Aviation Safety Agency' in B Marchetti (ed), *Administrative Remedies in the European Union: The Emergence of a Quasi-Judicial Administration* (Giappichelli, 2017) 21.
Cassese, S, 'Modern Kings: Non-elected Bodies in Modern Democracies', paper presented at the CREA Conference, Ancienne École Polytechnique Paris, 1998.
—— 'European Administrative Proceedings' (2004) 68 *Law and Contemporary Problems* 21.
Chamon, M, 'EU Agencies Between *Meroni* and *Romano* or the Devil and the Deep Blue Sea' (2011) 48 *Common Market Law Review* 1055.
—— 'EU Risk Regulators and EU Procedural Law' (2014) 5 *European Journal of Risk Regulation* 324.
—— 'The Empowerment of Agencies under the Meroni Doctrine and Article 114 TFEU: Comment on United Kingdom v. Parliament and Council (Short Selling) and the Proposed Single Resolution Mechanism' (2014) *European Law Review* 380.
—— 'The Institutional Balance, an Ill-Fated Principle of EU Law?' (2015) *European Public Law* 371.
—— *EU Agencies: Legal and Political Limits to the Transformation of the EU Administration* (Oxford University Press, 2016).
Chapus, R, *Droit administratif général* (Montchrestien, 1988).
Chirulli, P and De Lucia, L, 'Specialised Adjudication in the EU Administrative Law: The Boards of Appeal of EU Agencies' (2015) 40 *European Law Review* 832.
Chiti, E, *Le agenzie europee. Unità e decentramento nelle amministrazioni comunitarie* (Cedam, 2002).
—— 'Administrative Proceedings Involving European Agencies' (2004) 68 *Law and Contemporary Problems* 219.
—— 'La disciplina procedurale della regolazione' (2004) 54 *Rivista Trimestrale di Diritto Pubblico* 679.
—— 'An Important Part of the EU Institutional Machinery: Features, Problems and Perspectives of European Agencies' (2009) 46 *Common Market Law Review* 1395.

—— 'L'accountability delle reti di autorità amministrative dell'Unione Europea' (2012) *Rivista Italiana di Diritto Pubblico Comunitario* 29.

—— 'European Agencies' Rulemaking: Powers, Procedures and Assessment' (2013) 19 *European Law Journal* 93.

—— 'In the Aftermath of the Crisis: The EU Administrative System Between Impediments and Momentum' (2015) 17 *Cambridge Yearbook of European Legal Studies* 311.

—— 'Is EU Administrative Law Failing in Some of Its Crucial Tasks?' (2016) 22 *European Law Journal* 576.

Chiti, MP, 'The Role of the European Court of Justice in the Development of General Principles and their Possible Codification' (1995) *Rivista Italiana di Diritto Pubblico Comunitario* 661.

—— 'Lo spazio giuridico europeo' (2001) *Rivista Italiana di Diritto Pubblico Comunitario* 979.

—— *Diritto Amministrativo Europeo*, 3rd edn (Giuffrè, 2008) 179–82.

—— 'Towards a New EU Regulation on Administrative Procedure?' (2011) 21 *Rivista Italiana di Diritto Pubblico Comunitario* 1.

—— 'Lo Spazio amministrativo europeo' in MP Chiti and A Natalini (eds), *Lo spazio amministrativo europeo. Le pubbliche amministrazioni dopo il Trattato di Lisbona* (Il Mulino, 2012) 1.

—— 'Il sistema delle fonti nella nuova disciplina dei contratti pubblici' (2016) *Giornale di Diritto Amministrativo* 436.

Christiansen, T and Dobbels, M, 'Non Legislative Rule Making after the Lisbon Treaty: Implementing the New System of Comitology and Delegated Acts' (2013) 19 *European Law Journal* 42.

Cintioli, F, 'Il sindacato del giudice amministrativo sulle linee guida, sui pareri c.d. precontenzioso e sulle raccomandazioni di ANAC' (2017) *Diritto Processuale Amministrativo* 381.

Clarich, M, 'Il riesame amministrativo delle decisioni della Banca Centrale Europea' (2015) *Rivista Italiana di Diritto Pubblico Comunitario* 1513.

Cohen-Eliya, M and Porat, I, 'Proportionality and the Culture of Justification' (2011) 59 *American Journal of Comparative Law* 463.

Coman-Kund, F, 'The Future EASA Regulation: Enhancing the Union's Aviation Safety System through "Agencification"?', *EU TARN Blog* (26 October 2017), available at http://eutarn.blogactiv.eu/2017/10/26/the-future-easa-regulation-enhancing-the-unions-aviation-safety-system-through-agencification/.

Conway, G, 'Recovering a Separation of Powers in the European Union' (2011) 17 *European Law Journal* 304.

Craig, P, 'Unreasonableness and Proportionality in UK Law' in E Ellis (ed), *The Principle of Proportionality in the Laws of Europe* (Hart Publishing, 1999) 85.

—— *Administrative Law* (Sweet & Maxwell, 2008).

—— 'Delegated Acts, Implementing Acts and the New Comitology Regulation' (2011) 36 *European Law Review* 671.

—— *EU Administrative Law*, 2nd edn (Oxford University Press, 2012).

—— 'The Stability, Coordination and Governance Treaty: Principle, Politics and Pragmatism' (2012) 37 *European Law Review* 231.

—— *The Lisbon Treaty: Law, Politics, and Treaty Reform*, 2nd edn (Oxford University Press, 2013).

—— 'A General Law on Administrative Procedure, Legislative Competence and Judicial Competence' (2013) 19 *European Public Law* 503.
—— '"Pringle" and Use of EU Institutions Outside the EU Legal Framework: Foundations, Procedure and Substance' (2013) 9 *European Constitutional Law Review* 263.
—— *EU Administrative Law*, 3rd edn (Oxford University Press, 2015).
—— *EU Law: Texts, Cases and Materials*, 6th edn (Oxford University Press, 2015).
—— *UK, EU and Global Administrative Law* (Cambridge University Press, 2015).
—— 'Comitology, Rulemaking and the Lisbon Settlement. Tensions and Strains' in CF Bergström and D Ritleng (eds), *Rulemaking by the European Commission* (Oxford University Press, 2016) 173.
—— 'Law, Fact and Discretion in the UK, EU and the USA', *La chaire, Mutations de l'Action Publique et du Droit public*, available at www.sciencespo.fr/chaire-madp/sites/sciencespo.fr.chaire-madp/files/paul_craig.pdf.
Craig, P, Hofmann, H, Schneider, J-P and Ziller, J (eds), *ReNEUAL Model Rules on EU Administrative Procedure* (Oxford University Press, 2017).
Curtin, D, 'Holding (Quasi-)Autonomous EU Administrative Actors to Public Account' (2007) 13 *European Law Journal* 523.
Curtin, D and Manucharyan, T, 'Legal Acts and Hierarchy of Norms in EU Law' in A Arnull and D Chalmers (eds), *The Oxford Handbook of European Union Law* (Oxford University Press, 2015) 103.
Daelemans, C, 'The Legitimacy and Quality of European Standards: The Legitimation of Delegation of Powers and Standard-Setting Procedures' in C Joerges, KH Ladeur and E Vos (eds), *Integrating Scientific Expertise into Regulatory Decision-Making: National Traditions and European Innovations* (Nomos Verlagsgesellschaft, 1997) 257.
de Búrca, G, 'The Principle of Proportionality and its Application in EC Law' (1993) 13 *Yearbook of European Law* 105.
—— 'Institutional Development of the EU: A Constitutional Analysis' in P Craig and G de Búrca (eds), *The Evolution of EU Law* (Oxford University Press, 1999) 55.
de Pretis, D, *Valutazione amministrativa e discrezionalità tecnica* (Cedam, 1995).
De Vergottini, G, 'Note sugli atti normativi e amministrativi dell'ordinamento comunitario europeo' (1963) *Rivista Trimestrale di Diritto Pubblico* 887.
Dehousse, R, 'Regulation by Networks in the European Community: The Role of European Agencies' (1997) 4 *Journal of European Public Policy* 246.
—— 'Misfits: EU Law and the Transformation of European Governance' in C Joerges and R Dehousse (eds), *Good Governance in Europe's Integrated Market* (Oxford University Press, 2002) 207.
della Cananea, G, 'The European Union's Mixed Administrative Proceedings' (2004) 68 *Law and Contemporary Problems* 197.
Deodato, C, 'Nuove riflessioni sull'intensità del sindacato del giudice amministrativo. *Il caso delle linee guida dell'ANAC*' (2017) *Federalismi.it*, available at www.federalismi.it/nv14/articolo-documento.cfm?Artid=33244&content=Nuove+riflessioni+sull%27intensit%C3%A0+del+sindacato+del+giudice+amministrativo&content_author=%3Cb%3ECarlo+Deodato%3C/b%3E.
Di Noia, C and Gargantini, M, 'Unleashing the European Securities and Markets Authority: Governance and Accountability after the ECJ Decision on Short Selling Regulation (Case 270/12)' (2014) 15 *European Business Organization Law Review* 1.
Ederveen, S, Gelauff, G and Pelkmans, J, 'Assessing Subsidiarity' in G Gelauff, I Grilo and A Lejour (eds), *Subsidiarity and Economic Reform in Europe* (Springer, 2008) 19.

Egan, M, 'Regulatory Strategies, Delegation and European Market Integration' (1998) 5 *Journal of European Policy* 485.
Egeberg, M, Trondal, J and Vestlund, NM, 'The Quest for Order: Unravelling the Relationship Between the European Commission and European Union Agencies' (2015) 22 *Journal of European Public Policy* 609.
Estella, A, *The EU Principle of Subsidiarity and its Critique* (Oxford University Press, 2002).
Everson, M and Vos, E, *European Agencies: What about the Institutional Balance?*, Maastricht Working Papers 4/2014 (2014).
Fabbrini, F, 'A Principle in Need of Renewal? The Euro-Crisis and the Principle of Institutional Balance' (2016) 50 *Cahiers de Droit Européen* 285.
Falcon, G, 'Qualche sottolineatura in tema di principi generali del diritto dell'Unione europea' (2017) 27 *Rivista Italiana di Diritto Pubblico Comunitario* 364.
Falke, J, 'Achievements and Unresolved Problems of European Standardization: The Ingenuity of Practice and the Queries of Lawyers' in C Joerges, KH Ladeur and E Vos (eds), *Integrating Scientific Expertise into Regulatory Decision-Making: National Traditions and European Innovations* (Nomos Verlagsgesellschaft, 1997) 187.
Fernandez-Maublanc, L, 'Le prétendu déclin du détournement de pouvoir' in *Études offertes à Jean-Marie Auby* (Dalloz, 1992) 239.
Ferran, E and Babis, V, *The European Single Supervisory Mechanism*, University of Cambridge Legal Studies Research Paper Series 10/2013 (2013).
Ferran, E, *European Banking Union: Imperfect, But It Can Work*, University of Cambridge Legal Studies Research Paper Series 30/2014 (2014).
Fisher, E, 'The European Union in the Age of Accountability' (2004) 24 *Oxford Journal of Legal Studies* 495.
—— *Risk Regulation and Administrative Constitutionalism* (Hart Publishing, 2007).
Franchini, C, *Amministrazione italiana e amministrazione comunitaria. La coamministrazione nei settori di interesse comunitario*, 2nd edn (Cedam, 1993).
—— 'Le fasi e i caratteri del processo evolutivo dell'organizzazione amministrativa europea' (2017) 27 *Rivista Italiana di Diritto Pubblico Comunitario* 375.
Fromont, M, 'Le principe de proportionnalité' (1995) *AJDA* 156.
Galetta, DU, *Principio di proporzionalità e sindacato giurisdizionale nel diritto amministrativo* (Giuffrè, 1998).
—— 'Attività e procedimento nel diritto amministrativo europeo, anche alla luce della risoluzione del Parlamento europeo sulla disciplina del procedimento per istituzioni, organi ed organismi dell'Unione europea' (2017) *Rivista Italiana di Diritto Pubblico Comunitario* 391.
Galetta, DU, Hofmann, HCH, Mir Puigpelat, O and Ziller, J, 'Context and Legal Elements of a Proposal for a Regulation on the Administrative Procedure of the European Union's Institutions, Bodies, Officies and Agencies' (2016) 26 *Rivista Italiana di Diritto Pubblico Comunitario* 313.
Gaudemet, Y, *Droit Administratif*, 21st edn (LGDJ, 2015).
Geradin, D, 'The Development of European Regulatory Agencies: What the EU Should Learn from the American Experience' (2004) 11 *Columbia Journal of European Law* 1.
—— 'The Development of European Regulatory Agencies: Lessons from the American Experience' in D Geradin, R Muñoz and N Petit (eds), *Regulation Through Agencies in the EU: A New Paradigm of European Governance* (Elgar Publishing, 2005) 215.
Geradin, D and Petit, N, 'The Development of Agencies at EU and National Levels: Conceptual Analysis and Proposal of Reform' (2004) 23 *Yearbook of European Law* 137.

Giannini, MS, *Lezioni di diritto amministrativo* (Giuffrè, 1950).
—— *Diritto amministrativo*, 3rd edn (Giuffrè, 1993) vol 1.
—— *Il potere discrezionale della pubblica amministrazione* (Giuffrè, 1993).
—— 'Potere di ordinanza e atti necessitati' in MS Giannini, *Scritti 1939–1948* (2 vol, Giuffrè, 2002).
—— 'Le ordinanze dispositive della proprietà privata (art. 7 L. 20 marzo 1865, n. 2248, All. E)' in MS Giannini, *Scritti 1949–1954* (3 vol, Giuffrè, 2003).
Giglioni, F, 'The European Banking Union as a New Model of Administrative Integration?' in E Chiti and G Vesperini (eds), *The Administrative Architecture of Financial Integration: Institutional Design, Legal Issues, Perspectives* (Il Mulino, 2015) 123.
Gilardi, F, *Delegation in the Regulatory State: Independent Agencies in Western Europe* (Elgar Publishing, 2008).
Griller, S and Orator, A, 'Everything Under Control? The "Way Forward" for European Agencies in the Footsteps of the *Meroni* Doctrine' (2010) 35 *European Law Review* 3.
Grimm, D, 'Does Europe Need a Constitution?' (1995) 1 *European Law Journal* 282.
Groenleer, MLP, *The Autonomy of European Union Agencies: A Comparative Study of Institutional Development* (Eburon, 2009).
Guillermin, G, 'Le principe de l'équilibre institutionnel dans la jurisprudence de la Cour de justice des Communautés européennes' (1992) 119 *Journal de Droit International* 319.
Habermas, J, 'Remarks on Dieter Grimm's "Does Europe Need a Constitution?"' (1995) 1 *European Law Journal* 303.
Hancher, L and Winters, BM, *The EU Winter Package, Briefing Paper* (Allen & Overy LLP, February 2017).
Harlow, C, 'Codification of EC Administrative Procedures? Fitting the Foot to the Shoe or the Shoe to the Foot' (1996) 2 *European Law Journal* 3.
Harlow, C and Rawlings, R, *Process and Procedure in EU Administration* (Hart Publishing, 2014).
Hofmann, HCH, 'Agency Design in the European Union' (2010) 28 *Windsor Yearbook of Access to Justice* 309.
Hofmann, HCH and Morini, A, 'Constitutional Aspects of the Pluralisation of the EU Executive Through "Agencification"' (2012) 37 *European Law Review* 419.
Hofmann, HCH, Rowe, GC and Türk, AH, *Administrative Law and Policy of the European Union* (Oxford University Press, 2011).
Hofmann, HCH and Türk, AH, *Legal Challenges in EU Administrative Law: Towards an Integrated Administration* (Elgar Publishing, 2009).
Hoffmann, LH, Lord, 'The Influence of the European Principle of Proportionality upon UK Law' in E Ellis (ed), *The Principle of Proportionality in the Laws of Europe* (Hart Publishing, 1999) 107.
House of Commons, *EU Agencies and Post Brexit Options*, Briefing Paper no 7957 (2017).
Jacqué, J-P, 'The Principle of Institutional Balance' (2004) 41 *Common Market Law Review* 383.
—— 'The Evolution of the Approach to Executive Rulemaking in the EU' in CF Bergström and D Ritleng (eds), *Rulemaking by the European Commission* (Oxford University Press, 2016) 21.
Jellinek, W, *Gesetz, Gesetzesanwendung und Zweckmäßigkeitserwägung* (Mohr Siebeck, 1913).

Joerges, C, Schepel, H and Vos, E, *The Law's Problems with the Involvement of Non-Governmental Actors in Europe's Legislative Process: The Case of Standadardisation under the 'New Approach'*, EUI Working Paper Law no 99/9 (1999).

Johnson, SM, 'Ossification's Demise: An Empirical Analysis of EPA Rulemaking from 2001–2005' (2008) 38 *Environmental Law* 767.

Jowell, J, 'The Two Faces of Proportionality', paper delivered at the Institute of Advanced Legal Studies, London, 23 November 2007.

Kańska, K, 'Towards Administrative Human Rights in the EU: Impact of the Charter of Fundamental Rights' (2004) 10 *European Law Journal* 296.

Kelemen, RD and Tarrant, AD, 'The Political Foundations of the Eurocracy' (2011) 34 *West European Politics* 922.

Kornprobst, B, 'L'erreur manifeste' (1965) *Recueil Dalloz* 121.

Krapohl, S, 'Credible Commitment in Non-Independent Regulatory Agencies: A Comparative Analysis of the European Agencies for Pharmaceuticals and Foodstuffs' (2004) 10 *European Law Journal* 518.

Kreher, A, 'Agencies in the European Community: A Step Towards Administrative Integration in Europe' (1997) 4 *Journal of European Public Policy* 225.

Kuhn, TS, *The Structure of Scientific Revolutions*, 2nd edn (International Encyclopedia of Unified Science, University of Chicago Press, 1962).

Kühnert, H, Böhler, P and Polster, S, 'A Tale of Delegation and Power: ACER and the Dichotomy of the Non-Delegation Doctrine and the Creation of a Genuine Internal Market in Electricity' (2017) 1 *European Competition and Regulatory Law Review* 47.

Kumm, M, 'Constitutionalising Subsidiarity in Integrated Markets: The Case of Tobacco Regulation in the European Union' (2006) 12 *European Law Journal* 503.

La Spina, A and Majone, G, *Lo Stato regolatore* (Il Mulino, 2000).

Lagasse, B, *L'erreur manifeste d'appréciation en droit administratif* (Bruylant, 1986).

Lamandini, M, 'The ESAs' Board of Appeal as a Blueprint for the Quasi-Judicial Review of European Financial Supervision' (2014) 11 *European Company Law* 290.

Lastra, RM, 'Banking Union and Single Market: Conflict or Companionship?' (2013) 36 *Fordham International Law Journal* 1190.

Lauwaars, RH, 'Auxiliary Organs and Agencies in the E.E.C.' (1979) *Common Market Law Review* 365.

Lavrjissen S and Hancher L, 'Networks on Track: From European Regulatory Networks to European Regulatory "Network Agencies"' (2009) 36 *Legal Issues of European Integration* 23.

Lavrijssen, S and Ottow, A, 'Independent Supervisory Authorities: A Fragile Concept' (2012) 39 *Legal Issues of Economic Integration* 419.

Ledda, F, 'Potere, tecnica e sindacato giudiziario' (1983) *Diritto Processuale Amministrativo* 371.

Lemasurier, J, 'La preuve dans le détournement de pouvoir' (1959) *Revue du Droit Public* 36.

Lenaerts, K, 'Some Reflections on the Separation of Powers in the European Community' (1991) *Common Market Law Review* 11.

—— 'Regulating the Regulatory Process: "Delegation of Powers" in the European Community' (1993) *European Law Review* 23.

—— '"In the Union We Trust": Trust-enhancing Principles of Community Law' (2004) 41 *Common Market Law Review* 317.

Lenaerts, K and Verhoeven, A, 'Institutional Balance as a Guarantee for Democracy in EU Governance' in C Joerges and R Dehousse (eds), *Good Governance in Europe's Integrated Market* (Oxford University Press, 2002) 35.

Levi-Faur, D and Jordana, J, 'The Rise of Regulatory Capitalism: The Global Diffusion of a New Order' (2005) 598 *Annals of the American Academy of Political and Social Science* 200.

Lo Schiavo, G, 'From National Banking Union to a Centralized Model of Prudential Supervision in Europe?' (2014) 21 *Maastricht Journal of European and Comparative Law* 110.

—— 'The Single Supervisory Mechanism: Building the New Top-Down Cooperative Supervisory Governance in Europe' in F Fabbrini, EH Ballin and H Somsen (eds), *What Form of Government for the European Union and the Eurozone?* (Hart Publishing, 2015) 111.

—— *The Role of Financial Stability in EU Law and Policy* (Kluwer 2017).

Maas, H, 'The Administrative Commission for the Social Security of Migrant Workers' (1967) 4 *Common Market Law Review* 51.

Magliari, A, 'I procedimenti amministrativi di vigilanza bancaria nel quadro del Single Supervisory Mechanism. Il caso dell'applicazione dei diritti nazionali da parte della BCE' (2015) *Rivista di Diritto Bancario* 1.

—— 'Administrative Remedies in European Financial Governance' in B Marchetti (ed), *Administrative Remedies in the European Union: The Emergence of a Quasi-Judicial Administration* (Giappichelli, 2017) 99.

Magnette, P, 'The Politics of Regulation in the European Union' in D Geradin, R Muñoz and N Petit (eds), *Regulation Through Agencies in the EU: A New Paradigm of European Governance* (Elgar Publishing, 2005) 3.

Majone, G, 'La crescita dei poteri regolativi nella Comunità europea' (1993) 25 *Rivista Italiana di Scienza Politica* 409.

—— 'The Rise of the Regulatory State in Europe' (1994) 17 *West European Politics* 77.

—— *The European Community as a Regulatory State* (Nijhoff, 1995).

—— *Regulating Europe* (Routledge, 1996).

—— 'The New European Agencies: Regulation by Information' (1997) 4 *Journal of European Public Policy* 262.

—— 'The Rise of the Regulatory State in Europe' in R Baldwin, C Scott and C Hood (eds), *A Reader on Regulation* (Oxford University Press, 1998) 192.

—— 'Europe's "Democratic Deficit": The Question of Standards' (1998) 4 *European Law Journal* 5.

—— *The Regulatory State and its Legitimacy Problems*, IHS Political Science Series no 56 (1998).

—— 'The Credibility Crisis of Community Regulation' (2000) 38 *Journal of Common Market Studies* 273.

—— *The Transformations of the Regulatory State*, AIR Paper (2010), available at www.osservatorioair.it/wp-content/uploads/2010/10/Paper_Majone_RegulatoryState_sept2010.pdf.

—— 'From the Regulatory State to a Democratic Default' (2014) 52 *Journal of Common Market Studies* 1216.

Mancini, F, *Democracy and Constitutionalism in the European Union, Collected Essays* (Hart Publishing, 2000).

Mancini, M, 'Dalla vigilanza nazionale armonizzata alla *Banking Union*' (2013) *Quaderni di Ricerca Giuridica* 5.

Marchetti, B, 'Administrative Justice Beyond the Courts: Internal Reviews in EU Administration' in B Marchetti (ed), *Administrative Remedies in the European Union: The Emergence of a Quasi-Judicial Administration* (Giappichelli, 2017) 1.

—— 'La tutela non giurisdizionale' (2017) *Rivista Italiana di Diritto Pubblico Comunitario* 423.

Marone, F, 'Le linee guida dell'autorità nazionale anticorruzione nel sistema delle fonti' (2017) *Rivista Trimestrale di Diritto Pubblico* 743.

Marzuoli, C, *Potere amministrativo e valutazioni tecniche* (Giuffrè, 1985).

—— 'Eccesso di potere' (2016) *Enciclopedia Treccani online*, available at www.treccani.it/enciclopedia/eccesso-di-potere_%28Diritto-on-line%29/.

Mashaw, JL, 'Accountability and Institutional Design: Some Thoughts on the Grammar of Governance' in MW Dowdle, *Public Accountability: Designs, Dilemmas and Experiences* (Cambridge University Press, 2006) 115.

Mattarella, BG, 'Il provvedimento' in S Cassese (ed), *Trattato di diritto amministrativo* (Giuffrè, 2000) vol I, 705.

—— 'L'attività' in S Cassese (ed), *Trattato di diritto amministrativo* (Giuffrè, 2000) vol I, 629.

—— 'Discrezionalità amministrativa' in S Cassese (ed), *Dizionario di Diritto Pubblico* (Giuffrè, 2006) vol III, 1993.

—— 'The Concrete Options for a Law on Administrative Procedure Bearing on EU Direct Administration?' (2012) 22 *Rivista Italiana di Diritto Pubblico Comunitario* 537.

Meads, R and Allio, L, 'A "Win-Win-Win" Scenario: Reaping the Benefits of an EU Law on Administrative Procedure' (2014) 5 *European Journal of Risk Regulation* 87.

Mee, S, 'Negotiated Rulemaking and Combined Sewer Overflows (CSOs): Consensus Saves Ossification' (1997) 25 *Boston College Environmental Affairs Law Review* 213.

Mendes, J, *Good Administration in EU Law and the Code of Good Administrative Behaviour*, EUI Working Papers Law 2009/09 (2009).

—— *Participation in EU Rule-Making: A Right-Based Approach* (Oxford University Press, 2011).

—— 'Delegated and Implementing Rule Making: Proceduralisation and Constitutional Design' (2013) 19 *European Law Journal* 22.

—— 'Law and Administrative Discretion in the EU: Value of Comparative Perspective', paper presented at the Comparative Administrative Conference, Yale, April 2016, available at www.law.yale.edu/system/files/area/conference/compadmin/compadmin16_mendes_law.pdf.

—— 'Discretion, Care and Public Interests in the EU Administration: Probing the Limits of Law' (2016) 53 *Common Market Law Review* 419.

—— 'The Making of Delegated and Implementing Acts: Legitimacy Beyond Institutional Balance' in CF Bergström and D Ritleng (eds), *Rulemaking by the European Commission* (Oxford University Press, 2016) 233.

—— 'Executive Rule-making: Procedures in Between Constitutional Principles and Institutional Entrenchment' in C Harlow, P Leino and G della Cananea (eds), *Research Handbook on EU Administrative Law* (Elgar Publishing, 2017) 371.

—— 'Bounded Discretion in EU Law: A Limited Judicial Paradigm in a Changing EU' (2017) *Modern Law Review* 443.

Mester, M, 'Independent NRAs in European Electronic Communications Policy-making and Regulation: The Road to BEREC and Beyond' (2010) 147 *Studia Iuridica Auctoritate Universitatis Pecs Publicata* 113.

Millett, PJ, Lord, 'The Right to Good Administration in European Law' (2002) *Public Law* 309.

Modugno, F and Manetti, M, 'Eccesso di potere amministrativo' (1989) 12 *Enciclopedia Giuridica* 2.

Möllers, TJ, 'Sources of Law in European Securities Regulation: Effective Regulation, Soft Law and Legal Taxonomy from Lamfalussy to de Larosière' (2010) 11 *European Business Organization Law Review* 379.

Moloney, N, 'European Banking Union: Assessing Its Risks and Resilience' (2014) 51 *Common Market Law Review* 1609.

—— *EU Securities and Financial Markets Regulation*, 3rd edn (Oxford University Press, 2014).

Moran, M, 'The Rise of the Regulatory State' in D Coen, W Grant and G Wilson (eds), *The Oxford Handbook of Business and Government* (Oxford University Press, 2010) 383.

Moravcsik, A, *The Choice for Europe: Social Purpose and State Power from Messina to Maastricht* (Cornell University Press, 1998).

Morbidelli, G, 'Linee guida dell'ANAC: comandi o consigli?' (2016) *Diritto Amministrativo* 273.

Napolitano, G, 'La risposta europea alla crisi del debito sovrano: il rafforzamento dell'Unione economica e monetaria. Verso l'Unione bancaria' (2012) 65 *Banca Borsa* 747.

Nehl, HP, 'Good Administration as Procedural Right and/or General Principle?' in HCH Hofmann and AH Türk (eds), *Legal Challenges in EU Administrative Law: Towards an Integrated Administration* (Elgar Publishing, 2009) 322.

Nicola, FG, 'Critical Legal Histories in EU Law' (2013) 28 *American University International Law Review* 1173.

Ottow, A, 'The New European Supervisory Architecture of the Financial Markets' in M Everson, C Monda and E Vos (eds), *European Agencies in Between Institutions and Member States* (Kluwer, 2014) 123.

Papadopoulou, L, Pernice, I and Weiler, JHH (eds), *Legitimacy Issues of the European Union in the Face of Crisis* (Hart Publishing, 2017).

Peers, S and Costa, M, 'Accountability for Delegated and Implementing Acts after the Treaty of Lisbon' (2012) 18 *European Law Journal* 427.

Pelkmans, J, 'The New Approach to Technical Harmonization and Standardization' (1987) 25 *Journal of Common Market Studies* 249.

—— *Subsidiarity Between Law and Economics*, Bruges Research Papers in Law no 1 (2005).

—— *Testing for Subsidiarity*, Bruges European Economic Policy Briefings no 13 (2006).

—— *The Case for 'More Single Market'*, CEPS Policy Brief no 234 (2011), available at http://aei.pitt.edu/29749/1/No%20234%20JP%20on%20EU%20Single%20Market.pdf.

Pelkmans, J and Luchetta, G, *Enjoying a Single Market for Network Industries?*, Notre Europe Studies and Report no 9 (2013), available at www.notre-europe.eu/media/singlemarketnetworkindustries-pelkmansluchetta-ne-jdi-feb13.pdf?pdf=ok.

Pelkmans, J and Renda, A, 'Single eComms Market? No Such Thing …' (2011) 2 *Communications and Strategies* 21.

Pelkmans, J and Simoncini, M, *Mellowing Meroni: How ESMA Can Help Build the Single Market*, Regulatory Policy, CEPS Commentaries no 1 (2014).

Pescatore, P, 'La fusion des institutions et des pouvoirs' (1966) 18 *Revue Internationale de Droit Comparé* 301.

Pierce, RJ, Jr, 'Rulemaking Ossification is Real: A Response to Testing the Ossification Thesis' (2012) 80 *George Washington Law Review* 1493.

Pisani-Ferry, J, Sapir, A, Véron, N and Wolff, GB, *What Kind of European Banking Union?*, Bruegel Policy Contribution 2012/12 (2012).

Ponzano, P, 'The Reform of Comitology and Delegated Acts: An Executive's View' in CF Bergström and D Ritleng (eds), *Rulemaking by the European Commission* (Oxford University Press, 2016) 37.

Posner, E, 'The Lamfalussy Process: Polyarchic Origins of Networked Financial Rule-making in the EU' in CF Sabel and J Zeitlin (eds), *Experimentalist Governance in the European Union* (Oxford University Press, 2010) 43.

Predieri, A, 'Le norme tecniche nello Stato pluralista e prefederativo' (1996) *Il Diritto Dell'economia* 251.

Previdi, E, 'The Organisation of Public and Private Responsibilities in European Risk Regulation: An Institutional Gap Between Them' in C Joerges, KH Ladeur and E Vos (eds), *Integrating Scientific Expertise into Regulatory Decision-Making: National Traditions and European Innovations* (Nomos Verlagsgesellschaft, 1997) 225.

Rasmussen, M, 'Establishing a Constitutional Practice of European Law: The History of the Legal Service of the European Executive, 1952–65' (2012) 21 *Contemporary European History* 375.

—— 'Rewriting the History of European Public Law: The New Contribution of Historians' (2013) 28 *American University International Law Review* 1187.

Ritleng, D, 'The Reserved Domain of the Legislature: The Notion of "Essential Elements of an Area"' in CF Bergström and D Ritleng (eds), *Rulemaking by the European Commission* (Oxford University Press, 2016) 133.

Rittberger, B and Wonka, A, 'Introduction: Agency Governance in the European Union' in B Rittberger and A Wonka (eds), *Agency Governance in the EU* (Routledge, 2012) 2.

Roldán, JM and Lannoo, K, *ECB Banking Supervision and Beyond, Report of a CEPS Task Force* (CEPS, 2014).

Romagnosi, GD, *Principi fondamentali di diritto amministrativo onde tesserne le istituzioni*, 3rd edn (Guasti, 1835).

Rose-Ackerman, S, 'Product Safety Regulation and the Law of Torts' in J Hunziker and T Jones (eds), *Product Liability and Innovation: Managing Risk in an Uncertain Environment* (National Academy Press, 1994) 151.

Rouvière, J, 'Réflexions sur l'erreur manifeste' in *Rapport public* (Conseil d'État, 1988) 65.

Ruffert, M, 'Personality under EU Law: A Conceptual Answer Towards the Pluralisation of the EU' (2014) 20 *European Law Journal* 346.

Sabel, CF and Zeitlin, J, 'Learning from Difference: The New Architecture of Experimentalist Governance in the EU' in CF Sabel and J Zeitlin (eds), *Experimentalist Governance in the European Union* (Oxford University Press, 2010) 1.

Sacchi Morsiani, G, 'Eccesso di potere amministrativo' in *Novissimo Digesto Italiano* (Utet, 1982) vol 3, 219.

Sandulli, A, 'Eccesso di potere e controllo di proporzionalità. Profili comparati' (1995) *Rivista Trimestrale di Diritto Pubblico* 329.

Sandulli A, *La proporzionalità dell'azione amministrativa* (Cedam, 1998).

Saurer, J, 'The Accountability of Supranational Administration: The Case of European Union Agencies' (2009) 24 *American University International Law Review* 429.

Schammo, P, 'The European Securities and Markets Authority: Lifting the Veil on the Allocation of Powers' (2011) 48 *Common Market Law Review* 1879.

—— 'EU Day-to-Day Supervision or Intervention-based Supervision: Which Way Forward for the European System of Financial Supervision?' (2012) 32 *Oxford Journal of Legal Studies* 771.

Schepel, H, *The Constitution of Private Governance: Product Standards in the Regulation of Integrating Markets* (Hart Publishing, 2005).

—— 'The New Approach to the New Approach: The Juridification of Harmonized Standards in EU Law' (2013) 20 *Maastricht Journal of European and Comparative Law* 521.

Schmidt-Assmann, E, *La Teoría General del Derecho Administrativo como Sistema* (Marcial Pons, 2003).

Schneider, J-P, 'A Common Framework for Decentralized EU Agencies and the *Meroni* Doctrine' (2009) *Administrative Law Review* 29.

Scholten, M, *"Independence vs. Accountability": Dilemma or Misconception* (2010), available at https://ssrn.com/abstract=1718584.

—— '"Independent, Hence Unaccountable"?' (2011) 4 *Review of European Administrative Law* 5.

—— *The Political Accountability of EU and US Independent Regulatory Agencies* (Brill Nijhoff, 2014).

—— 'Publication Review: M Chamon, *EU Agencies: Legal and Political Limits to the Transformation of the EU Administration* (Oxford University Press 2016)' (2017) 42 *European Law Review* 139.

Scholten, M and van Rijsbergen, M, 'The *ESMA-Short Selling* Case: Erecting a New Delegation Doctrine in the EU upon the *Meroni-Romano* Remnants' (2014) 41 *Legal Issues of Economic Integration* 389.

Schout, A, 'Inspecting Aviation Safety in the EU: EASA as an Administrative Innovation?' in E Vos (ed), *European Risk Governance: Its Science, Its Inconclusiveness and Its Effectiveness*, Connex Report Series no 6 (2008) 257.

—— 'Assessing the Added Value of an EU Agency for Aviation Safety' (2011) 31 *Journal of Public Policy* 363.

Schütze, R, *From Dual to Cooperative Federalism: The Changing Structure of European Law* (Oxford University Press, 2009).

—— '"Delegated" Legislation in the (New) European Union: A Constitutional Analysis' (2011) 74 *Modern Law Review* 661.

Schwarze, J, 'The Principle of Proportionality and the Principle of Impartiality in European Administrative Law' (2003) *Rivista Trimestrale di Diritto Pubblico* 53.

—— 'Judicial Review of European Administrative Procedure' (2004) 68 *Law and Contemporary Problems* 85.

Scoca, FG, 'Profili sostanziali del merito amministrativo' (1981) *Nuova Rassegna* 1376.

——, 'La discrezionalità nel pensiero di Giannini e nella dottrina successiva' (2000) *Rivista Trimestrale di Diritto Pubblico* 1045.

Scott, C, 'Accountability in the Regulatory State' (2000) 27 *Journal of Law and Society* 38.

Scott, J, 'In Legal Limbo: Post-Legislative Guidance as a Challenge for European Administrative Law' (2011) 48 *Common Market Law Review* 329.

Scott, J and Sturm, S, 'Courts as Catalysts: Rethinking the Judicial Role in New Governance' (2007) 13 *Columbia Journal of European Law* 565.

Seidenfeld, M, 'Why Agencies Act: A Reassessment of the Ossification Critique of Judicial Review' (2009) 70 *Ohio State Law Journal* 251.

Senden, L, *Soft Law in European Community Law* (Hart Publishing, 2004).

Shapiro, M, 'The Problems of Independent Agencies in the United States and the European Union' (1997) 4 *Journal of European Public Policy* 276.

Shapiro, SA, 'Outsourcing Government Regulation' (2003) 53 *Duke Law Journal* 389.

—— 'Rulemaking Ossification and the Debate over Reforming Hard Look Review' (2015) 41 *Administrative and Regulatory Law News* 13.

Simoncini, M, 'Governing Air Traffic Management in the Single European Sky: The Search for Possible Solutions to Safety Issues' (2013) 38 *European Law Review* 209.

—— 'The Erosion of the *Meroni* Doctrine: The Case of the European Aviation Safety Agency' (2015) 21 *European Public Law* 309.

—— 'Legal Boundaries of European Supervisory Authorities (ESAs) in the Financial Markets: Tensions in the Development of True Regulatory Agencies' (2015) 34 *Yearbook of European Law* 319.

Simoncini, M and Straetmans, G (eds), 'Sixty Years Later: Rethinking Competing Paradigms for EU Law in Times of Crisis' (2017) 9 *Perspectives on Federalism*, Special Issue no 2.

Snyder, F, 'The Effectiveness of European Community Law: Institutions, Processes, Tools and Techniques' (1993) *Modern Law Review* 19.

—— 'Soft Law and Institutional Practice in the European Community' in S Martin (ed), *The Construction of Europe, Essays in Honour of Emile Noël* (Kluwer, 1994) 197.

Somek, A, *Individualism: An Essay on the Authority of the European Union* (Oxford University Press, 2008) 114.

Sorace, D, 'Una nuova base costituzionale europea per la pubblica amministrazione' in MP Chiti and A Natalini (eds), *Lo spazio amministrativo europeo. Le pubbliche amministrazioni dopo il Trattato di Lisbona* (Il Mulino, 2012) 45.

Spagnuolo, F, 'La nozione europea di poteri pubblici' (2011) *Giornale di Diritto Amministrativo* 1289.

Stefan, O, 'European Union Soft Law: New Developments Concerning the Divide Between Legally Binding Force and Legal Effects' (2012) *Modern Law Review* 879.

—— 'Hybridity Before the Court: A Hard Look at Soft Law in the EU Competition and State Aid Case Law' (2012) 37 *European Law Review* 49.

Stewart, R, 'The Reformation of American Administrative law' (1975) 88 *Harvard Law Review* 1667.

Strauss, PL, 'The Rulemaking Continuum' (1992) 41 *Duke Law Journal* 1463.

Ter Kuile, G, Wissink, L and Bovenschen, W, 'Tailor-made Accountability Within the Single Supervisory Mechanism' (2015) 52 *Common Market Law Review* 155.

Terpan, F, 'Soft Law in the European Union: The Changing Nature of EU Law' (2015) *European Law Journal* 68.

Thatcher, M, 'The Creation of European Regulatory Agencies and Its Limits: A Comparative Analysis of European Delegation' (2011) 18 *Journal of European Public Policy* 790.

Torchia, L, 'La regolazione del mercato dei contratti pubblici' (2016) *Rivista della Regolazione dei Mercati* 72.

Travi, A, 'Il giudice amministrativo e le questioni tecnico-scientifiche: formule nuove e vecchie soluzioni' (2004) *Diritto Pubblico* 439.

Tridimas, T, *The General Principles of EU Law*, 2nd edn (Oxford University Press, 2006).

—— 'Financial Supervision and Agency Power: Reflections on ESMA' in N Nic Shuibhne and LW Gormley (eds), *From Single Market to Economic Union, Essays in Memory of John A. Usher* (Oxford University Press, 2012) 55.

Tröger, TH, 'The Single Supervisory Mechanism: Panacea or Quack Banking Regulation? Preliminary Assessment of the New Regime for the Prudential Supervision of Banks with ECB Involvement' (2014) 15 *European Business Organization Law Review* 449.
Türk, AH, 'Oversight of Administrative Rulemaking: Judicial Review' (2013) 19 *European Law Journal* 126.
Ule, CH, 'Zur Anwendung unbestimmter Rechtsbegriffe im Verwaltungsrecht' in O Bachof et al (eds), *Forschungen und Berichte aus dem Öffentlichen Recht, Gedächtnisschrift für Walter Jellinek* (Isar Verlag, 1955).
—— *Verwaltungsprozeßrecht. Ein Studienbuch* (Beck, 1978).
Van Cleynenbreugel, P, '*Meroni* Circumvented? Article 114 TFEU and EU Regulatory Agencies' (2014) 21 *Maastricht Journal of European and Comparative Law* 64.
Van Cleynenbreugel, P and Demoulin, I, 'The EP's "European Standards" Resolution in the Wake of *James Elliott Construction*: Carving Ever More Holes in the Pandora's Box?', *European Law Blog* (25 September 2017), available at http://europeanlawblog.eu/2017/09/25/the-eps-european-standards-resolution-in-the-wake-of-james-elliott-construction-carving-ever-more-holes-in-pandoras-box/.
Van den Bergh, R, 'The Subsidiarity Principle in European Community Law: Some Insights from Law and Economics' (1994) 1 *Maastricht Journal of European and Comparative Law* 337.
van Gestel, R, 'European Regulatory Agencies Adrift? Case 270/12' (2014) 21 *Maastricht Journal of European and Comparative Law* 188.
—— 'Primacy of the European Legislature? Delegated Rule-Making and the Decline of the "Transmission Belt" Theory' (2014) 1 *Theory and Practice of Legislation* 1.
van Gestel, R and Micklitz, HW, 'European Integration Through Standardization: How Judicial Review is Breaking Down the Club House of Private Standardization Bodies' (2013) *Common Market Law Review* 145.
van Gestel, R and van Golen, T, 'Enforcement by the New European Supervisory Agencies: Quis Custodiet Ipsos Custodes?' in K Purnhagen and O Rott (eds), *Varieties of European Economic Law and Regulation, Liber Amicorum for Hans Micklitz* (Springer, 2014) 757.
Verkuil, PR, 'Comment: Rulemaking Ossification: A Modest Proposal' (1995) 47 *Administrative Law Review* 453.
Vidal, R, 'L'évolution du détournement de pouvoir dans la jurisprudence administrative' (1952) *Revue du Droit Public* 275.
Villata, R and Ramajoli, M, *Il provvedimento amministrativo*, 2nd edn (Giuffrè, 2017).
Vincent, JY, 'L'erreur manifeste d'appréciation' (1971) *Revue Administrative* 407.
Volpato, A, 'The Harmonized Standards Before the ECJ: *James Elliott Construction*' (2017) 54 *Common Market Law Review* 591.
von Bogdandy, A, Arndt, F and Bast, J, 'Legal Instruments in European Union Law and their Reform: A Systematic Approach on an Empirical Basis' (2004) 23 *Yearbook of European Law* 91.
Vos, E, 'EU Food Safety Regulation in the Aftermath of the BSE Crisis' (2000) 23 *Journal of Consumer Policy* 227.
—— 'Reforming the European Commission: What Role to Play for EU Agencies?' (2000) 37 *Common Market Law Review* 1113.
—— 'Independence, Accountability and Transparency of European Regulatory Agencies' in D Geradin, R Muñoz and N Petit (eds), *Regulation Through Agencies in the EU: A New Paradigm of European Governance* (Edward Elgar Publishing, 2005) 120.

—— 'European Agencies and the Composite EU Executive' in M Everson, C Monda and E Vos (eds), *European Agencies in Between Institutions and Member States* (Kluwer, 2014) 11.

Wakefield, J, *The Right to Good Administration* (Kluwer, 2007).

Weatherill, S, 'The Limits of Legislative Harmonization Ten Years after *Tobacco Advertising*: How the Court's Case Law has Become a "Drafting Guide"' (2011) 12 *German Law Journal* 827.

Webb Yackee, J and Webb Yackee, S, 'Testing the Ossification Thesis: An Empirical Examination of Federal Regulatory Volume and Speed, 1950–1990' (2012) 80 *George Washington Law Review* 1414.

Weiler, JHH, 'The Community System: The Dual Character of Supranationalism' (1982) 1 *Yearbook of European Law* 267.

—— 'The Transformation of Europe' (1991) 100 *Yale Law Journal* 2403.

Weismann, P, 'The European Financial Market Supervisory Authorities and Their Powers to Issue Binding Decisions' (2012) 27 *Journal of International Banking Law and Regulation* 495.

Welter, H, *Le contrôle juridictionnel de la moralité administrative: étude de doctrine et de jurisprudence* (Sirey, 1929).

Witte, A, 'The Application of National Banking Supervision Law by the ECB: Three Parallel Modes of Executing EU Law?' (2014) 21 *Maastricht Journal of European and Comparative Law* 89.

—— 'Standing and Judicial Review in the New EU Financial Markets Architecture' (2015) 1 *Journal of Financial Regulation* 1.

Woehrling, JM, 'Le contrôle jurisdictionnel du pouvoir discrétionnaire en France' (1999) 52 *La Revue Administrative* 75.

Wolfers, B and Voland, T, 'Level the Playing Field: The New Supervision of Credit Institutions by the European Central Bank' (2014) 51 *Common Market Law Review* 1463.

Wymeersch, E, *The Single Supervisory Mechanism or 'SSM', Part One of the Banking Union*, ECGI Working Paper Series in Law 240/2014 (2014).

Yantaganas, XA, *Delegation of Regulatory Authority in the European Union: The Relevance of the American Model of Independent Agencies*, Jean Monnet Working Paper 3/2001 (2001).

Yesilkagit, K and Christensen, J, 'Institutional Design and Formal Autonomy' (2010) 20 *Journal of Public Administration Research and Theory* 53.

Ziller, J, 'Le principe de proportionnalité' (1996) *AJDA* 185.

—— *Alternatives in Drafting EU Administrative Procedure Law* (Policy Department C: Citizens' Rights and Constitutional Affairs, 2011).

—— 'Is a Law of Administrative Procedure for the Union Institutions Necessary?' (2011) *Rivista Italiana di Diritto Pubblico Comunitario* 699.

Index